Praise for *Mapping Innovation*

As soon as I see—in my twitter feed or at *Harvard Business Review,* or anywhere else—that Greg Satell has written a new piece, I know that I am going to learn something new and it is going to be fun to read. In particular, Satell writes brilliant stuff about what it actually takes to design and implement an innovation strategy. It's the kind of stuff I find useful to discuss with my students in my class and the executives I coach.

> —Robert Sutton, Professor of Business and Engineering at
> Stanford University, IDEO Fellow, author of *Scaling up*
> *Excellence, Weird Ideas That Work* and *The No Asshole Rule*

Innovation in a startup isn't the same as innovation in a large company, just as pursuing a fundamental discovery in a scientific lab isn't the same as building an application on top of an initial insight. In *Mapping Innovation,* Greg Satell helps us make sense of it all and apply the right strategies to the right problems. It's a great read too.

> —Steve Blank, lecturer, Stanford University and UC Berkeley
> Haas Business School, author of *The Startup Owner's Manual*

Greg Satell has a deep instinct about how innovation and technology are changing business. His unique writing perspective makes us all smarter by his inquiry into the inner workings of the innovation experience. We all learn from his journey of discovery.

> —Dr. James Canton, CEO, Institute for Global Futures,
> author of *Future Smart*

Greg is a superb blend of integrity, creativity, and professionalism. Insightful, responsive, and diligent, he always makes sure he gets the facts straight. In my field, where life and death hang in the balance, that's really important and I appreciate it immensely.

> —Ron DePinho MD, President, MD Anderson Cancer Center

In my role as Chief Strategist for a $10 billion enterprise, innovation is always top of mind and Greg Satell provides a wonderful, practical guide in *Mapping Innovation.* More than just clever gimmicks or buzzwords, it presents a simple, easy-to-use framework derived from some of the world's most innovative organizations. Greg knows his stuff from firsthand, upstream business experience too. For me that's key.

> —Rishad Tobaccowala, Chief Strategist, Publicis Groupe

Greg is a talented writer, which comes naturally given his wide-open thinking and overall fantastic strategic perspective that is refreshingly different.

—Suzy Deering, Chief Marketing Officer, eBay

The trick to innovation is balancing serendipity with design, of creating a well-planned space for the unexpected. Greg has walked that thin line well. His principles are simultaneously pragmatic and welcoming to unexpected ideas from unexpected quadrants. That is the kind of reality your innovation process demands.

—Alph Bingham, cofounder and former
President and CEO, Innocentive

Many people write about innovation. Greg Satell is one of my favorites. He combines thorough research and innovative viewpoints with a practical style that makes his work relevant to practitioners. Greg's work has always been an insightful and enjoyable source for my own thinking.

—Alex Osterwalder, inventor of the Business Model Canvas, author
of *Business Model Generation* and *Value Proposition Design*

I have long been a fan of Greg Satell's writings on innovation and, for the past five years or so, we have used him as a source of innovation inspiration and good ideas in the joint executive program on Driving Strategic Innovation, that is a partnership between MIT's Sloan School of Management and IMD.

What sets Greg apart from other observers of the innovation scene is his broad range of vision and references, his practical experience, and the effectiveness of his writing. There are few people I know who can weave these three attributes together as well as Greg has done. I think he has made a mark on social media and through his *Forbes* and *Harvard Business Review* writing that has made him one of the more visible commentators on innovation related issues today, and I would look forward to any innovation project that he is associated with.

—Bill Fischer, Professor of Innovation Management, IMD,
author of *Reinventing Giants* and *The Idea Hunter*

Greg Satell is a thoughtful, insightful, and entertaining writer. His articles always make me think. I would read and recommend any book Greg writes.

—Saul Kaplan, founder and Chief Catalyst, The Business Innovation Factory, author of *Business Innovation Factory*

There are many writers these days trying to explain the impact of technology and why "it might be different this time." Greg Satell's writing *is* different because he covers not just the surface activity but the implications of technology's influence on how people interact with machines, algorithms, and each other; how this affects the way business is done; and why that matters for the present and the future.

His work is both stimulating and thought-provoking. On my own website, in which I curate writing of interest to clients, friends, strangers and, most of all, me, I have found that Greg's articles invariably generate more page views and commentary than those of any other author/thought leader I post. I would love to see him expand his thoughts into a book-length effort.

—Jonathan Low, partner at Predictive LLC, former Deputy Assistant Secretary for Work and Technology at the Department of Labor, author of *The Invisible Advantage*

MAPPING INNOVATION

A PLAYBOOK FOR NAVIGATING A DISRUPTIVE AGE

GREG SATELL

New York Chicago San Francisco Athens London Madrid
Mexico City Milan New Delhi Singapore Sydney Toronto

1 2 3 4 5 6 7 8 9   LCR   22 21 20 19 18 17

ISBN   978-1-259-86225-0
MHID   1-259-86225-9

e-ISBN   978-1-259-86224-3
e-MHID   1-259-86224-0

Library of Congress Cataloging-in-Publication Data

Names: Satell, Greg, author.
Title: Mapping innovation : a playbook for navigating a disruptive age / Greg Satell.
Description: New York : McGraw-Hill, 2017.
Identifiers: LCCN 2016055010 (print) | LCCN 2017013334 (ebook) | ISBN
    9781259862243 () | ISBN 1259862240 () | ISBN 9781259862250 (alk. paper) |
    ISBN 1259862259
Subjects: LCSH: Technological innovations--Management. | Diffusion of
    innovations--Management. | Research, Industrial. | New products.
Classification: LCC HD45 (ebook) | LCC HD45 .S286 2017 (print) | DDC
    658.5/14--dc23
LC record available at https://lccn.loc.gov/2016055010

McGraw-Hill Education books are available at special quantity discounts to use as premiums and sales promotions or for use in corporate training programs. To contact a representative, please visit the Contact Us pages at www.mhprofessional.com

To my wife, Liliana, and daughter, Ashley,
who I hope one day will read her Daddy's book

CONTENTS

FOREWORD

I've spent my entire career focused on innovation working as a scientist at a single company, IBM. Many might conclude that means that it's all been part of a single thread, yet nothing would be further from the truth.

Like countless other scientists and engineers who came before me, I found it necessary over the years to often rethink and retool my own focus and skill set to accomplish tasks that had evolved dramatically as to what was required to succeed. Along the way, I also learned the importance of knowing my own limitations, and the criticality of then seeking out those with complementary skills to buttress my own.

Further along in my career, as I moved into executive management, I found that many of the lessons I had learned along the way applied equally to how I helped lead and set the tone of my organization, with the additional challenge of applying those lessons at scale. It is this latter facet of driving innovation—helping to fit solutions to problems rather than championing one particular strategy or method—that is the focus of the chapters that follow, and has similarly been the focus of my career at IBM.

I first came to IBM in 1979 as an intern completing my PhD in solid state physics. It was like being a kid in a candy store. I saw the stockroom piled high with equipment that I would have otherwise spent a year writing funding requests and justifications for. So unlike many of my colleagues who took jobs at academic institutions, I decided to pursue my path in industry.

A year later I began my career at IBM in the chemistry group of the Physical Sciences department. I had interviewed at many other research organizations, but I chose IBM given its decades-long commitment to basic research, as well as my sense of it being a flat organization that thrived on "Innovations That Matter." That metric for a successful innovation was particularly attractive to me. I saw it as the ultimate validation—placing my work in a highly competitive marketplace and seeing it thrive on its own merits.

I began my career in Physical Sciences, which was then the "blue sky" innovation center of the IBM universe, with scientists and engineers working in extraordinarily diverse fields. I came to be the lone physicist in a group of chemists because of my expertise in solid state materials, which was well aligned to the chemistry team's interest in amorphous semiconductors, an exciting and emerging field at the time. Often introduced at meetings as the sole member of the team not having an advanced degree in chemistry, it earned me a lot of good-natured abuse, but I learned more about the true nature of innovation there than at any other time in my career.

My first epiphany was that chemists, those odd folks from that "other" specialization, were not from the "dark side." They actually had a great deal to add to my core work. In fact, they enabled me to debunk several decades of literature that obstructed progress in my own field of interest. It was that collaboration that led to the creation of a new generation of silicon germanium (SiGe) semiconductors, which were long theorized about but had never before been successfully developed.

Obviously that was a big moment in my career, but even more importantly it taught me the value of diversity. So I then hunted down two of our best electrical engineers, and we rapidly created the first viable SiGe transistors, setting a slew of records along the way. That achievement in the end had demanded innovation spanning chemistry, physics, electrical engineering, microscopy, chemical analysis, and manufacturing. Yet still I knew the work was not yet done. I joined IBM to create "Innovations that Matter," and for all of our technical success, we still hadn't achieved that.

To achieve real success, at some point you simply need to bite the bullet and see if anyone cares about your "baby." As it turned out, Wi-Fi—wireless technology—was just beginning to emerge commercially, but costs were prohibitive given the fairly exotic semiconductors it employed at that early time in its development. By contrast, the SiGe technology we developed was based on traditional low cost silicon manufacturing. We saw the potential to produce wireless technology that was vastly superior in cost performance to anything anyone had believed possible at the time.

Still, we lacked experience with consumer electronics. So once again we broadened our innovation ecosystem, by meeting with a wide variety of potential commercial partners. Ultimately we allied with a Harris Semiconductor spinout, Intersil. Working together, we focused on making Wi-Fi pervasive, and SiGe sales took off when it proved to be an enabling technology for low-cost Wi-Fi. Even today, two decades later, SiGe technology is now found in virtually every device and technology manufactured.

I share this story because these experiences were highly formative for me and continue to shape how I see innovation. I graduated with a degree in physics focused on materials science, but in order for me to help take a basic discovery in my field and make it a pervasive, important technology, I had to push beyond my own horizons and collaborate with a highly diverse set of individuals and companies, all bringing their technical skills and business acumen together to achieve a common goal.

That is the lesson that IBM taught me. I am forever grateful for that, and it is what I endeavor to pass on. It is also an idea that pervades the chapters that follow.

I hope you enjoy them.

—Dr. Bernard S. Meyerson
Chief Innovation Officer, IBM

ACKNOWLEDGMENTS

Nobody truly writes a book alone, and this one is no exception. Many people helped along the way by sharing their time, advice, and encouragement. I'm more grateful than you can imagine.

First, I'd like to thank my mother, Penny Satell Berman, as well as Maureen Ryan and Mark Boncheck for their help with the initial proposal. Few realize how much work goes into a book even before the writing starts, and their advice and support were invaluable.

Many people also helped me by lending their experience and expertise, in some cases, looking over sections to make sure I got my facts right. One of the things that I tried to do in this book is, whenever possible, let the innovators share their stories directly with the reader. That was only possible because some of the world's best innovators took the time to speak with me. These include (in no special order): Eric Haller, Michael Troncale, Saul Kaplan, Steve Blank, Alex Osterwalder, Christopher Blake, Bernie Meyerson, Irving Wladawsky-Berger, Randy Terbush, Alph Bingham, Nabil Sakkab, George Crabtree, Angel Diaz, Dharmendra Modha, Charlie Bennett, Fabio Rosati, Christian Gheorghe, Lynda Chin, Giulio Draetta, Ron DePinho, Raj De Datta, Samuel Moore, and Tim Kastelle. Christopher Blake, Jason Freidenfelds, Samuel Moore, and Tim Tyrell-Smith were also enormously helpful in connecting me to executives at their respective companies.

I would also like to thank my former colleagues at KP Media, who taught me more about innovation than anyone before or since, especially: Anya Dovgal, Olga Sych, Vitaly Sych, Alexander Tismenetsky, Oksana Sohor, Vitaly Gorduz, Herakliusz Lubomisrky, Oleksiy Kolupaev, Yulia McGuffie, Magda Mazur, Svetlana Udod, Pavel Zhdanov, Elena Viter, Olga Shchur, Katya Vorapayeva, Alona Tokar, Yuriy Ivashenko, Dasha Ivashenko, Maxim Kulakov, Max Tkachuk, and, of course, KP's founder, Jed Sunden, who made it all possible.

Finally, I'd like to thank my agents, Jill Marr and Sandra Dijkstra, as well as my editor, Cheryl Ringer, and the entire team at McGraw-Hill.

Most of all, I would like to thank my wife, Liliana, and my daughter, Ashley, without whose love and encouragement I wouldn't have gotten far beyond the first page.

The "Mother of All Demos"

*The Encyclopedia Britannica could be reduced to the
volume of a matchbox. A library of a million volumes
could be compressed into one end of a desk.*

—VANNEVAR BUSH (1945)

On December 9, 1968, a research project funded by the U.S. Department of Defense launched a revolution. The focus was not a Cold War adversary or even a resource-rich banana republic, but rather to "augment human intellect," and the man driving it was not a general, but a mild-mannered engineer named Douglas Engelbart.

It's hard to fully grasp what happened that day without understanding the context of the time. In those days, very few people ever saw a computer. They were, in large part, mysterious machines to be used only by a select priesthood who were conversant in the strange mathematical languages required to communicate with them. The tasks they performed were just as obscure, carrying out complex calculations for scientific experiments and managing mundane back-office tasks for large organizations.

But here was Engelbart, dressed in a short-sleeved white shirt and a thin black tie, standing in front of a 20-foot-high screen and explaining in his low-key voice how "intellectual workers" could actually *interact* with computers. What's more, he began to *show them*. As he began to type a document on a simple keyboard, words started to appear, which he could then edit, rearrange, and add graphics and sound to, while all the time navigating around the screen with a small device he called a mouse. Nobody had seen anything remotely like it ever before.

The presentation would prove to be so consequential that it is now called "The Mother of All Demos." Two of those in attendance, Bob Taylor and Alan Kay, would go on to further develop Engelbart's ideas into the Alto, the first truly personal computer, at Xerox's famed Palo Alto Research Center (PARC). Later, Steve Jobs would take many elements of the Alto to create the Macintosh.

So who deserves credit? Engelbart for coming up with the idea? Taylor and Kay for engineering solutions around it? Jobs for turning it all into a marketable product that created an impact on the world?

Maybe none of them. Engelbart got the ideas that led to "The Mother of All Demos" from Vannevar Bush's famous essay, "As We May Think,"[1] so maybe we should consider Bush the father of the personal computer. But why stop there? After all, it was John von Neumann who invented the eponymous architecture that made modern computers possible. And that, in turn, relied on Alan Turing's breakthrough concept of a "universal computer." Or maybe we should credit Robert Noyce and Jack Kilby for developing the microchip that powered the digital revolution? Or Bill Gates who built the company that made much of the software that allowed businesses to use computers productively?

The story doesn't seem any clearer when we try to look at the events that led to modern computing as a linear sequence going forward. Turing never set out to invent a machine. He was, in fact, trying to solve a problem in mathematical logic, the question of whether all numbers are computable. He created his idea of a universal computer—now known as a Turing machine—to show that it was possible to create a device that could "compute all computable numbers," but ironically in doing so he proved that all numbers are not computable. His work was an extension of Kurt Gödel's famous incompleteness theorems, which showed that logical systems themselves were broken. It was these two insights about the illogic of logical systems and the incomputability of numbers that led to the powerful logic of modern computers that we see all around us every day. Confusing, to be sure.

The waters muddy even further when we try to gauge the impact of personal computing. We know that Xerox built the first Alto in 1973 and Apple launched the Macintosh with great fanfare in 1984, but as late as 1987 the economist Robert Solow remarked, "You can see the computer age everywhere but in the productivity statistics."[2]

And, in fact, economists didn't start seeing any real economic impact from information technology until the late 1990s—*nearly 30 years after* "The Mother of All Demos." So what happened in the interim?

It seems that any time we try to understand an innovation through events, the story only gets more tangled and bewildering. And it doesn't get any clearer if we look at the innovators themselves. Some were highly trained PhDs, but others were college dropouts. Some were introverts. Others were extroverts. Some worked for the government, others in industry. Some worked in groups, but others largely alone.

Yet that brings us to any even more important question: How should we pursue innovation? Some companies, like IBM, invest heavily in basic research and always seem to be able to invent new businesses to replace the old ones that inevitably run out of steam. Others, like Procter & Gamble, are able to effectively partner with researchers and engineers outside their organizations to develop billion-dollar products. Apple became the world's most valuable company by limiting the number of products it sells and relentlessly focusing on the end user to make things that are "insanely great." Google continuously experiments to develop a seemingly endless stream of new innovations. Which path should you pursue?

Fortunately, there is an answer, and it starts with asking the right questions to define the problems you seek to solve and map the innovation space. From there, it is mostly a matter of choosing the right tools for the right jobs to develop an innovation playbook that will lead to success in the marketplace. This book will show you how to do that.

What Is Innovation?

In *The Little Black Book of Innovation*, Scott Anthony defines innovation as "something different that has impact."[3] That seems like a reasonable definition. After all, to innovate we need to come up with something different—if not a completely new invention, then a process for using an existing technology in a new way. That would cover significant technologies, like the Internet and the World Wide Web, while also making room for services like Uber and Facebook that harness those earlier inventions for new purposes.

And clearly, innovation needs to have an impact. Yet how are we to judge that? Did Engelbart's "Mother of All Demos" have an

INTRODUCTION: THE "MOTHER OF ALL DEMOS"

impact in 1968? Maybe it did on the people who were there to witness it, but few others. But Anthony insists that innovations need to have a *measurable impact*,[4] which didn't happen until 1984, with the launch of the Macintosh, or possibly even later, in the late 1990's, when the effect of personal computers could be detected in productivity numbers. So does that mean that Steve Jobs was an innovator and Engelbart was not? That certainly doesn't sound right. Maybe the Macintosh was the impact of "The Mother of All Demos." But that would mean that Engelbart didn't become an innovator until 16 years after he completed the work and that, in fact, Steve Jobs is responsible for making Engelbart's work important and not the other way around. That doesn't sound right either.

This is not, to be sure, a new debate, but one that's been raging for over a century. In 1939 Abraham Flexner published an article in *Harper's Magazine* entitled "The Usefulness of Useless Knowledge,"[5] in which he recounted a conversation he had with the great industrialist George Eastman. He asked Eastman who he thought was the man most useful to science, to which Eastman replied that he felt it was Marconi, the inventor of radio. Flexner then argued that Marconi was inevitable, given the work of Maxwell and Hertz, who discovered the basic principles that made radio possible. Further, he argued that these men were driven not by practicality—or as Anthony would put it, by the impact of their work—but merely by curiosity.

Flexner went on to describe an institution he was building in Princeton, New Jersey, called the Institute for Advanced Study, in which minds like John von Neumann as well as Albert Einstein, Kurt Gödel, and many others could pursue any subject they liked in any manner they chose, without any responsibility to teach or publish or show any impact at all from their work.

It was there that von Neumann developed a computer with a revolutionary new architecture that could store programs. He devised his new machine using other ideas once thought useless, like the vacuum tubes invented by Vladimir Zworykin in the 1920s. This design, now known as the von Neumann architecture, was open sourced and led to the development of the first commercial computers that were sold to businesses. Just about every computing device in the world is still organized according to the scheme that von Neumann came up with in 1945.

Today, hundreds of scholars come to the Institute for Advanced Study each year to work on abstract problems like string theory and abstract geometry. Will there ever be a measurable impact from their work? We probably won't know for decades, but clearly there is an incredible amount of innovative thinking about some very tough problems going on there.

So a better definition for innovation would be "a novel solution to an important problem." But that leads to the question: Important to whom? Well, first to a particular industry or field. Engelbart's work was innovative because it was both new and considered incredibly important to the field of computer science, for which it created an entirely new paradigm. Also, innovations are important to the next innovator. Engelbart made Taylor and Kay's work on the Alto possible, which made Steve Jobs's work on the Macintosh possible, which in turn helped unleash the creativity of millions of others.

That's why it's so hard to understand where innovation begins and ends. The truth is that any significant innovation involves an incredible diversity of problems that need to be solved, from theoretical and engineering challenges to manufacturing and distribution hurdles. There is no silver bullet, and no one person—nor even a single organization—can provide all the answers alone.

Still—and this is a crucial point—we all must pursue our own path to innovation alone. We have to choose what problems we intend to solve, whom we will work with, the manner in which we will work with them, and how we will bring our solutions to market. Those are decisions that we need to make, and no one else can do it for us.

This book will show you how to map the innovation space in order to make those decisions in a more rational, informed manner. It will also help you build a strategy around those decisions that can help you win in the marketplace.

A New Era of Innovation

As we have seen, innovation is far more difficult and complex than most people give it credit for. It takes more than a single big idea to change the world, and it can take decades after the initial breakthroughs for the true impact of an idea to become clear.

Still, in some ways we've had it easy. Our basic computer architecture has not changed since John von Neumann created it in 1945. Moore's Law, the regular doubling of chip performance that Gordon Moore postulated in 1965, has effectively given innovators a road map for developing new technology. Since the 1970s, engineers have depended on it to tell them how to focus their efforts. Other key technologies, such as the lithium-ion batteries that have made mobile devices predictably smaller and more powerful with each generation, have been in use since 1991. Over the last quarter century, these technologies have dramatically improved, but the basic paradigm of their design has not changed in any significant way.

The next decade or two, however, will look more like the fifties and sixties than it will the nineties or the aughts. We'll essentially be starting over. Moore's law, that trusty old paradigm that we've come to depend on, will likely come to an end around the year 2020, as transistors become so small that quantum effects between molecules will cause them to malfunction. Lithium-ion batteries will hit theoretical limits soon after that. They will be replaced by fundamentally new technologies, like quantum computing, neuromorphic chips, and new materials for energy storage that nobody really knows how to work with yet.

At the same time, new fields such as genomics, nanotechnology, and robotics are just beginning to hit their stride, leading to revolutionary new cures, advanced materials, and completely new ways to produce products. Artificial intelligence services like IBM's Watson, Amazon's Echo, and Google Assistant will become thousands of times more powerful and change the way we work and collaborate—with machines as well as each other. I've talked to many of the people developing these revolutionary technologies and, despite the amazing potential of the breakthroughs, each time I've been struck by how much work there is still to do. We're just beginning to scratch the surface.

Over the past 25 years, we've struggled to keep up with the pace of change. But over the next few decades, we will struggle to even understand the nature of change as fundamentally new technologies begin to influence the way we work, live, and strive to innovate. It will no longer be enough to simply move fast, we will have to develop a clear sense of where we're going, how we intend to get there, and what role we will be able to play. We'll need, in other words, to learn how to map innovation.

* * * * *

The purpose of this book is threefold. First, it will help you get a better understanding of innovation by dispelling destructive innovation myths. Innovations don't happen just because someone comes up with one big idea. It takes many ideas to solve an important problem, and that requires a collective effort.

Second, this book will give you valuable tools to help you frame the problems that are important to you. As you will see, it is only by framing problems effectively that you can find the approach most likely to solve them. Finally, it will help explain how innovation in the digital age is different from what it was in previous generations. Simply put, technology has given us powerful new tools, and we need to learn how to use them effectively.

In Part 1, we will see that, contrary to the innovation fairy tales we often hear of single flashes of insight and "Eureka!" moments, innovation is never a single event, and that rather than following a linear path, effective innovators combine the wisdom of diverse fields to synthesize information across domains. If a problem is difficult enough, it needs to borrow from multiple fields of expertise. Innovation, more than anything else, is combination.

Part 2 offers a powerful framework, the "innovation matrix," that will help you map the innovation space and define your innovation approach. It explains that first, we have to ask the right questions— How well is the problem defined? and, How well is the domain defined?—to help determine the innovation strategy that will be most likely to yield results.

It will also give you a set of tools to navigate the often confusing— and jargon laden—world of innovation and find the right path for you and your organization. You will be shown how to access pathbreaking new research, pursue open innovation strategies, develop new business models, and seek out new horizons without forsaking your core business.

Part 3 focuses on the challenges of innovating in the digital age. In earlier generations, we could get by with just a few collaborators with whom we worked closely. Today, however, we must use platforms to access ecosystems of talent, technology, and information in order to tackle the increasingly complex problems we face. Finally, Chapter 9 will explain how, as we enter a new era of innovation, collaboration itself is becoming a source of competitive advantage.

In the Afterword, I show you how to use the principles explained in this book to create your own innovation playbook.

So let's get started.

PART ONE

HOW INNOVATION REALLY HAPPENS

It's more complicated than you may think.

CHAPTER ONE

Innovation Is Never a Single Event

The future is already here—it's just not very evenly distributed yet.
—WILLIAM GIBSON

In 1927 Albert Einstein and Niels Bohr engaged in a series of debates at the fifth Solvay Conference held in Brussels that year. These debates, although largely unnoticed at the time by the general public, would determine the future of physics. It was there that Albert Einstein famously said, "God does not play dice with the universe," to which Niels Bohr retorted, "Einstein, stop telling God what to do."

Bohr's quip was much more than a clever line, but a tipping point in the world of physics toward a quantum world of probabilities rather than the deterministic universe that Einstein preferred. The debate soon enveloped their disciples, including Erwin Schrödinger, Werner Heisenberg, and many others. The concepts being proposed were strange—even outlandish—wild ideas about the possibilities of cats being both dead and alive at the same time and particles taking on their properties only after they were observed. Although few outside the physics community took much notice, for those inside that exclusive club it was like watching the Ali-Frazier fights, a clash of titans that would change the course of history.

And indeed it did, although it would take more than a quarter century. In time, though, engineers understood enough of what Einstein and Bohr were talking about to create some basic components, such as the transistor and, later, the microchip. These, in turn, created their impact though countless other engineers, who figured out how to refine them further, manufacture them in bulk, and use them to make better products.

Even then, it was another decade until the "Mother of All Demos," which wasn't so much of a theoretical breakthrough or a practical invention—it took a team of dozens for Engelbart's version of a "personal computer" to work—as it was a change in conception. Computers at the time were merely calculating machines, but Engelbart saw the potential for them to be interactive devices that could "augment human intellect." He envisioned architects using them to design buildings and professionals using them to design reports.[1] This, like quantum mechanics, seemed outlandish at the time, but is of course a perfectly normal facet of everyday life now.

At Xerox PARC, Engelbart's disciples, Bob Taylor and Alan Kay, were able to create a working version of his vision fairly quickly. In 1973, the Alto was built, and a few thousand were produced, but only Xerox employees used the machines. It wasn't until 1984 that Steve Jobs and Apple launched the Macintosh and the general public was introduced to Engelbart's vision. Jobs was also able to add further refinements, like a much cheaper and more user-friendly mouse and a library of fonts. Jobs's version wasn't just accessible, but actually fun to use!

Like Engelbart, Jobs's great accomplishment was not of engineering, but of vision. While Xerox sought to combine Alto with other innovations—such as the Ethernet and the laser printer—into a big expensive system that would create "the office of the future," Jobs saw a consumer product that people would buy for their homes. Soon after, Microsoft launched its Windows software that could run on cheap PCs, and before people knew it, the PC revolution had arrived.

Yet still, in 1987, when the PC revolution was in full swing, economist Robert Solow remarked, "You can see the computer age everywhere but in the productivity statistics."[2] As we have already seen, it wasn't until the late 1990s—30 years after the "Mother of All Demos"—that we saw a measurable impact from computers. Why so long?

The problem is that computers don't really do anything by themselves. People need to use them to transform the work of their industry or field, and that takes more than just a change in technology—it takes a change in behavior. People have to see how technology can solve their problems. If, for example, an executive is used to a secretary typing his letters and memos, then he is unlikely to care much about an easy-to-use word processing program. And if he believes that crunching numbers is something for the accounting department to do, then a spreadsheet application won't hold any attraction for him either. It is only when people see how technology can add value to their lives that it can truly create an impact.

The computer industry is, of course, unusually complex, and for information technology to make an impact, it needs to be adopted and applied to other complex processes across many different fields and industries. So it might seem that information technology is an exceptional case in which it takes a while for the usefulness of new discoveries to become clear.

But consider the story of Alexander Fleming, a brilliant but sometimes careless scientist, who returned to his lab after a summer holiday in 1928. Upon his arrival, he found that the bacteria cultures he had been growing had been contaminated by a mysterious fungus, which eradicated all the colonies in its path and destroyed weeks of work.

Most people would have simply started over, but Fleming switched his focus from the bacteria to the fungus itself. First, he identified the mold as *Penicillium rubrum** and called the bacteria-killing substance it secreted "penicillin." Then he tested it against a variety of bacteria cultures to make sure the first accidental contamination was not a fluke. Seemingly in a single stroke, Fleming had created the new field of antibiotics. At least, that's how the story is usually told.[3]

The truth, however, is vastly different. After Fleming published the results in a scientific journal, his discovery went largely unnoticed for a full decade. It wasn't until 1939 that a completely different team altogether, led by Howard Florey, a pathologist, and Ernst Chain, a biochemist, discovered Fleming's paper and immediately understood its significance. Florey at the time was the chair of the William Dunn School of Pathology at Oxford and had a large team at his disposal with a variety of skills, including Norman Heatley, who was a whiz at constructing sophisticated apparatus out of everyday odds and ends he found around the lab.

As it turned out, the three had the perfect combination of skills to solve the penicillin problem. Contrary to the myths surrounding

---

* He slightly misidentified the mold. It was actually a close cousin, *Penicillium notatum*.

Alexander Fleming, his discovery couldn't have cured anyone. While the "mold juice" secreted by the penicillin fungus could kill bacteria in the lab, it would have been absolutely useless for treating patients. (Imagine going to a doctor with an infection and being told that he intended to squeeze some "juice" out of a fungus and inject it into you.)

The problem with penicillin was twofold. First, it was notoriously unstable and nobody knew how to isolate, purify, and store it in a stable form. Second, it was very difficult to make in quantity. Chain, a first-rate biochemist, figured out how to solve the first problem and created a stable form of penicillin that could be used in a clinical environment. Heatley then got to work on the second problem, concocting a fermentation apparatus from objects he pulled together from around the lab.

The team then began experimenting on mice that were infected with large doses of the streptococcus bacteria. After 16 hours, all of the 25 mice given no treatment were dead, but 10 days later, 24 out of the 25 treated with penicillin were in perfect health.[4] Given the fact that at the time there was no effective treatment for bacterial infection at all, these were astounding results! Soon Florey and his team began looking for a human subject to test penicillin on.

They found a willing participant in Albert Alexander, a 44-year-old constable who had a severe infection from a scratch he had gotten working in his rose garden. By the time Florey's team found him, he was already at death's door. Yet within a day of receiving penicillin shots, Alexander showed dramatic improvement. His fever came down to normal, the swelling subsided, and he seemed on the way to recovery. Unfortunately, Florey's supply of penicillin was soon exhausted, the infection returned, and Constable Alexander eventually died about a month after treatment began.[5]

Clearly, penicillin had to be produced in massive quantities, and that was far beyond the capabilities of the Oxford lab. It had been a constant struggle for Florey to keep his lab funded for normal operations, much less find additional money for expansion. To make matters worse, World War II had begun, making it even harder to attract funding, despite the incredible results his lab was showing. Florey, on the brink of one of the greatest discoveries of the twentieth century, was unable to get the support he needed to take it any further.

Luckily, he had been sharing his results with someone he knew at the Rockefeller Foundation, and the organization proved willing to provide further funding for research into new fermentation methods that could mass-produce the drug. Florey and Heatley flew to the United States and, working in conjunction with American labs, made two additional discoveries. The first was that fermenting penicillin with corn steep liquor could significantly increase the yield.[6] The second was that they found a strain of the mold, later identified as *Penicillium chrysogenum*, which was vastly more powerful than the one first identified in Fleming's lab.[7] These were major advances, but they still needed access to industrial-scale facilities to produce large supplies on a consistent basis.

Finally, in 1943, with World War II raging, the War Production Board enlisted 21 companies to produce penicillin supplies for the war effort, saving countless thousands of lives. It wasn't until after the war, in 1945—almost two decades after Fleming's initial discovery—that penicillin became available to the general public.

*　*　*　*　*

We tend to think of innovation as arising from a single brilliant flash, but the truth is that it is a drawn-out process involving the discovery of an insight, the engineering of a solution, and then the transformation of an industry or field. That's almost never achieved by one person or even within one organization. To truly understand innovation, we need to break it down into its constituent parts: discovery, engineering, and transformation. Each of these requires distinct expertise, capabilities, and processes, so we need to approach each differently.

Discovering New Insights

Science is a process of discovery and so is often more romantic than practical. As Marie Curie put it, "A scientist in his laboratory is not a mere technician: he is also a child confronting natural phenomena that impress him as though they were fairy tales."[8] Great scientists are essentially great dreamers. That's why until fairly recently scientists were generally men of means. Historically, it was only those who had resources and leisure time that could pursue their passion for discovery. Most scientists, even today, don't seek or expect practical consequences of their work. Rather, they strive to expand horizons.

The typical work product of science is a series of papers and lectures that most people will never read nor hear. Even historic discoveries like the physics of Einstein and Bohr provide no practical benefit at the time they are uncovered. They are explorations, not inventions.

That's one reason that very few businesses invest in fundamental research. Another is known as *the problem of appropriability*. Simply put, a fundamental discovery in a field like quantum mechanics has very broad implications, so it is unlikely that a single firm investing in exploratory research will be able to appropriate all of the benefits from their efforts.

Still, fundamental research is key to successful innovation. To understand how, just look at an iPhone. Sure, it's made by Apple, a profit-seeking business, but take a deeper look and you'll see that almost all of the basic technology came out of federally funded research programs. The basic stored program architecture—the von Neumann architecture—was developed at the Institute for Advanced Study in Princeton to aid the development of the hydrogen bomb. The lithium-ion battery came from research funded by the Department of Energy. GPS and the Internet were both developed by the Department of Defense, as was Siri, the iPhone's intelligent personal assistant. Practically the only thing that wasn't developed by the U.S. government is the World Wide Web, which was invented at CERN, funded by the European Union.[9]

This is no accident, but part of a grander design that has its roots in the run-up to World War II. Vannevar Bush, a prominent academic, engineer, and entrepreneur (he cofounded Raytheon, which today is a $20 billion business), convinced President Roosevelt that bullets and bombs alone would not win the war. He argued that the United States would also have to mobilize its scientists to develop more advanced weaponry. Immediately seeing his point, Roosevelt established the Office of Scientific Research and Development (OSRD) and put Bush in charge.

As head of the OSRD, Vannevar Bush led government into the science business, funding enormous research projects that led to the development of the proximity fuze, radar, and, most famously, the atomic bomb. The agency also had a hand in strong-arming pharmaceutical firms to manufacture penicillin. There's no question that the OSRD programs had a profound, if not decisive, impact on the outcome of World War II.

In 1944, as the outcome of the war became clear, the question arose about what form, if any, scientific funding should take in peacetime. President Roosevelt, just before his death, asked Bush to write a report about how to organize future funding for science. That report, called *Science, The Endless Frontier*, was presented to President Harry Truman in 1945. It proposed the formation of a new government agency to direct government funds for basic research. Bush laid out his reasoning:

> Basic research leads to new knowledge. It provides scientific capital. It creates the fund from which the practical applications of knowledge must be drawn. New products and new processes do not appear full-grown. They are founded on new principles and new conceptions, which in turn are painstakingly developed by research in the purest realms of science.[10]

It was a profound statement. Bush was arguing that industriousness and hard work are not enough to produce prosperity. You also need to uncover new knowledge about how the world works. He also argued, persuasively, that government funding for basic research would be key to national competitiveness, writing, "there must be a stream of new scientific knowledge to turn the wheels of private and public enterprise." His proposal envisioned a partnership of government, academia, and private industry.

Bush noted that most research performed in industry and government was of an applied rather than a theoretical nature. He also argued that without vigorous funding for basic research to expand the frontiers of knowledge, advances in technical applications would be limited, endangering our national security, health, and economic well-being. The architecture he envisioned would fund research at outside institutions, rather than within government or industry. Grants would be given out on a multiyear rather than an annual basis to provide stability, and research would be published openly to ensure dissemination of knowledge. The report led directly to the creation of the National Science Foundation (NSF) and indirectly to other scientific efforts such as the Defense Advanced Research Projects Agency (DARPA), National Institutes of Health (NIH), and research programs at the Department of Energy (DOE).

* * * * *

Today, just about every industry you can imagine has been shaped by Bush's vision. Smartphones, as noted above, are largely built on federally funded technologies, and so are other products of information technology. Most of the blockbuster drugs developed over the last half century stem from research funded by the NIH. Google itself began as an NSF funded project.

So while few of us spend much time thinking about fundamental research, it is absolutely essential to the innovation process. As we will see in Chapter 9, there are new efforts underway to integrate the efforts of research scientists more closely with those of other innovators.

Engineering New Solutions

While researchers expand horizons by discovering new phenomena, engineers harness those phenomena to create novel solutions to important problems. It is at this point that we recognize scientific discoveries as potentially being useful.

Yet the relationship is never direct or one-to-one because useful technologies are, in fact, combinations of ideas. For example, today's computers owe a great debt to Einstein and Bohr, but also to Gödel's theorems, Alan Turing's work on a universal computer, and the information theory of Claude Shannon, just to name a few. Often the string of events is long and tenuous.

An entrepreneur or corporate executive must sift through mountains of research to identify the rare discoveries that can lead to a viable product. Even then, there is an enormous amount of refining to be done. Markets need to be tested, production methods devised, distribution kinks worked out, and even then, most new products end up failing in the marketplace.

How an Obscure Discovery Became a Cancer Breakthrough

To understand how difficult it is to turn a discovery into a marketable product, let's look at cancer immunotherapy, a cutting-edge treatment that the journal *Science* named the "Breakthrough of the Year for 2013."[11] Early results show that it can extend the life of terminally ill cancer patients for years, if not indefinitely. Many go on to live normal lives, seemingly cancer free. Immunotherapy is widely considered to be nothing less than a miracle cure.

It began much less auspiciously, though, as an obscure discovery by some French researchers who, in 1987, found a previously unknown receptor called CTLA-4. An American scientist at the

University of California, Berkeley, James Allison, thought that this newly discovered molecule might figure prominently into what had become his life's work.

As a graduate student, Allison had become enamored with the immune system. "T cells had just been discovered," he told me. "I was just fascinated by the whole idea of it. These cells would just cruise around and kill stuff for you and not hurt you." After receiving his PhD in biochemistry from the University of Texas at Austin in 1973, Allison began to research the mysterious workings of the immune system.

At the time, little was known about how our bodies fight disease, which is what made the discovery of T cells so intriguing. How do these cells decide what to attack and what to leave alone? What causes our bodies to go from a quiet ecosystem, with our own cells peacefully coexisting with millions of symbiotic bacteria that are beneficial to our health, to a war zone with T cell warriors arming up to eradicate unwanted intruders? How do they tell the difference between friend and foe? When Allison first started in the field, nobody knew the answers to any of these questions, which is what made it such an exciting field.

As new discoveries came in, the pieces of the puzzle started to come together. Most of the time, our immune system is largely dormant, with very few T cells in circulation. But when a malicious intruder is detected, it springs into action. One molecule (called B7), acts as an ignition switch and primes the system. Another (called CD28) acts as a gas pedal. Like a racing car coming out of a pit stop, the level of acceleration is massive—our bodies can go from having just a few dozen specialized T cells to hundreds of thousands of them in a matter of days.

Allison's first major success was the discovery of the structure of CD28 (the gas pedal), so the French researcher's discovery of the CTLA-4 receptor, which was similar in structure to CD28, was of particular interest to him. Could it be that the immune system had two gas pedals? Were they used to fight different types of invaders, or did they work together to send the immune system into hyperdrive? These questions were endlessly debated by scientists.

Yet none of it made any sense to Allison. His research showed that the mysterious molecule that the French had discovered didn't appear until after the immune response had already started. If anything, he thought, it's not a gas pedal, but a brake. It seemed to him that it was something our body uses to bring the immune response to a halt. So he took his hunch to the lab and, after his research confirmed it, he published his results in 1992. It turned out to be an enormous insight.

A further breakthrough came in 1994 when Allison's colleague, Sarah Townsend, showed that the B7 ignition switch inhibits tumors. This led Allison to believe that a glitch in our immune system inhibits our ability to fight cancer. He also thought that if he could help the body to calibrate the regulation of T cells, he could treat cancer in a revolutionarily new way.

First, he guessed that you need some tumor cells to die for the immune system to target cancer cells. That would cause the ignition switch to fire and the gas pedal to accelerate the immune response. However, it seemed that the brakes were being applied too early, inhibiting our natural defense's ability to fight the cancer effectively.

So just as he had done his entire life, Allison got started figuring out the problem. He reasoned that "stepping on the gas" by stimulating the immune system would lead to problems, because it would cause T cells to attack everywhere. But if he could just take off the brakes to an immune response already in progress, he might be able to create a positive effect. The results, which he published in 1996, were nothing short of astounding.

The mice that were injected with an antibody that blocked the CTLA-4 "brakes" on the immune system showed a rapid reduction in their tumors, and most of them were still cancer free 70 days later. What's more, the mice he treated showed immunity when injected with new cancer cells. The outcome surprised even Allison himself. "I was expecting it to slow the tumors a little bit, but the tumors completely melted away," he says. It was, obviously, a major breakthrough.

For his entire career, Jim Allison had been happy as a lab scientist. He wasn't seeking fame or fortune. He was just in love with, as he puts it, "figuring things out." A breakthrough of these proportions, however, thrust him into a new role. "I consider myself a basic scientist," he told me, "but when I saw this I said, 'Boy, this thing has got to get translated into an effective treatment.'"

Soon he found himself flying around the country presenting his revolutionary results. He met with scientists at a dozen companies and sometimes was asked back to show his discovery to higher-ups.

Nevertheless, much like Howard Florey's experience with penicillin, he had trouble convincing anyone to fund the translation of his discovery into a usable cure. The answer always came back the same—no. "It was depressing," he told me. "I knew this discovery could make a difference, but nobody wanted to invest in it."

The executives had good reasons for their reticence. Other immunological approaches for cancer had been tried countless times, and they all had failed. What Allison was proposing also ran counter to the more targeted approaches coming into vogue. "We weren't really treating cancer, just fiddling with switches," he says. "The attitude was, 'You're not targeting, you think you're just going to take the brakes off and it's going to work?'" As so often happens with a radical new innovation, Allison's approach was so different that many in the field had trouble accepting it.

Another reason pharmaceutical companies were hesitant to invest in Allison's research is that drug development is a very risky business. In 2014, only 45 drugs were approved by the FDA.[12] Of those, McKinsey estimates, only one-third will be successful in the marketplace.[13] That's after hundreds of millions were already spent on clinical trials and millions more spent to market drugs.

So it's understandable that pharmaceutical companies would be wary, even with a very promising discovery like Allison's. After nearly three years of trying to sell his idea, not to mention the decades he had spent building his reputation as a top-notch research scientist, Allison was coming up empty. Finally, in 1999, a small biotech company in Princeton, Medarex, saw potential and agreed to invest in his approach. It proved to be a wise investment.

* * * * *

By 2004, Allison had moved to the Memorial Sloan Kettering Cancer Center in New York City, where, just a few floors down, clinical trials for a drug called Ipilimumab, or "Ippy" for short, that had been developed based on his research was now in Phase 1 testing.

Around the same time, Sharon Belvin, just 22 years old, found that she had a very aggressive form of skin cancer.[14] Despite being in otherwise good health—she was an avid runner—the prognosis was devastating. The melanoma had already spread to her lungs, and doctors only gave her a 50 percent chance of survival. As she ran through the usual treatment options of surgery, chemotherapy, and radiation, nothing seemed to slow the cancer's spread.

It was then that Belvin's physician, Jedd Wolchok, suggested that she participate in the clinical trial testing "Ippy." Out of options, she agreed without hesitation. She began 90-minute treatments every three weeks. The side effects were so mild that she said to her husband, "Why could they have not started me on this, rather than making me suffer through chemo?"

After just four rounds of treatment, the tumor in her lung had shrunk by 60 percent. Some months later, she found out that she was in remission. Today, Belvin is in her midthirties, a mother of two, a personal trainer, and cancer free.

* * * * *

When Dr. Wolchok first told her that she was in remission, he asked Belvin if she wanted to meet the man who had invented the cure that saved her life. She said yes, and the doctor called Jim Allison to ask him to come downstairs. As soon as Allison walked into the emotionally charged room, it became clear why Wolchok had invited him. His eyes immediately filled with tears.

It was a singular moment, but not a single event. Dr. Allison's insight didn't come to him in a single flash but was the product of decades of studying how the immune system functions. As he described it to me, the idea that you could cure cancer by taking the brakes off of the immune system was something that he slowly put together as the disparate pieces of evidence came in. It arose out of not only his own efforts, but those of colleagues, postdoctoral students, and many others. In fact, one analysis of his work concluded that it relied on work conducted by 7,000 scientists at 5,700 institutions over a hundred-year period.[15]

In 2011, Ipilimumab, the drug based on Allison's work, was approved by the FDA, and it is now marketed under the brand name Yervoy by Bristol-Myers Squibb, which acquired Medarex for $2.4 billion in 2009, largely on the strength of Allison's idea. It is saving the lives of terminal patients who, just a few years ago, would have little hope.

Today, the field of cancer immunotherapy that Allison spawned has become well established, with teams of doctors around the country working to find other switches they can flip to unleash our bodies' natural defenses on cancer cells. One of these approaches, which injects polio virus into patients' brains to stimulate an immune response against a particularly aggressive form of cancer called glioblastoma, was featured on *60 Minutes*. It has since been fast-tracked for FDA approval.[16] Another recent trial showed that combining Allison's Ipilimumab with a similar drug boosted response from under 30 percent to almost 60 percent.

Jim Allison is now one of the most celebrated scientists on the planet. He has won a Lasker Award, a Breakthrough Prize, and is considered to be a shoo-in for a Nobel Prize. Yet the work is far from over.

Cancer immunotherapy has only been approved for a small number of cancers, and many patients do not respond to the treatment. Why? Nobody knows yet. It also remains to be seen if immunotherapy can be combined with other approaches to treat a wider range of cancers. Where once Allison stood alone, he is now joined by thousands of other scientists and physicians. As is so often the case, one innovation can open the door for many others.

Allison has since moved to MD Anderson Cancer Center in Houston, where immunotherapy has become a key aspect of its "moonshots" program. "Immunology is now the fourth pillar of cancer therapy, along with surgery, radiation, and chemotherapy," he explains. The problem is that we've got to understand how these work together in combination. That's what we're doing at MD Anderson. We now know that we actually can cure cancer."

* * * * *

Of course, the pharmaceutical industry is intensively regulated, and with good reason. Before the FDA, a multitude of concoctions were marketed as miracle cures. Even today, there are many "alternative medical clinics," located outside the United States, that promise miraculous results to desperate people. Still, the stringent drug standards clearly slow down innovation.

So let's look at Google's efforts to build autonomous cars, which don't face the same restrictions. Google didn't begin the effort from scratch. Rather the project grew out of the DARPA-funded Grand Challenge, which invited researchers from around the world to build self-driving cars for a $1 million prize. Google hired the winning team of the 2005 Grand Challenge to develop a commercial version.

Yet operating in an everyday environment is profoundly different than in a contest. So for more than a decade Google has been refining the car further to operate in traffic and identify obstacles and pedestrians. To date, its autonomous vehicles have driven over two million miles and is now being tested in four U.S. cities. Still, the company doesn't expect to start selling its cars to the public for at least a few more years.

Even then, there are still many questions to be answered. Who will buy a self-driving car? How much will they be willing to pay? How will Google differentiate itself from competitors like Tesla, Uber, and Mercedes-Benz that are also working on versions of the technology? Even a breakthrough product needs to find a market and demonstrate its value before it can be considered a successful innovation. Remember, Xerox really did create the "office of the future" with its Star system; it just wasn't able to turn it into a profitable business.

Clearly, it takes more than a single big idea to change the world. As Scott Berkun has put it, "Big thoughts are fun to romanticize, but it's many small insights coming together that bring big ideas into the world."[17]

Transforming Industry and Society

Even when an innovative solution is developed, the job is still not complete. For an idea to truly have an impact, it needs to become widely adopted, which means that it needs to replace an existing model already in use if it is to transform an entire industry or field. And that process of transformation is every bit as challenging and important as the discovery and innovation that precede it.

To understand why it takes so long to go from an engineered solution to a tangible impact on society, consider the case of electricity, the basic principles of which were discovered by Michael Faraday and James Clerk Maxwell in the early 1800s, but it wasn't until the end of that century that those principles began to bear fruit.

Thomas Edison invented his famous lightbulb in 1879, and three years later opened his Pearl Street Station in lower Manhattan. It was the first commercial electrical distribution plant, and by 1884 it was servicing over 500 homes. Until that point, electrical light was mostly a curiosity. While a few of the mighty elite could afford to install generators in their homes—J. P. Morgan was one of the very first—it was well out of the reach of most people. Electrical transmission changed all that. In the years to come, much of the country became electrified.

Still, as Stanford economist Paul David explained in a highly cited paper,[18] electricity didn't have a measurable impact on productivity until the early 1920s. Until then, to paraphrase Robert Solow, you could see electricity everywhere but in the productivity statistics. Once again, the evidence clearly demonstrates that it takes a lot more than a single big idea to change the world.

The first version of any innovation is always inefficient, and Edison's power station was no different. While electrical lighting had a clear qualitative advantage over gas lighting—it was brighter, cleaner, and much safer—getting costs down was a problem from the start. Running copper wires under city streets, for example, was expensive. So Edison was constantly tinkering with his power station and distribution system to increase efficiency.

As he did this, George Westinghouse acquired the rights to Nikola Tesla's patent for a competing system that ran on AC current and could transmit power farther and cheaper, using newly designed transformers that would "step up" voltage that could run over thinner, cheaper wires. The voltage would then be "stepped down" before it entered residences and businesses.

That's what began the famous "war of the currents."[19] In the ensuing years, Edison and Westinghouse fought a vicious battle for supremacy in power distribution, and both worked feverishly to hone their operations, improve quality, and lower costs. In the end, Edison was forced to merge with competitor Thomson-Houston to form the General Electric Company.

Yet as the battle was raging, prices dropped precipitously and distribution improved. Soon power was being transported hundreds of miles from large-scale power plants to end users. This ability to increase scale reduced costs further, and by 1910, electric power was available to just about any business that wanted it. Still, electricity did not progress in a vacuum but had to compete with existing technologies that were already in use. There were many thousands of factories running on ordinary steam engines at the time. If electrical power was to be adopted, it needed to become financially viable.

The factories of the time were not like those we see today. They were multistory buildings organized around a massive central steam engine that would drive a single shaft, which would then turn a number of belts running at the same speed. These belts, in turn, would drive the machines attended by the workers. The most obvious solution would be to replace the steam engine with a modern electrical motor. But this would only make sense if the benefits would outweigh the costs of junking the old engine and installing an electrical motor. Often, they did not, and adoption for many years was fairly slow.

When new factories were built, however, the calculation was somewhat different. In those cases, the owners of the factory would only need to pay for the electrical motor plus the difference between electrical and steam power. As the new technology became cheaper, that became an easier decision to make, and soon most new factories were using electrical power.

It took some time, but eventually it became clear that factories could be designed in ways that would make better use of electrical power. First, instead of one large motor, smaller ones could be designed to work with each machine. This was not only more energy efficient, it obviated the need to build braces to support a huge shaft running through the building, cutting factory construction costs dramatically. Also, because each machine had its own motor, the entire factory didn't have to stop if one machine broke down or needed maintenance. Without the need for machines to be close to the central shaft, single-story factories soon became the norm, reducing construction costs even further.

But perhaps the most important change was how machines were arranged in factories. Now managers were free to design workspaces that optimized each task and able to experiment and improve production processes. That, in turn, allowed them to share information about what methods and techniques worked best, and efficiency was propelled further. This created a need for more highly trained workers who could make decisions and take responsibility. Firms that adopted new practices expanded faster while those that clung to the old ways went out of business. Manufacturing would never be the same again.

* * * * *

As Robert Gordon explained in *The Rise and Fall of American Growth*,[20] by the 1920s—40 years after Edison opened the electrical plant on Pearl Street—the revolution that Faraday, Edison, and others had wrought was in full bloom. Productivity was soaring and would continue to do so for a half century.

Yet more efficient factories were just the start. The impact from complementary technologies was even greater. For example, household appliances vastly reduced the backbreaking work that needed to be done in the home, allowing women to enter the workforce.

Air conditioners opened up the American South to industrialization. Refrigeration greatly reduced spoilage and improved diets. It also allowed for farms to ship their produce across the country. Radio—and later television—transformed how information flowed, as did telephones. Average people would learn about—and could act upon—even distant events in nearly real time.

By 1940—60 years after Edison opened his Pearl Street Station and more than a century after Michael Faraday invented the dynamo and the electric motor—the revolution was complete. Households had access to the full complement of modern conveniences that we do today. Six years later, the first digital computer—the ENIAC—was built and a new revolution began.

* * * * *

We tend to think of innovation as a single event, but that's never true. While Edison gained fame and fortune for his inventions—and rightly so—there were countless others, from factory architects to managers and accountants to workers themselves, who created a revolution around electricity. As much as we may try to identify a single person or action, what we find is an ecosystem of literally thousands of people.

Without Faraday and his dynamo and electric motor, the inventions of Edison, Westinghouse, and Tesla would not be possible. Those solutions, in turn, needed to be applied to specific problems, like factories, home appliances, radio, and television to create measurable impacts on society. Computers, in this light, are merely the next step in the continuum.

Now we can understand why it took so long for information technology to show up in the productivity statistics. Even though computers were widely available in the 1980s, enterprises themselves needed to be transformed around them. Executives used to dictating memos to their secretaries and getting numbers crunched by the accounting department needed to develop new habits and channel them effectively. New processes needed to be devised, new skills needed to be learned, and people needed to change their conceptions of how to do their jobs.

So, if we want to understand how innovation really happens, we can't look at single events and attempt to draw conclusions from them. To truly create an impact, we need to tap into entire ecosystems of discovery, engineering, and transformation.

Clearly, none of these elements can exist in isolation. And even within the specialized fields that make up the rich innovation tapestry, disparate threads must come together. Innovation arises, in fact, when the right people, ideas, and events combine to create something truly new and useful. If we want to innovate effectively, we need to look beyond linear sequences of events and take a broader view. Rather than striving to dream things up out of thin air, we need to look around us to see what we can combine to create novel solutions to important problems.

If a problem is difficult enough, it needs to borrow from multiple fields of expertise. Innovation, more than anything else, is combination. So when anybody offers us the "one true path" to innovation, we should always be suspicious. Innovation is, quite clearly, not a path but an ecosystem.

CHAPTER TWO

Innovation Is Combination

*Combinatory play seems to be the essential
feature in productive thought.*

—ALBERT EINSTEIN

The story of Fleming's discovery of innovation is particularly compelling because it aligns so well with the common conception of how discoveries happen: a chance observation, a flash of insight, and Eureka!—the world is transformed. We've already seen that the process is far more complex than that, but if we look a little closer, we'll see that even the discovery itself owes a lot to combining ideas.

To understand how, consider the case of Ignaz Semmelweis,[1] a young doctor working in a maternity ward in Vienna General Hospital in the 1840s, who noticed a much higher mortality rate from childbed fever in one clinic than another. Through some smart deductive reasoning, he figured out that the doctors in one clinic were delivering babies straight after working with cadavers, while the other clinic was mostly staffed with midwives who did not perform autopsies. He surmised that the cadavers must have been contaminating the doctors in some way. To test the theory, he instituted a strict regime of hand washing and immediately saw miraculous results. Mortality rates came crashing down.

Alas, from there, things did not go well. Doctors, like many high-status professionals, are often not receptive to changing their habits. Too make matters worse, his hand washing idea conflicted with the prevailing "miasma theory" of the day, which held that an imbalance

21

of humours combined with "bad air" caused disease, rather than bacteria and other germs. So the medical establishment, rather than showering Semmelweis with adulation for showing that childbed fever could be greatly reduced by the simple practice of hand washing, castigated him mercilessly. He was, simply put, treated like a quack, and it drove him to madness. Eventually, Semmelweis was committed to a mental hospital, where he died in 1865, ironically of an infection he contracted there.

It was only after his death that, through the work of scientists like Louis Pasteur and Joseph Lister, the germ theory of disease came into wide acceptance. That, in effect, was why Alexander Fleming was studying bacteria in the first place and, when he discovered penicillin by accident, he found it important enough to study the bacteria-killing mold and publish his results. If not for the work of Pasteur, Lister, and others to establish a new paradigm, Fleming's work would not have been possible.

In *The Structure of Scientific Revolutions*,[2] Thomas Kuhn called the discoveries like Fleming's "normal science." He wrote:

> When the individual scientist can take a paradigm for granted, he need no longer, in his major works, attempt to build his field anew, starting from first principles and justifying the use of each concept introduced. This can be left to the writer of textbooks. . . . Normal science consists in the actualization of that promise, an actualization achieved by extending the knowledge of those facts that the paradigm displays as particularly revealing, by increasing the extent of those facts and the paradigm's predictions, and by further articulation of the paradigm itself.[3]

And that's exactly what we saw in the development of penicillin. Semmelweis's work didn't have any relevance within the paradigm of miasma theory, which is why the medical community was so reluctant to accept hand washing in hospitals. To do so would have called into question the entire body of accepted knowledge at the time. Yet when the paradigm of germ theory became accepted, the new facts that Fleming discovered not only fit with the theory, but extended it by supporting its predictions. Later, Florey and Chain extended it further by producing a workable version of penicillin and beginning clinical experiments.

Creating a new paradigm is enormously difficult because it requires us to throw out ideas we thought were working and making a positive impact. For doctors to accept germ theory, they would have to admit to themselves that they weren't doing their patients any good and, in fact, were killing them. That's a hard pill to swallow and, as Kuhn explains, before a new paradigm can be accepted, a period of professional crisis ensues:

> Because it demands large-scale paradigm destruction and major shifts in the problems and techniques of normal science, the emergence of new theories is generally preceded by a period of pronounced professional insecurity. As one might expect, that insecurity is generated by the persistent failure of the puzzles of normal science to come out as they should. Failure of existing rules is the prelude to a search for new ones.[4]

Again, that's exactly what we saw happen in the case of Semmelweis and childbed fever. According to the miasma theory, the women were dying due to environmental factors. But it increasingly became clear that no such factors were common to the women dying from childbed fever. If anything, the epidemics seemed to be tied to certain doctors rather than any environmental factor. The facts simply didn't match the accepted framework.

Kuhn explained that at first these mismatches are seen as "special cases" and professionals in the field find a way to work around them. Rules, after all, tend to have exceptions. But as these types of anomalies build up over time, the existing paradigm comes under increasing pressure and a new one eventually has to emerge, usually pushed forward by a new generation of professionals not tied to the old model. This is what Kuhn called "revolutionary science."

To get a better understanding of how this works, let's look at three significant paradigm shifts that fit the description of "revolutionary science": Darwin's natural selection, Einstein's relativity, and Watson and Crick's discovery of the structure of DNA.

Darwin and the Theory of Natural Selection

Charles Darwin was born in 1809 to a prominent family where much was expected of him. His paternal grandfather, Erasmus Darwin, was a noted physician and intellectual who produced significant works on botany and zoology. He was also considered an important poet and even wrote a famous verse about evolution, the field for which his grandson would achieve renown. His mother's side of the family was no less accomplished. Josiah Wedgwood, Darwin's maternal grandfather, was an industrialist who created the famous ceramics empire that still bears his name. His father, Robert Darwin, like his grandfather, was a prominent physician.

Throughout his early life, Charles never seemed to able to devote himself to a single field of study. When young Charles was 16, he became an apprentice to his father before attending the University of Edinburgh Medical School, but he found the medical lectures boring and grew queasy at the sight of blood. His disappointed father suggested the church as an alternative and, with the object of becoming a clergyman, Darwin entered Christ's Church at Cambridge in 1828. There he remained a mediocre student but became an enthusiastic amateur naturalist. Much like at Edinburgh, he never showed much interest in his formal studies.

He did, however, show an insatiable curiosity about the natural world. At Edinburgh, Darwin became friendly with a professor of zoology, Robert Grant, and joined a group of students who gathered and classified specimens called the Plinian Society. Later, at Christ's College, he became an avid insect collector and geologist and even had some of his findings published. While at Christ's Church, he also struck up a close friendship with John Stevens Henslow, a prominent geologist and botanist who introduced him to Robert FitzRoy, the 26-year-old captain of the *HMS Beagle*.

Fitzroy, as it happened, was looking for a naturalist for his upcoming voyage. There were three requirements for the job: the person in question would have to have some expertise in geology, a background in zoology, and would have to come from a family of means, as the post came without salary. Darwin fit the bill and was accepted on the voyage, which sailed in 1831. For once, his extracurricular activities led to an opportunity rather than a disappointment.

* * * * *

At the time, there were two prevailing theories about evolution. The first was the orthodox, biblical view. Yet despite the predominance of the biblical paradigm, there was a growing suspicion that life evolved over time. Much as Kuhn described, it was getting harder and harder to neatly fit all the new facts being uncovered into the existing biblical paradigm. So a variety of scientists began to propose alternative theories.

Darwin's voyage came at an auspicious time for a new theory of evolution. There was increasing suspicion in the scientific community that something was amiss, yet there remained no plausible explanation. Darwin himself had mixed feelings about the subject and, it's important to remember, he undertook his mission on the *HMS Beagle* to observe, not to theorize. His first notes on natural selection came after the journey, not before or during. A Silicon Valley entrepreneur today might even call Darwin's famous theory a "pivot."

While on the voyage, Darwin and FitzRoy, the Captain of the *HMS Beagle,* made fast friends, probably in no small part due to the similarity in their ages. At the beginning of the voyage, the young captain gave the young naturalist a book, *Principles of Geology,* by Charles Lyell. The book advocated a new view, *uniformitarianism,* that contradicted orthodox biblical doctrine. While the prevailing view at the time was that the earth had formed a long time ago, Lyell made the case that not only had it formed gradually, but it was still being shaped.

It was Lyell's influence, along with the amazing variation in the wildlife he saw on the voyage, that got Darwin thinking seriously about evolution.

* * * * *

When Darwin returned to England in 1836, he began a series of notebooks to record his ideas about evolution. A chance breakthrough came when he happened to read the work of an economist, Thomas Malthus, who observed that populations grow faster than the means to support them. That's what convinced him that all living things are perpetually locked in a struggle for survival. In Darwin's own words:

> In October 1838, that is, fifteen months after I had begun my systematic enquiry, I happened to read for amusement Malthus on *Population,* and being well prepared to appreciate the struggle for existence which everywhere goes on from long and continued observation of animals and plants, it at once struck me that under these circumstances favorable variations would tend to be preserved and unfavorable ones to be destroyed. The result of this would be the formation of a new species. *Here, then I had at last got a theory from which to work.* [emphasis added][5]

This last element, a paper on economics and not biology, was the tipping point. In the struggle to survive, those with advantageous variations would pass those traits to their offspring. And if, according to Lyell, the world was in a constant state of flux, new species would form in response to changes in environment.

So by 1838, all the elements of the theory were in place. It is a testament to both his thoroughness and to the controversy surrounding the subject that Darwin didn't publicly reveal his results till two decades later. Darwin published *On the Origin of Species*, the book that explained his theory of natural selection, in November of 1859.

Darwin's book was widely read and hotly debated. Finally, there was a workable theory that could account for the evolutionary hypothesis. However, it became one of the most important scientific theories in history not by its own merits alone, but through combination with other ideas.

First, Gregor Mendel's work on genetics both extended and strengthened Darwin's theory. Mendel had published the results from his experiments in 1865, just shortly after Darwin published *The Origin of the Species*, but much like Fleming's paper on penicillin, it went largely unnoticed until early in the twentieth century, when the same principles were rediscovered by other scientists.

Later, Darwin's ideas were combined with Fleming's invention of antibiotics when it became clear that bacteria were evolving resistance to penicillin—a problem that continues to this day—and new drugs needed to be developed. Thanks to Darwin, scientists had a very clear paradigm to aid them in finding a solution. Darwin's ideas are also combined with computer science to develop genetic algorithms for use in applications designed to find optimal solutions to complex problems, such as logistics software..

So basically, anytime that you take antibiotics or shop at a major retailer like Walmart you are making use of Darwin's theory combined with something else.

Einstein and His "Miracle Year"

While today his name is synonymous with genius, as a child growing up in Germany, Einstein was unexceptional. He was neither a prodigy nor a dullard, neither rich nor poor. He was intelligent and did well in school, especially in math (despite legends to the contrary, he never failed math or any other subject). However, he was mostly just a normal child from a normal middle class home, if a bit quirky. There was nothing to suggest that he would grow up to be much different than millions of other bright young boys.[6]

Much like Darwin, the young Einstein showed an insatiable curiosity about a variety of topics. He devoured all of the math and science books that he could get his hands on and read important works on philosophy. Although impenetrable even for most adults, Einstein had an immediate affinity for Immanuel Kant's *Critique of Pure Reason* and worked his way through all 800 dense pages. That led him to the works of Scottish philosopher David Hume and others.

He was later to cite the profound effect that Hume would have on his work, especially with regard to relativity.[7] Hume was so skeptical of our ability to understand the universe that he even described the notion that the sun will rise tomorrow as no more provable than the possibility that it won't. One of Einstein's greatest strengths as a scientist was that he was able to discard accepted paradigms when they got in the way of solving a problem.

What was most important about Einstein's youth is that he engaged in an intriguing thought experiment. He imagined what it would be like to ride a beam of light. It was the kind of fantasy that is common in teenagers. If he was born a century later, we can imagine a young Einstein going to Star Trek conventions and learning to speak Klingon. What was not so common, however, was that he continued to think about the idea for a decade and, as we will see, the childhood fantasy would culminate in one of the greatest scientific discoveries in history.

★ ★ ★ ★ ★

Upon graduation from high school, Einstein entered Zurich Polytechnic. Although no longer a child, Einstein still had not given up his fascination of riding on a beam of light. Now a physics student, he began to study the properties of light seriously, which led him to the work of James Clerk Maxwell, the famous Scottish scientist who, in 1864, published his famous equations on electromagnetism. It was these that established that electricity, magnetism, and light were all equivalent phenomena and described their behavior.

Unfortunately, the young Einstein's interest in Maxwell's revolutionary ideas, combined with his natural rebelliousness, led him into conflict with his professor, Heinrich Weber, who favored a much more traditional approach. The antagonism between the two resulted in Einstein graduating near the bottom of his class and, Einstein later suspected, led to his difficulty in finding an academic job after he had finished his coursework.

After he graduated from Zurich Polytechnic in 1900, Einstein entered a dark period. Unable to find work, he spent much of his time drinking coffee and discussing philosophy with friends at meetings they called the "Olympia Academy." Einstein's letters during this time showed enormous anguish. In a letter to his sister in 1898, he wrote:

> What depresses me most is the misfortune of my poor parents who have not had a happy moment for so many years. What further hurts me deeply is that as an adult man, I have to look on without being able to do anything. I am nothing but a burden to my family. . . . It would be better off if I were not alive at all.[8]

Finally, in 1902 Einstein found a job at the Swiss patent office. His father had died earlier that same year, before there was even a hint that his son would amount to anything more than a midlevel civil servant. Yet if the elder Einstein had lived just a few years longer, he would have seen his son change the world. In 1905 Einstein would unleash a series of papers on the world that were so astounding—and paradigm shifting—that it is now referred to as his "miracle year."

$$\ast \quad \ast \quad \ast \quad \ast \quad \ast$$

Einstein's first "miracle year" paper, published in March 1905, argued that light was made up of discrete packets called quanta. Until then, it was thought that light traveled exclusively in waves. It was this paper that created the study of quantum mechanics (a field that Einstein, ironically, could never bring himself to accept) and would unleash a century of amazing discoveries that continues to this day. What made it even more miraculous is that the paper contained no facts that were not well established in the physics community at the time. It was a product of pure insight.

The topic Einstein's paper discussed was *black body radiation*. In 1901, just four years before Einstein's miraculous year, Max Planck made a breakthrough by describing the phenomenon with a simple formula: $E = h\nu$, which introduced the strange and indecipherable quantity known as Planck's constant.

What is interesting here is Planck's explanation of the constant. He described the energy as being *quantized*, meaning that it was broken into discrete parts, but regarded it as a mathematical convenience, not a physical explanation. Planck still strongly believed that light was purely a wavelike phenomenon, and so did the rest of the physics community. It was an established paradigm.

Besides Planck's constant, there was another recent discovery that figured into Einstein's thinking. Philipp Lenard, who had been studying cathode rays, noticed that they passed through most materials easily. However, when projected at dense metals they would cause electrons to fly off. He also observed that at higher frequencies more electrons would scatter, but higher intensities would only cause the electrons to fly out at greater speed. This implied that cathode rays were made up of particles, not of waves as Planck and others believed.

We know this phenomenon as the *photoelectric effect*, and it explains how plants create energy in the food we eat and how we get sunburned at the beach. We see it at work all around us but don't really notice it. For instance, we can feel heat from low frequency infrared radiation, but it won't darken our skin or give us skin cancer. Yet when we lie out on the beach we can get sunburned from the ultraviolet rays even if it isn't very hot that day. It's the type of radiation rather than how strong it is that creates the effect.

Einstein's great insight was that Planck and Lenard were talking about the same thing. He showed that Planck's constant also applied to Lenard's cathode rays. From there it was relatively simple to show that what Planck had thought was a simple mathematical constant is actually a physical reality. Light doesn't travel *as if* it was broken up into discrete little packets of energy, but is *actually* made up of discrete little packets of energy that Einstein called *quanta*.

It's hard to read the last sentence and not ask, "What's the big deal?" Einstein really hadn't *discovered* anything, at least not in the sense that Columbus *discovered* America. Not only did he not make any new observations, but the observations he discussed were well known and actively discussed among physicists. Planck's constant and Lenard's photoelectric effect were major discoveries—both would win Nobel Prizes—not obscure facts buried in the footnotes of some little-known journal. The evidence was there for anyone to see.

Here we see the true genius of Einstein—and the influence that David Hume's skepticism had on his work. Everybody else was bound by the earlier paradigm and convinced that electromagnetic radiation was a purely wavelike phenomenon. Einstein was the only one who dared to ask whether what everybody thought to be true was, in fact, false.

In effect, by being able to see past the earlier paradigm, he was the only one who *imagined* that there could be quanta. From there, he just needed to go through the evidence and check his facts, ask himself some further questions, and check facts some more. Any one of hundreds of physicists could have done the work, but it took Einstein's genius to recognize that there was work to be done.

* * * * *

By identifying quanta, Einstein brought about a revolution in physics that continues to this day. However, he still had not received his doctorate, which is why the next paper was far more conventional. He devised a method to determine the number of molecules in a liquid, where before it had only been possible to do so for gases. While his previous attempts at a dissertation had failed, this one succeeded, and he became Dr. Einstein (although amazingly, he still wouldn't secure an academic position until four years later, in 1909, when he had already become a celebrated scientist).

A few weeks after his dissertation, Einstein firmly established once and for all the existence of atoms and molecules (at the time, it was still a matter of some debate). Again, his method was purely theoretical, using information that was available to anyone at the time.

Before the year was halfway over, Einstein had earned his doctorate, changed the fundamental understanding of electromagnetism, and proved the existence of atoms. If he had stopped there, his accomplishments would surely have won him a place in history. But all of that paled in comparison to his fourth and final paper that year, which would change the way we view the very fabric of the universe—his special theory of relativity.

* * * * *

Relativity was not an altogether novel concept. Copernicus and Galileo discussed it in the sixteenth century. A decade before Einstein published his famous paper, in 1895, the Dutch physicist Hendrik Lorentz used Maxwell's equations to form a theory that argued that time and space might not be quite absolute. The term "principle of relativity" was mentioned in 1898 by Henri Poincaré.

So, once again, the basic ideas that led to Einstein's great discovery were very much in the air. Even he would later say that if he hadn't come up with his theory of relativity, someone else would have. Still, no one else seemed to be able to break free of the existing paradigm that time and space were constant, stable quantities (and most people even today are still unaware that they are not).

In retrospect, the concept of relativity is fairly straightforward, especially to one who spent 10 years thinking about what it would be like to ride a beam of light.

> ▸ A boy riding a beam of light would also see light.
> ▸ If Maxwell's equations were accurate, then light travels at a constant speed.
> ▸ So the light he saw wouldn't be able to just stand still.
> ▸ Speed is the movement through space over time.
>
> *Therefore, if the speed of light is constant, then time and space must be relative.*

As strange as it may appear, relativity is something that we experience all the time without realizing it. When we travel on a plane at roughly half the speed of sound, we can carry on conversations as we normally would. Sound seems to travel the same way when we fly as it does when we are on the ground. What Einstein did was show how far-reaching the consequences really are that time and space are not absolute, but relative quantities that can change.

One consequence of Einstein's realization is that as things speed up and time slows down, objects contract and get heavier. This revelation led Einstein to realize a further consequence of his new theory: if the energy of motion was converted into mass, then energy and mass must be equivalent. After he sent off his paper, he added a new section that described this relationship mathematically according to Maxwell's equations governing electromagnetism. The result is an equation that has come to symbolize the power of physics itself: $E = mc^2$.

* * * * *

Clearly, Einstein was a master of combination. He took theories of scientists like Maxwell, Planck, Brown, and Lenard, filtered them through Hume's skepticism, and then applied his own incredibly active imagination to show that ideas that most scientists regarded as impossible were, in fact, true.

It's also clear that Einstein's ideas, combined with others, have made much of our modern world possible. As we saw in the last chapter, our basic computer technology is based on the ideas of Einstein, combined with those of Bohr and others. GPS satellites need to be calibrated according to Einstein's relativity equations, so whenever you use your smartphone to get you where you're going, you have Einstein to thank. As string theorist and popular author Michio Kaku has pointed out, these days even generals at the Pentagon need to be briefed on relativity.[9]

Watson, Crick, and the Discovery of DNA

When James Watson met Francis Crick at Cambridge University in 1951, it would prove to be one of the most effective combinations in history.

The two couldn't have been more different. Watson, an American prodigy born in Chicago, was only 23, but entered college at the tender age of 15 and had already earned his PhD. He also had done important postdoc work on bacteriophages (viruses that insert themselves into the genes of bacteria). Crick, an English native from Northampton, was more of a late bloomer. Already 35 years old, he originally earned his PhD in physics but had switched to biology and was still a graduate student. Nevertheless, when by chance they were assigned an office together, the two hit it off. As Crick would later write, "He was the first person I had met who saw biology the way I did. . . . I decided that genetics was the really essential part, what the genes were and what they did."[10]

In a sense, their journey together had begun a year before, when Linus Pauling announced his discovery of the alpha helix—the three-dimensional geometry of the protein keratin, using a new technique of x-ray diffraction.[11] It was this breakthrough that, through a strange confluence of events, would help bring Watson and Crick together and guide them to make a discovery of historic proportions.

Most of the compounds we learn about in high school chemistry are fairly simple. They contain only a handful of atoms that fit together neatly, guided by fairly straightforward interactions among electrons and protons. So H_2O, the formula for water, implies a bent V shape as the much larger oxygen atoms push the far more diminutive hydrogen atoms closer together.

Proteins, however, are almost impossibly complex. They form long chains out of smaller molecules called amino acids, creating elaborate twists and turns as they do. It is their complicated structure that allows proteins to provide such a wide array of functions in living organisms. Some, like hydrolases, function as enzymes that break down food in our digestive system. Others, like hemoglobin, transport other molecules, like oxygen, around our bodies. Keratin is a structural protein that makes up our hair and nails and also forms a tough outer layer that protects our skin cells.

For years, Pauling had been making models of what keratin might look like on an atomic level, but he failed to identify a geometry that agreed with what the fuzzy x-ray photographs were telling him. Finally, in 1948, as he lay sick in bed with a bad cold while serving as a visiting professor at Oxford, Pauling had an epiphany.

He imagined a spiral staircase structure—a helix—in which the long molecule twisted around itself. Although it seemed unlikely, his gut told him that it fit all the data he had been collecting on keratin over the years. To confirm his suspicions, he traveled to Cavendish Laboratory at Cambridge, which had the world's most sophisticated x-ray crystallography center. He published his paper on the alpha helix after he got home to Pasadena, California, on February 28, 1951. Pauling would be awarded the Nobel Prize for his work in 1954.

* * * * *

It was in this environment that Watson met Crick at Cavendish. They were both convinced that DNA held the key to the genetic code. At the time, this notion was far from accepted, but scientists had begun to suspect that DNA was the central player.

Two other scientists, Maurice Wilkins and Rosalind Franklin, were doing pathbreaking work in x-ray crystallography at King's College, London, which is what drew Watson to nearby Cambridge. And Pauling's work on proteins had shown that unraveling the mysteries of complex molecules was possible.

But Pauling had also given them something more—his method. Rather than spending all of his time in the laboratory, Pauling used his imagination to build models based on what was already known about the protein. He would then go to the x-ray crystallography evidence to see if the geometrical structure he had dreamed up conformed to the images made from the reflections of the x-rays bouncing off the molecule. It was a far cry from the step-by-step process that most scientists preferred, but Watson and Crick felt that it fit them—and the problem at hand—to a tee. Crick would later write:

> What Pauling did show us was that exact and careful model building could embody constraints that the final answer had in any case to satisfy. Sometimes this could lead to the correct structure, using only a minimum of then direct experimental [x-ray] evidence. This was the lesson that we learned and that Rosalind Franklin and Maurice Wilkins failed to appreciate in attempting to solve the structure of DNA.[12]

They also had each other and their complementary talents. Watson was an expert on the logic of cellular processes and had a good feel for how a genetic material would have to function. Crick, on the other hand, with his background in mathematical physics, was able to make sense of the vague images that x-ray crystallography produced. Most of all, they were well suited to each other, both happy to spend countless hours discussing hunches and endless possibilities.

At the time, many facts were known about DNA. It was well established, for example, that it was made of long chains of deoxyribose sugar molecules with phosphate groups attached. These phosphate groups, in turn, came in two flavors: purines—adenine (A) and guanine (G)—and pyrimidines—thymine (T) and cytosine (C). So, just as Pauling had done with keratin, the two got to work grouping the various elements together into geometric structures that would abide by the physical constraints of the chemical bonds, the logic of what was known about cellular processes, and the evidence from the x-ray crystallography images. The pair tested countless possibilities, but nothing seemed to fit all the data.

They unearthed an additional clue when they came across the work of Erwin Chargaff, a biochemist at Columbia University who discovered something that would be immensely important for their search. While the composition of DNA would change depending on the organism and where it was found, the proportion of the phosphate groups (A, T, C, and G) stayed exactly the same: the amount of adenine was always equal to the amount of thymine, and the amount of guanine was always equal to cytosine (A = T and C = G).

It was this insight that led the pair to believe that the key to DNA was how the phosphate groups bonded with each other, and, after two years of painstaking work, Watson and Crick came up with a structure that worked. They built a model with a double helix, with the sugar forming the backbone and the phosphate groups forming the "steps" by bonding with another phosphate group on the other side (A bonding to T and C bonding to G).

What made this structure interesting was that each side would form a code for a particular amino acid, the building blocks of proteins).[13] It also implied a copying mechanism, because each complementary side would be a template for the other. If, for instance, there was a T on one side of the helix, it could only bond with an A on the other side. The structure explained both how DNA coded for proteins and how it played a role in heredity. It proved to be a major breakthrough that ushered in the new field of genetics. The pair was awarded the Nobel Prize for their work in 1962.

Much like Einstein, the two had uncovered no new facts, but rather combined evidence that others had uncovered to come up with a completely new model. However, unlike Einstein, there were no incredible leaps of imagination. They mostly just plowed through the possibilities until they found something that worked. In today's parlance, we might say that they "iterated" a solution.

Why We Fail to Adapt

Unlike Semmelweis's hand washing idea, the discoveries of natural selection, relativity, and the structure of DNA were accepted fairly quickly. In fact, to many scientists they seemed obviously right the moment they were published, even though, with the exception of Darwin, all came from unknown scientists of negligible achievement. How was it that these scientists were able to see what far more accomplished scientists could not? In other words, why are Kuhn's paradigms so powerful?

We tend to think that we experience the world as it is. We see and hear things, store them away as knowledge, and then take new facts into account. Yet that's not what we really do.

In fact, we filter out most of what we experience. In effect, we forget most things so we can focus on what we feel is of prime importance. This effect is cumulative. What we think of as knowledge is really connections in our brains called synapses, which develop over time. These pathways strengthen as we use them and degrade when we don't. Or, as scientists who study these things like to put it, the neurons that fire together, wire together—a principle known as Hebbian plasticity.

So, as we go through life and learn the ways of the world, we become less able to imagine new possibilities. Our mental models become instinctive, and standard practices become "the right way to do things." This effect becomes even stronger and more pervasive if we see our mental models as being responsible for our success. At some point, best practices are no longer just a set of tools to promote operational efficiency, but become full-fledged mental models that become hardwired in our brains. To violate them offends our sense of how the world is supposed to work.

What's more, while our previous experiences tend to blind us to new developments, those around us will help reinforce common beliefs. In fact, a series of famous experiments done at Swarthmore College in the 1950s showed that we will conform to the opinions of those around us even if they are *obviously wrong*.[14]

In the real world, though, few of the issues we face are so clear-cut. We tend to cling to our beliefs because they have worked for us. As Thomas Kuhn explained, new paradigms don't emerge whole, but first arrive as a series of quirky anomalies that are easy to dismiss as "special cases" that we can work around. This usually works pretty well for a while, and things go on much as before. Even if we notice that something is awry, that things aren't quite what we thought they were, we will most likely forget about it and get back to business. After all, not only do we believe in our present working model, so do those around us. The world is a messy place, and every rule has exceptions. Life goes on.

A final barrier to shifting paradigms is that change incurs real costs. How much time, effort, and resources do we want to expend on a hunch? Especially when our own instincts and those around us tell us that our present course is the right one. People who gain prominence in their field are not only proud of their accomplishments, but also of how they achieved them. It was their dedication to the path they traveled that earned them the accolades they came to enjoy.

So part of the answer to the puzzle that Darwin, Einstein, and Watson and Crick present is that they were better able to come up with innovative new ideas because they weren't especially prominent. They had no record of accomplishment to fall back on and protect. So it was easier for them to explore new ideas. For them, these weren't merely "special cases" or small anomalies to be worked around and forgotten, but exciting new paths to travel.

Another commonality is that all of these scientists spent seemingly idle time letting their imaginations run wild. Darwin had a five-year voyage on the *Beagle* to simply observe nature and think about what he saw. Einstein's "miracle year" occurred while he was in virtual exile as a clerk in a patent office and hashing over ideas at cafés as part of the "Olympia Academy" he formed with his friends. Watson and Crick, much to the annoyance of their colleagues, seemed to spend their time trading wild ideas rather than doing experiments.

Most of all—and this is a crucial point—they did not confine their explorations to their own fields. It's hard to see how Darwin could ever have come up with his famous theory if he had confined his interests to biology. It was, in fact, a book on geology that first got the ball rolling. And his breakthrough moment came while reading the work of Thomas Malthus, an economist. Biology, geology, and economics are three very different fields with relatively little in common. But by combining them Darwin was able to attain groundbreaking new insights. Without any one of those three elements, it is doubtful he would have achieved what he did.

In much the same way, Einstein credited the insights of philosopher David Hume with helping him to formulate his theory of relativity. Watson and Crick combined insights from biology, chemistry, and x-ray crystallography to solve their puzzle. Everybody else who was working on the problem, many more talented and distinguished than Watson and Crick, were focusing on just one aspect of it.

In fact, when we look at any breakthrough of significance, we never seem to find a linear path, but instead a synthesis of several diverse domains. For example, Larry Page and Sergey Brin of Google developed their famous algorithm by borrowing the system of cites used in academic publications to come up with a profoundly better way to search the Internet. While there were many engineers far more talented than Steve Jobs working to develop new computers, he was the one to fuse technology and design to create products unlike anyone had ever seen before.

Dharmendra Modha, who heads up the team at IBM developing neuromorphic chips, a revolutionary technology based on the human brain that we will discuss in more detail in Chapter 7, compares the process of innovation to the children's story "Stone Soup," in which hungry travelers tell villagers that they are cooking "stone soup" and get them all to contribute to the task. By the end of the story, their empty pot containing nothing more than an ordinary stone is transformed into a hearty meal.

In Modha's case, he started out with a just a general idea of what he wanted to achieve, and then went about collecting additional insights from others. Given that he needed to borrow from widely disparate domains, including not only his chosen field of computer science, but also neuroscience, network theory, and others, there was literally no one on earth who could do it alone. Nevertheless, what he ended up with was truly transformative. As he put it to me, with a bit of a glint in his eye, "In our case, we got lucky and the 'soup' ended up really being something special."

If a problem is difficult enough, it needs to borrow from multiple fields of expertise. To break free of an existing paradigm, we need to search beyond the realm in which it was established. Innovation, more than anything else, is combination, which is why if we are to create anything truly important, we need to travel down multiple paths.

Yet that doesn't mean innovation is a random pursuit. We need a clear sense of where we're going and some concrete ideas on how to get there. To do that, we need to map innovation.

PART TWO

MAPPING THE INNOVATION SPACE

*A simple, clear framework
to drive innovation.*

CHAPTER THREE

The Innovation Matrix

If I had 20 days to solve a problem,
I would spend 19 days to define it.
—ALBERT EINSTEIN

Innovation has become like a religion in business today, with "innovate or die" as its mantra. When an organization succeeds, people attribute its good fortune to superior innovation. When it fails, people say it lacked the ability to innovate, no matter how many new products or initiatives it launched. The message is simple: you need to disrupt to survive.

So it shouldn't be surprising that there is no shortage of people offering silver bullets and promising a "secret sauce" that will unlock the creativity in your organization. They preach disruption, open innovation, Lean LaunchPad, or whatever else is the flavor of the day with the passion and surety of evangelical ministers. Yes, all of those things can be effective, but only if you are facing the specific type of problem that they were designed to solve.

The truth is that there is no one true path to innovation. As we have already seen, innovation takes many forms. Compare any two great innovators, and they inevitably do things very differently. If you choose to emulate one, you are in a sense rejecting the other, who may have been equally or even more successful. The only real path forward is to define the problems you seek to solve and build your own innovation playbook.

To understand the problem, let's look at the case of Apple. There are few companies that can boast innovative success like Apple can. Products like the iPod, the iPhone, and the iPad weren't just wildly successful in the marketplace, they redefined entire categories. If there is one organization a company manager dreams about being like, it's probably Apple.

And Tim Cook, Apple's CEO, has very clear ideas about what it takes to create breakthrough products. "It's people who care enough to keep thinking about something until they find the simplest way to do it," he says. "It's caring enough to call the person who works over in this other area, because you think the two of you can do something fantastic that hasn't been thought of before. It's providing an environment where that feeds off each other and grows."[1] Sounds like good advice.

Cook also has very clear ideas about what not to do, such as creating innovation labs, which he thinks is a really bad idea, going as far as to say, "A lot of companies have innovation departments, and this is always a sign that something is wrong when you have a VP of innovation or something. You know, put a for-sale sign on the door."

That sounds like it makes sense, too, but then you look at Google and building an innovation lab is exactly what it has done with its "X" division. Microsoft and IBM also have research divisions and have successfully innovated for decades, across multiple technology cycles. Today, those companies continue to push the envelope with pathbreaking new products like Google's self-driving cars, Microsoft's HoloLens, and IBM's Watson cognitive computing system. Apple, meanwhile, still relies on the iPhone, launched in 2007, for roughly two thirds of its revenue.

So, how should we pursue innovation? Should we hand it over to the guys with white lab coats, an external partner, a specialist in the field, crowdsource it, or explore fundamental questions within a particular field?

What we need is a clear framework for defining innovation problems and the strategies most likely to resolve them.

Like any journey, the best way to start is by creating a map. Maps, of course, are not answers in themselves because they always offer more than one path to our destination. They do, however, help us choose the path that's best for us. Sometimes, we will opt to take the highway in order to travel at the optimum speed. Other times, perhaps at rush hour, we will take the scenic route in order to avoid traffic. Or maybe we want to take another route altogether because we have a secondary task in mind, like picking up dinner on the way home.

Innovation works in much the same way, except it is often the destination itself that varies. Some firms market their products to consumers, others to enterprises that themselves have a considerable amount of expertise in their particular fields. Some seek to gain the upper hand in a competitive market, while others are looking to create an entirely new category. When it comes to innovation, it is not enough to try to get there faster; you first need to define where "there" is.

Another important aspect of innovation is that organizations vary widely in their capabilities. Some are large enterprises with considerable resources, while others are nimble upstarts. Some have considerable scientific and technical expertise, while others are master marketers. Still others excel at creating effective partnerships to access capabilities they lack internally.

So looking for "one true path" to innovation is nothing more than a distraction. It is more likely to set us on a wild goose chase and waste lots of time and money than anything else. What we need is to identify *our own path to innovation* and then gather the tools we need to get where we want to go.

The Innovation Matrix

The best place to start mapping the innovation space is by asking two crucial questions:

1. **How well is the problem defined?** When Steve Jobs, who was a master at defining a clear product vision, set out to build the iPod, he framed the problem as "1,000 songs in my pocket." That simple phrase defined not only the technical specifications, but the overall approach. Unfortunately, some problems, like how to create a new paradigm for computer chip technology, a next generation technology for energy storage, or a revolutionary cure for cancer, aren't so easy to delineate. So your innovation strategy will have to adapt, depending on how well the problem can be framed.

2. **Who is best placed to solve it?** Once Jobs defined the iPod problem, it was clear that he needed to find a hard drive that could store 1,000 songs and still fit into a device that you could hold in your pocket. After a few years of looking, he found out that Toshiba had created a five-gigabyte drive that was about the size of a silver dollar and immediately authorized a $10 million check to secure exclusive rights to the technology.[2] From there, creating the iPod was merely a

matter of putting Apple's considerable design and engineering talents into gear.

Often, however, the proper domain isn't so cut-and-dried, and it isn't immediately clear who is best equipped to pursue a solution. Other times, after working on the problem for a while, it becomes clear that a more diverse set of skills is needed to solve the problem.

Once you start asking these questions, you'll find that they clarify the issues very quickly. Either there is a simple answer, or there isn't, and that can be enormously helpful in defining an approach.

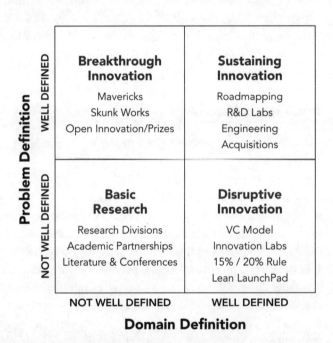

FIGURE 3.1 The Innovation Matrix

As the innovation matrix in Figure 3.1 shows, once you have thought about how well defined both the problem and the domain are, you can narrow down your options for an innovation strategy to one of just four quadrants: basic research, breakthrough innovation, sustaining innovation, and disruptive innovation. Let's look at each one in more depth.

1. Basic Research

When your aim is to discover something completely new, neither the problem nor the domain is well defined. For the most part, basic research is funded by the government and undertaken by academic institutions because of the problem of appropriability. Simply put, fundamental research is likely to result in a broad range of applications—Vannevar Bush once described it as "seed corn"—so any individual firm is unlikely to be able to appropriate much of the benefit.

As Nobel laureate George Smoot put it, "If we only did applied research, we would still be making better spears," and the opportunities to be unlocked by fundamental new discoveries are enormous.[3] Take a look at any fixture of modern life, from the laser scanners that clerks use at the grocery store to the blockbuster drugs that cure us when we are sick, and the initial insights were provided by publicly funded exploratory research. We all benefit from the energy boom created by hydraulic fracking, but few realize that as well was originally a federal research project. Firms like Apple and Samsung design and manufacture smartphones, but as we saw in Chapter 1, nearly every component, including the lithium-ion battery, the basic architecture, the Internet, GPS navigation, and many other things came either directly from government labs or as the result of government grants.

The fact is, every year tens of thousands of scientific papers are published, and each one has the potential to lead to a breakthrough new product or even an entirely new industry. Clearly, any business able to capitalize on these breakthrough ideas can forge a significant competitive advantage.

Some firms, like IBM and Microsoft, invest in basic research because they believe it both helps them attract world-class talent and allows them to see 5, 10, or 20 years down the road, yet they are rare exceptions. Very few are able—strategically or financially—to work on that kind of time scale. Still, you don't need a billion-dollar research program to benefit from basic research. As I noted above, most exploratory research is publicly funded and openly published, so it is mostly a matter of identifying and accessing the types of discoveries that can give your business a leg up.

One way that firms identify and access crucial research in the public domain is to simply monitor what's going on in the academic world, by sending internal researchers to conferences and working closely with the offices of technology transfer at government agencies. In the pharmaceutical industry, the monitoring process can be incredibly elaborate. Perry Nisen, CEO at Sanford Burnham Prebys Medical Discovery Institute, points out that his former employer, GlaxoSmithKline, has thousands of people working in R&D and assigns experts to specific areas of interest. Some of these experts spend their entire careers focusing on a single specialty.[4]

However, most companies don't have those kinds of resources and need to take a more ad hoc approach. Eric Haller, EVP and global head at Experian DataLabs, emphasizes creating a culture of discovery. "We pay for our data scientists to go to the conferences of their choice, encourage them to publish white papers, and we have weekly seminars so that they can share what they've learned," he says, but his company doesn't assign formal areas of focus.

The key, emphasizes Jeff Welser, lab director at IBM's Almaden Research Center, is to be seen as an active participant and not just a spectator. "Being immersed is incredibly critical," he stresses. "You need to have people active at conferences, writing papers and helping the field advance. You have to put value in to get value out."

Another way that some firms get the inside track is to partner directly with academia so that they don't have to wait for results to be published publicly. Daniel Hook, managing director of Digital Science, explains that these are structured differently than government grants and that while corporate partnerships are often more flexible, they can also be more demanding. "Generally more is asked of researchers in a private partnership, such as consulting with internal researchers" he says. "There are also often milestones put in place that determine whether funding continues." Companies sponsoring research also usually insist on first right of refusal for any commercialization of the research and require approval prior to publication.

Giulio Draetta, Director for MD Anderson's Institute for Applied Cancer Science, believes that making sure incentives are aligned is crucial to making academic partnerships work. He advises first to "put in place a system that recognizes contribution based on having achieved an agreed-upon task," such as identifying a particular molecule or receptor in cancer studies.

Partnering with academia can also be done at a much smaller scale. Daniel Hook of Digital Science points to Elsevier, which offers small prizes, usually just a few thousand dollars, for scientific achievement. IBM's Welser told me that he advises smaller firms to "look to cultivate relationships with a couple of professors. I would also think seriously about geography and build up relationships with universities in your area that you can drop in on and interact with," he says.

One pitfall for firms looking to mine research in the academic world is the basic cultural divide between academic scientists who are doing basic exploratory work and those who are focusing on research of a more applied nature. Often, scientists themselves don't agree on which approach is more fruitful. For example, Sanford Burnham's Nisen told me, "I try to find people, physician scientists especially, who understand unmet clinical needs and can verbalize the pharmacological effect that we can work back from. From there, we can go searching through the science to find useful solutions to the problem."

Yet MD Anderson's Draetta takes the opposite view. He says, "I still think that the greatest discovery comes from exploratory research in which there is not a specific target. Starting with a specific disease in mind is more high percentage, but the real break-throughs come from basic discoveries," and points to the recent advances in cancer immunotherapy as a prime example. As we saw in Chapter 1, James Allison wasn't searching for a cure for anything. He was simply curious about how the immune system worked and wanted to add to the world's knowledge. Nevertheless, his work led to a multibillion-dollar business.

As we have already seen, the development of a breakthrough product, whether it is an electronic device, a miracle cure, or something else, usually involves hundreds of people, including researchers, engineers, designers, marketers, accountants, and many other specialized areas of expertise, but it all starts with the discovery of a new phenomenon, and that means the process always begins with basic science.[5] While few firms are able to actively invest in this type of exploration, every organization can benefit from better visibility into what's going on in fields of study that may affect their industry.

In my conversations with scientists and executives engaged in basic research, there was one thing I heard over and over again: to gain access to top-quality research, *you have to be seen as a participant rather than just an observer.* Firms that are successful in this area publish openly, attend scientific conferences, and actively contribute to the expansion of knowledge, whether through their own internal research or by in-kind support, such as offering the use of their facilities or data to cash-strapped scientists. Contrary to what many think, that doesn't take a multimillion-dollar research lab or even a high-flying partnership with a major university. Sometimes, it is enough merely to be seen as engaged and supportive of advancement in a particular field.

As Woody Allen put it, "80 percent of success is just showing up."

2. Breakthrough Innovation

The primary objective of basic research is exploration, which is why very few private firms choose to invest in it. Although history has shown there is a handsome return to basic research in the long run, most companies simply aren't able to operate on that type of time horizon. So most organizations focus on solving problems that they can clearly define.

Still, as we have already seen, even well-defined problems can be devilishly hard to solve. Clearly, it wasn't that Alexander Fleming didn't understand the problems with his penicillin discovery. He was perfectly aware that it was unstable, hard to manufacture, and completely useless as a therapeutic drug; he just didn't have the skills needed to solve them. Theories of evolution were widely discussed decades before Darwin came up with his theory of natural selection. The problem that Watson and Crick tackled, the structure of DNA, was not only well known, but there was a rabid competition among a number of top-notch scientists to see who would get there first.

As we have also seen, to solve really tough problems you need combinations of ideas, but what kinds of combinations are likely to be most effective? That's the question that a team of researchers set out to explore when they analyzed 17.9 million scientific papers to see what made for the most highly cited papers. Their results showed a clear pattern. The most impactful discoveries came from combining deep expertise in closely related fields with just a smidgen of knowledge from some unlikely place. As the authors of the study wrote, "The highest-impact science is primarily grounded in exceptionally conventional combinations of prior work yet simultaneously features an intrusion of unusual combinations. Papers of this type were twice as likely to be highly cited works. Novel combinations of prior work are rare, yet teams are 37.7% more likely than solo authors to insert novel combinations into familiar knowledge domains."[6]

And that's entirely consistent with what we have already seen. Howard Florey was a pathologist and Ernst Chain was a biochemist, exactly the kind of skills you would expect to be working on a pharmaceutical problem. But it was the combination of those skills with the mechanical wizardry of Norman Heatley that made a viable solution to the penicillin problem possible. Einstein cited David Hume, a philosopher, as one of the crucial influences that led to his discovery of special relativity. Darwin's theory of natural selection sprung to life after he read a paper by Thomas Malthus, an economist.

The one possible exception to the rule was Watson and Crick's discovery of the structure of DNA, but upon closer inspection it seems to apply there as well. Remember, the two chose to work at Cavendish specifically because it was one of the few places in the world that had a sophisticated x-ray crystallography lab. At the time, combining that technique with any other was unconventional, and Watson and Crick were particularly adept at scouring the literature for everything that was known about DNA.

So clearly, to solve really tough problems you have to cast your net far and wide to find the one elusive piece of the puzzle that does not lie in a conventional domain. Steve Jobs said that a calligraphy class ended up being key to how he designed products.[7] Charlie Bennett, the father of quantum information theory, told me that one thing that set him on his course to developing the ideas for a quantum computer was how DNA turned genetic information into proteins.[8] "If molecules could compute, why not subatomic particles?" he thought. You never know where a valuable insight can come from.

One story I heard, albeit secondhand, illustrates the point particularly well. A technology firm was given a $1 million budget to design a sensor to detect water pollutants in minute concentrations, which is an extremely complicated task. At the team's first meeting, the chip designers got right down to work discussing the problems they would have to solve and immediately realized how daunting a challenge it was going to be. After about 45 minutes of intense discussion, the marine biologist assigned to their team walked in, apologized for being late, and dropped a bag of clams on the table. Upon seeing the puzzled looks on the chip designers' faces, the marine biologist explained that clams can detect pollutants at concentrations of just a few parts per million, which would cause their shells to open. So they didn't actually need to build an expensive sensor to detect pollutants, just a cheap one that could detect when clams opened their shells. The idea not only saved an enormous amount of time, effort, and money, they also ate the clams for dinner!

Now clearly, using clams is not something a team of chip designers would be likely to come up with on their own, but for a marine biologist, the ability of clams to detect pollutants is common knowledge. That's what happens when you get people of varied skills, perspectives, and experiences together, they tend to come up with solutions that would be unlikely to arise in any single domain.

That's why many organizations have found it useful to set up a "Skunk Works" facility that is specifically designed to encourage multidisciplinary teams with diverse but specialized expertise to work closely together. IBM used this strategy to develop the PC in record time back in the 1980s. More recently, Google established its Google X division to pursue "moonshots." As we will discuss in more depth in Chapter 9, there is a growing trend of setting up consortia that combine the domains of government labs, academic institutions, and manufacturers in the private sector to tackle our toughest problems. For instance, President Obama's National Network for Manufacturing Innovation (NNMI) creates hubs to develop new manufacturing technologies in specific areas, like 3D printing or silicon photonics. The Joint Center for Energy Storage Research (JCESR) at Argonne National Laboratory is working to find new breakthrough technologies to replace the lithium-ion batteries that power our laptops, mobile phones, and electric cars. MD Anderson Cancer Center has established the Institute for Applied Cancer Science to help transform exciting new research into effective treatments. "For us, it's imperative to create a true 'team of teams,' where research scientists, physicians, and drug developers would work hand-in-hand," Ron DePinho, president of MD Anderson, told me.

Another way to solve a difficult problem is to simply offer a prize for anyone—no matter what their field or qualification—who can solve it. This is not, in fact, a new idea, but dates back to 1714, when the British Parliament offered £20,000 to the first person who could figure out how to measure longitude at sea. Later Napoléon I offered 12,000 francs to anyone who could devise a way to preserve food that could sustain his army in the field. The result was the method of canning we still use today.[9]

More recently, DARPA has issued Grand Challenges that give million dollar prizes for breakthrough new technologies like self-driving cars and advanced robots. The XPRIZE Foundation, a nonprofit, awards prizes for solving a number of insanely tough problems, like building an economically viable spaceship, designing a car that can get 100 mpg, and developing a tricorder device that can diagnose illness, just like on *Star Trek*. An upcoming prize, to be awarded in 2020, focuses on tackling climate change by transforming CO_2 emissions into useful products.[10] Again, these are devilishly hard problems and there's no telling where the solution may come from, but offering a prize casts a wide net. These types of contests routinely attract far more investment than the value of the prize.

As we will see in Chapter 5, the InnoCentive platform applies these same principles to allow organizations to post problems that have stumped them and offer a bounty to anyone who can provide them with a solution. Often it turns out that what is considered to be an intractable challenge in one field has been solved long ago in another. Procter & Gamble has found this strategy so effective that it has built its own platform, called Connect + Develop, to invite people across the world to solve problems that it can't lick on its own.

The mantra of the open source software community is "with enough eyeballs, all bugs are shallow," and I think that's true of problems in every field. When you get stuck, you need to bring a more diverse set of skills, perspectives, and experiences to meet the challenge.

3. Sustaining Innovation

Every technology needs to get better. Every year, our cameras get more pixels, computers get more powerful, and household products become "new and improved." Many scoff at this type of "incremental innovation," believing it lacks excitement and impact, but it's extremely important. Take lithium-ion batteries, the technology that powers our smartphones, laptops, and electric cars. The principles of these batteries were first discovered in 1979, and by the early 1990s, Sony began using them for personal electronics like camcorders. Since then, energy densities in lithium-ion batteries have improved by a factor of 6 and costs have dropped by a factor of 10, making our ultra-sleek iPhones and laptops possible.[11] Imagine how inconvenient it would be if the smartphones we carry around every day had to be six times larger.

Incremental advancement has been even more impressive in other technologies. Consider the case of DRAM, the working memory in our computers that allows us to continually pull information from our hard drives and work on it without rebooting. DRAM was originally developed by IBM in 1966 and has improved incrementally since then. On the face of it, that's not very impressive. Yet incremental innovation works the same way as compounding interest in your IRA. Even a small amount of advancement a year can create dramatic effects over a period of decades. If our current laptops still used the same version of DRAM invented in 1966, they would weigh 250,000 tons![12]

Large organizations tend to be very good at this type of innovation, because conventional R&D labs and outsourced suppliers are well suited for it. Another facet of sustaining innovation that makes traditional organizations strong performers is that the process fits nicely into a conventional strategic roadmapping process. Essentially, you pursue sustaining innovations by identifying objectives and then undertaking the actions you need to achieve them, whether that means a traditional R&D engineering process, accessing technology you need through suppliers, or acquiring companies that have developed technologies that can benefit your strategy.

To understand how sustaining innovation works, let's look at Experian, the global information services giant that *Forbes* named one of the world's most innovative companies in 2015.[13] When Eric Haller started at the company as a vice president on the Strategic Development team in 1994, the contours of the business were pretty clear. The credit reporting industry was rapidly consolidating, and Experian, the product of a recent merger of the British company CCN and the credit operations of the American conglomerate TRW, was poised to take a leadership position.

However, there were major challenges. Credit reporting had historically been a relatively sleepy business, with lots of mom-and-pop operations collecting data on consumers and offering it to banks, retailers, and other businesses to help them make decisions about whether or not to extend credit. Traditionally, this was done over the phone. A client would simply call the credit agency, and a clerk would pull up a paper file and share the consumer's credit history. Now, the industry was being rapidly transformed by powerful digital technologies, which could store and analyze mountains of data far more efficiently than ever before.

Both CCN and TRW had been on the forefront of this transformation, and Experian's management believed that the combined company had an enormous opportunity to dominate in the new digital environment. The executive management team developed a road map for Experian's strategy, which they called "Data Solutions and Decisions Systems" or "DS squared" for short, to exploit the opportunities they saw in the marketplace (Figure 3.2). It encompassed four key functional areas (data, analytics, decisions, and delivery) across four key verticals (financial services, retail, telecom, and automotive). The firm also saw a great opportunity to use its data and analytical capabilities to sell services across all verticals.

	FINANCIAL SERVICES	RETAIL	TELECOM	AUTOMOTIVE
	Marketing Services			
Data	Integration of Experian data with customer's decision rules algorithms to streamline credit approval process			
Analytics	Deepen core competency through investment in talent and continuous improvement			
Decisions	Adapt to rapidly changing information technology environment by working with suppliers to upgrade systems			
Delivery	Improve speed and convenience of decisions through working with suppliers to upgrade technology			

FIGURE 3.2 Experian DS Squared Strategy

Experian's Haller says of that time, "We knew that each key segment of the 'DS squared' value chain represented opportunity for Experian. But the biggest opportunities were recognizing the synergies that exist when you pull all the pieces together. Turning data into decisions—we believed that would be really big." With the strategy set, the main challenge ahead was to execute it flawlessly.

The company already had strong customer relationships in each of the core verticals, so the innovation strategy focused on the four key functional areas. The most obvious opportunity was to deepen its market leading capabilities in data and analytics. It was, after all, Experian's ability to collect enormous amounts of data about consumers' creditworthiness and transform that data into reliable credit scores through sophisticated analytics that had been key to its success. However, in the rapidly changing technology environment of the 1990s, upgrading Experian's IT systems to facilitate better decision making and faster delivery of reports to its customers was just as important.

A lot of Experian's strategy involved basic blocking and tackling. For example, Experian did not develop IT solutions itself, but worked with suppliers to ensure that its systems were the absolute best in the industry. In analytics, the job was mostly to continue recruiting the best talent in the industry and motivate them to do their best work. In large part, successful execution of the strategy required the company to do what it always had, just continue to do it better and better.

However, Experian also came up with some creative ways to substantially improve service. For example, each of its corporate customers had different criteria for extending credit. Experian would send credit scores to the customers' servers, and the corporate customers' systems would apply rules management algorithms to decide whether a particular consumer met their standards for creditworthiness. However, Experian's management team saw that they could streamline the process by hosting corporate customers' rules management algorithms on their own servers. This would allow a clerk in a retail store to simply send a patron's identifying information to Experian and receive a credit decision, based on that retailer's own criteria, in minutes.

Other opportunities arose through Experian's aggressive acquisition strategy. As the industry continued to consolidate in the late 1990s, the company acquired more than half a dozen competitive firms to broaden its footprint. Yet it also noticed that the data and analytics capabilities of its former competitors often could be incorporated into Experian's own systems and markedly improve performance.

As Experian proceeded with its strategic road map, it also recognized a completely new opportunity. With all of the sophisticated new services the company was delivering, as well as increasing demand for faster credit decisions, its corporate customers across all verticals needed help adapting. So the company created a consulting group to assess its customers' needs and devise solutions, which became a further point of differentiation and brought in additional revenues.

All of this may seem somewhat prosaic. Nothing Experian did involved any spellbinding insights or earth-shattering epiphanies, but that's how sustaining innovation works. Apple, for example, is a superior sustaining innovator. It didn't invent the digital music player, the smartphone, or even the tablet computer. Still, the company improved on earlier designs to such an extent that its products seemed like something completely new. In a similar vein, Toyota mostly makes cars that are much like any others, except better.

In Experian's case, the cumulative effect of all the things it did to improve its product and its business led to astounding results. In the five years between 1994 and 1999, the company's revenues quadrupled, from $250 million to $1 billion, and it not only took a leading position in the credit reporting industry, but also became a recognized global leader in providing information services for marketers, healthcare providers, insurance companies, and governments.

4. Disruptive Innovation

In 1997, Harvard professor Clayton Christensen published his book *The Innovator's Dilemma* and introduced the world to disruptive innovation. His key insight was that firms often fail not because they are incompetent—many of the companies he studied had excellent management, reinvested profits back into their companies' products, and catered to their customers' needs—but in fact because they were actually *too good* at what they did. What he found was that after a certain point, sustaining innovation creates products and services that are actually better than what the market is demanding, which opens up an opportunity for a competitor to change the basis of competition.

Consider the case of Xerox, the firm that invented the market for copiers. It sold the best copiers, at impressive margins, to the biggest corporate accounts. In order to maintain its leadership position, the company invested heavily in research so that it was constantly coming out with copiers that could produce more copies. That's what its customers were demanding, and the company worked hard to deliver it.

However, by the 1970s Xerox began to face stiff competition from Japanese firms, like Canon and Ricoh, that were selling copiers that produced fewer copies, slower and with worse quality. Yet the Canon and Ricoh copiers were *good enough*, especially for small and midsize companies that couldn't afford a high-performance copier from Xerox.

These copiers also had some other advantages besides attractive pricing. For example, they were much smaller than Xerox's high-performance copiers and didn't require an entire copy room to operate them. After a while, even big companies decided that there were advantages to being able to have a small copier on every floor rather than one for an entire office building and, as the quality and performance of the Japanese copiers improved, Xerox's market share plummeted.

So a disruptive innovation, according to Christensen, is a product that changes the basis of competition because it performs worse according to traditional parameters, but better against new parameters that previously weren't regarded as important (in the case of the copier business, size and price). He also pointed out that these types of innovators also tend to target either light consumers or nonconsumers of a category (for example, small and medium-sized businesses versus Xerox's large corporate clients) and introduce a new business model to the market. (Xerox made its money on the volume of copies; the Japanese simply sold or leased their products.)

However, another way to view disruptive innovation is as an existing technology put toward a new purpose. This, for the most part, is equivalent to Christensen's definition, but operationally, it opens up opportunities to ask, "What new markets can we adapt existing technology to?" Successful disruptors like Uber and Airbnb, for example, added very little, if anything, to existing technological capabilities. Their innovational insight consisted of using fairly ordinary technology to disrupt a market with a new business model.

Another facet of disruptive technologies is that the process of developing them is profoundly different than in any of the other four quadrants. They succeed mostly by the virtue of a new business model rather than developing fundamentally new capabilities. It is, in fact, their radically different business models that make them so hard for incumbent firms to compete with without undermining their own profitability. (We will discuss how to develop disruptive new business models in the next chapter).

Disruptive innovation differs from the other three quadrants operationally as well. Rather than the deliberative and thoughtful process by which you would run a traditional business or research operation, a disruptive strategy is fundamentally iterative. It is not a purposeful march toward a set of tangible strategic objectives, but thrives on experimentation and agility. That's why it is an innovation strategy most often employed by start-ups financed by venture capital rather than established firms.

With that said, some large enterprises have devised effective strategies to pursue disruptive innovations. Both 3M, the company that pioneered Scotch Tape and Post-it Notes, and Google use a version of the 15 percent or 20 percent rule, in which employees are encouraged to devote a fixed portion of their time to projects unrelated to their jobs. 3M derives up to 30 percent of its revenue from products launched in the past five years. Google has released an array of disruptive products, from Google Docs and Google News to Chromebooks.

Recently, Experian has learned that it can use disruptive innovation to gain a competitive edge as well. When Eric Haller returned to the company in 2007 after a seven-year hiatus during which he worked with a number of start-ups, he realized that although the company was increasingly successful, it was also missing out on a lot of opportunities. The problem, as he saw it, was that the company was "trapped in its P&L." For any new line of business to be pursued, it had to meet strict profitability guidelines. That's a sensible risk management strategy, but it also limited the firm's ability to experiment and pursue nascent opportunities where there was no existing market to measure.

"Opportunities today are greater and they come faster, so you have to move faster or you miss them," Haller told me. "You simply have to be more agile now than you did when I started in the nineties. We were missing important opportunities because we couldn't calculate an internal rate of return." Haller proposed to Experian's executive management that it create a separate division, called Data-Labs, to pursue these types of disruptive opportunities.

"When we first started," he remembers, "it was just a team of data scientists along with a few product consultants. We went to customers, too, and talked to them about unresolved problems in their business and effectively offered to problem solve for free, with the understanding that we would own any intellectual property that resulted from the engagement. We would then build something, incubate it, and eventually turn it over to the business units to scale it up."

The DataLabs operation, started in 2011, is now just six years old, but it has already had a measurable impact on the company's performance. In the United States alone it has launched 8 products, each with over a million dollars in profits, and it has another 12 in development. The small five-person team that Haller started with has grown to 40 data scientists across three data labs located in the United States, the United Kingdom, and Brazil.

However—and this is a crucial point—Experian has never abandoned the sustaining innovation strategies it pursued in the early 1990s. In fact, as we will see in the next chapter, the ability to roadmap and pursue continuous improvement is essential to scaling the businesses that DataLabs develops. The new division is specifically focused on pursuing disruptive innovations by searching for new problems that the company can solve with its existing capabilities. It doesn't operate as a standalone business or have any targets for financial performance. Its mission is to identify new opportunities, build solutions around those opportunities, and develop new capabilities, because that's what innovation labs excel at. They are great for incubating businesses, but can't function the same way conventional business units do.

Unfortunately, in recent years innovation labs have become so fashionable that many companies have launched them without thinking them through. Rather than a being used to fulfill a specific function, they are often launched as a cure-all that is supposed to somehow magically solve an entire organization's innovation failures. Not surprisingly, innovation labs set up this way rarely succeed.

To innovate effectively, you have to choose the right tool for the right job. That's the essence of building a successful innovation strategy. Instead of thinking about innovation as a search for the "one best way," we need to start thinking about it as building a portfolio of solutions aimed at solving the specific portfolio of challenges that a particular organization faces.

Building an Innovation Portfolio

As I noted in the beginning of this chapter, there is no "one true path" to innovation. We all must find our own way. Every enterprise is a unique combination of business model, strategy, and culture. We need to resist the urge to adopt a particular innovation strategy just because it worked somewhere else or because that's how we solved the last problem. You have to use the right tool for the right job.

At the same time, every organization faces a variety of challenges, so we also shouldn't limit ourselves to just one quadrant of the innovation matrix. While focus is important, we need a portfolio of strategies. Apple, for instance, is mainly a sustaining innovator, but iTunes was certainly an important disruptive innovation. And while Google may very well be the greatest disruptive innovator on the planet, as we will see in Chapter 6, it is also highly focused on improving its core products through sustaining innovations. In fact, that's where it concentrates 70 percent of its resources.

To see what an effective innovation portfolio looks like, let's take another look at Experian.

The Experian Innovation Matrix

Take a look at the matrix in Figure 3.3, and you'll notice that a key to Experian's success is a highly focused portfolio of innovation strategies. While it is indeed a vast enterprise, with revenues of $4.5 billion,[14] that doesn't leave much room for the billion-dollar budgets that the tech giants and pharmaceutical companies enjoy. Nevertheless, it maintains a vigorous innovation regime and achieves strong profit margins topping 26 percent.

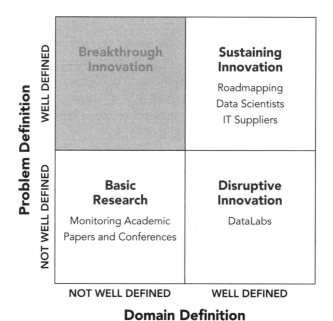

FIGURE 3.3 Experian Innovation Matrix

One key to its success is that its portfolio of innovation strategies is specifically geared to the challenges it faces.

The Four Quadrants
BASIC RESEARCH

As we saw earlier in this chapter, Experian doesn't invest in basic research but is still able to identify and access cutting-edge scientific discoveries by closely monitoring academic papers and conferences. It also employs a highly trained cadre of PhD level data scientists and encourages them to publish openly and holds weekly seminars in which the latest findings, along with potential applications, are discussed.

So, although there is no basic research budget at Experian, it still manages to be an active member of the scientific community and establish relationships with top minds in the field. Remember, most scientific discoveries are government financed and in the public domain. You don't actually need to own the intellectual property, you just need to identify and access the discoveries that can benefit your business.

BREAKTHROUGH INNOVATION

While Experian is an extremely successful innovator, it is also highly disciplined and doesn't take on problems that can't be solved in an actionable time frame. However, much like it does with basic research, the company actively monitors developments in data science and related fields. It also takes a multidisciplinary approach to its consulting business, working closely with experts in the industries it serves.

Still, you can see how the elements to achieve a breakthrough are there, if the right business opportunity arose. Experian already has considerable technical expertise in data science and has invested for decades in building the systems to deliver it efficiently. It has also, throughout its history, built increasingly collaborative relationships with its corporate customers across a variety of industries, which would be a valuable asset if the need arose to create a solution to a problem that straddled Experian's expertise and the domain of one of its clients' industries.

SUSTAINING INNOVATION

Most of the innovation that goes on at Experian, as in most organizations, isn't particularly sexy. It talks with customers, seeks to understand their problems, and applies the talents within its organization to solve them. It also works with outside suppliers to ensure that its systems are state-of-the-art, so that its employees are empowered to serve customers at the highest possible level.

Still—and again I cannot stress this point enough—it is these types of innovations that produce the most value. It is because of sustaining innovations that we can carry our smartphones—which would once have been considered supercomputers—in the palm of our hands. It's why our laptops don't need to weigh 250,000 tons. Even once-in-a-generation breakthroughs like Jim Allison's discovery of cancer immunotherapy needs sustaining innovation to move from being a promising possibility for a small minority of terminal patients to a standard therapy that can end unimaginable suffering for the vast majority.

DISRUPTIVE INNOVATION

Disruptive innovation at Experian happens at its DataLabs, which pursue opportunities in areas where no clear business model yet exists. There are no guidelines for financial performance, no preconceived notions of what a "good" information services business should look like, and no boundaries for what the data scientists can explore. Rather, the job of the DataLabs is to solve unresolved problems for customers and see if a business can be built around them.

By the standards of conventional business practice, that doesn't sound like a winning proposition, but for Experian it certainly is. The DataLabs are spinning out a continuous stream of profitable businesses that are sent to the other divisions to scale up. What it lacks in concrete business objectives, it makes up for with concrete business results.

How It All Works Together

What is most important to understand about Experian's innovation portfolio is how it all works together. If all you pursue is sustaining innovations, you leave too many promising opportunities on the table. At the same time, if you only pursue disruptive innovations, you will never get your business to scale profitably. Experian has become such an uncommonly successful innovator because it has been able to integrate both disruptive and sustaining innovations and power them both through its active involvement in the scientific community.

Another important thing to notice about Experian is how its innovation portfolio changed over time. After the merger between CCN
and TRW that created Experian, its industry was rapidly consolidating and much of its efforts were focused on increasing scale, running
its business efficiently, and providing continually improving service
to its corporate customers. Those things are still obviously important, but in order to continue to grow the company needs to seek out
new markets, which is the primary function of the DataLabs. At the
same time, data science is entering something of a renaissance, so it's
becoming increasingly important for Experian to stay in touch with
basic research going on in the academic community.

Yet the phenomenon of shifting innovation portfolios applies not
only to Experian, but to the marketplace as a whole. In the 1950s
and '60s, for example, many important technologies, such as digital
computers and xerography, were just beginning to emerge, so there
was enormous value in basic research and breakthrough innovation.
Firms like IBM and Xerox were able to dominate their industries for
decades through superior technology.

For the past 25 years, however, the basic technological
paradigms have been fairly standard and disruptive innovations—
well-understood technologies applied to new markets—became a
much more fruitful path to follow. Yet as I noted in the Introduction,
it is very likely that we are now entering a new era of innovation that
will be more similar to what we saw in the '50s and '60s than the '90s
or the aughts.

Old paradigms, such as Moore's Law and lithium-ion batteries, will reach their theoretical limits in the next 5 to 10 years. That
means that nascent technologies, including largely new areas such
as genomics, nanotechnology, and robotics, will play important and
maybe even decisive roles in value creation. This is likely to cause
innovation portfolios to shift again. You can't win in the marketplace by fighting the last war; you have to constantly look to the next
one and adjust your innovation portfolio accordingly, much like you
might change the asset mix in an investment portfolio from time
to time.

That's why it's important to continually innovate how we innovate
and deepen our knowledge of the rich tapestry of strategies available
to us. In the next four chapters we'll look at four broad categories
of innovation strategies: business model innovation, open innovation, innovating the core, and innovation at scale. It is very unlikely

that you could—or should—pursue all of them at the same time. Yet as you read through, you should not only think about whether they apply to your present situation, but try to imagine what potential problem or opportunity might arise and make one of them a valuable addition to your innovation portfolio.

CHAPTER FOUR

Developing New Business Models to Disrupt the Marketplace

*No business plan survives first
contact with the customer.*

—STEVE BLANK

By 2006 we knew we had a serious problem. Our company's onetime flagship product, called *Afisha*, was in a steady decline, and it was becoming all too clear that something had to be done. The problem was nobody had an idea exactly what. Operationally, nothing had really changed. We still believed in our product and our people. But what had once been a market leader that generated large profits that fueled the growth of our company had slowly but surely lost its market position.

Afisha was the brainchild of our company's founder, Jed Sunden, an American who had come to Ukraine to catalog Jewish cemeteries in 1995. Sensing opportunity in the former Soviet Republic, he decided to stay and launched the *Kyiv Post*, an English language weekly newspaper that quickly became known for hard-hitting, independent journalism. That was, in itself, a significant development in a country where just a few short years before the Communist party had controlled the primary news sources. As it built its reputation for strong reporting and integrity, the *Kyiv Post* became popular not only with the growing community of expatriate businessmen, but also with local Ukrainians looking for reliable news. It also helped them hone their English language skills, an asset becoming increasingly important for young Ukrainians looking to build a career.

When *Afisha* came out in 2000, it was an immediate hit. At its core, it was simply a guide to restaurants, nightlife, and other entertainment, but as with the *Kyiv Post*, Sunden made sure to stock it with strong editorial talent. Its restaurant, music, and movie columnists quickly became tastemakers in Kyiv, while its sex advice column, written by editor-in-chief Anna Dovgal but published under the pseudonym "Eva Bardot," achieved a cult status. Ad dollars soon came rolling in.[1]

In 2006, all of the elements that had made *Afisha* successful were still in place, but the business environment had changed significantly. The ad market, which had been worth less than $100 million in 2000, including TV, print, radio, and billboards, was now quickly approaching $1 billion. Strong multinational publishers like Hearst, Hachette, and Rodale had begun investing heavily into Ukrainian versions of top international titles like *Cosmopolitan*, *Elle*, and *Men's Health*. *Afisha*, although still popular with readers, was no longer a dominant brand. That diminished our ability to command top ad rates, while, at the same time, the booming media market sent our editorial costs through the roof.

I had joined the company two years before, when Jed had asked me to come and help improve operations. I spent two years revamping the company's sales and marketing efforts and also brought in a new digital team, including a user-experience expert from Poland's top web portal, Onet.pl, to enhance performance in our digital businesses. By 2006, those efforts had paid off. Our Russian language newsmagazine, *Korrespondent*, along with our web portal, *Bigmir*, were now undisputed market leaders, highly profitable, and growing robustly.

However, *Afisha* was a different kind of problem. Its columnists were just as popular as they had always been, and the same sales and marketing practices that had been implemented throughout the rest of the company had been applied there. Reviving the business would take more than the operational fixes I had been working to install over the past two years. *Afisha* needed a new business model.

The Anatomy of a Business Model

Remember, in the Innovation Matrix, we put disruptive innovation in the lower right quadrant because disruptive innovations have well-defined domains but poorly defined problems. In other words, they are essentially solutions looking for problems to solve, which is why they almost always require a new business model.

That's exactly the problem we had at *Afisha*. Our product was still popular with consumers, but the job it had normally done for advertisers, which was to provide a platform for their advertisements, was now being done better by the international magazine brands like *Cosmopolitan* and *Men's Health*. We were confident in our ability to put out a quality product, but we couldn't hope to compete with the caché those brands offered. Furthermore, because of international agreements, many advertisers were mandated, or at least strongly encouraged, to buy our competitors' products.

Another problem was that *Afisha* had mostly relied on free distribution in restaurants, clubs, and other venues. This strategy had served us well in the early days, when none of the publishers in Ukraine had strong distribution networks. Now, however, the international brands had increased circulation many times over, so the amount we could distribute at eateries and nightspots wasn't enough to be competitive. Also, because we had built our brand as a free product, distributors didn't want to carry us at newsstands. Worst of all, rising production costs were making free distribution an increasingly untenable financial proposition, especially considering the numbers of copies we would have to print to be competitive against the international brands. In sum, we were in quite a fix.

It was clear that we needed to figure out a different way of doing things—and fast. So Jed and I called a meeting of our senior managers to brainstorm new solutions. Some of what we came up with was fairly straightforward. It was decided that we would redesign the magazine to put more emphasis on editorial content rather than listings for restaurants, clubs, and events. With our revamped digital operation, we also saw various ways we could improve the website to increase our revenues there. Still, we knew that neither of these steps would create the kind of impact that was required. We didn't articulate the words "business model innovation" at the time—I don't think we were more than vaguely aware of the term—but that's what we needed.

A business model is often confused with a business plan. In truth, they are very different animals.

A *business plan* is basically a financial projection, in essence, an extended version of a quarterly budget. That can be very valuable, essential even, for an existing business. It helps you to understand the basic dynamics and underlying financial logic of your enterprise, quantify various assumptions and alert you to areas where adjustments need to be made.

A *business model*, however, provides the conceptual rather than the financial logic of your business by spelling out a coherent logic for how you create, deliver, and capture value. So to innovate a business model, you need to find a way to significantly improve on one of those elements for a given market.

Afisha, for example, created value through editorial content and advice on where to go in the city of Kyiv. It delivered that value through a free distribution magazine and a website. It captured value primarily through advertising sales. As I noted above, we were still confident in our ability to create value, but our models for delivering and capturing value were clearly broken.

So, in addition to improving our product through magazine and website redesigns, we came up with two additional ideas. The first was that we would offer licenses to publish *Afisha* in other cities. This would improve our ability to deliver value through expanded distribution. It would also help us capture additional value through licensing fees and the expanded advertising sales we would gain from building a national network.

The second idea was a bit far-fetched. It involved trying to revive our Afisha card program. Before I get to what our idea was, let me explain a little bit about the program. Although the vast majority of our distribution was free, we did have a small number of paying subscribers, all of whom received an Afisha card as part of their subscription. Merchants who participated in the program gave discounts to cardholders in return for some promotional space in the magazine.

The idea we had, which was not well thought through, involved creating an event calendar to go with the Afisha card and allowing merchants to promote events in the magazine and on the website in return for giving additional value to cardholders. For instance, a bar could offer reduced drink prices for a few hours; a retail store could hold a special shopping event; or a club could offer free admission for a night. We thought that this could increase the value of a subscription and reduce our reliance on free distribution. There was also a possibility, however remote, that someone might actually pay us to provide additional promotion for an event. To be honest, it was a bit of a goofy idea, but we were desperate and it seemed like a low-risk move. We figured that if we could get at least one decent event a week, it might be worth doing.

Here's what the two ideas looked like in terms of creating, delivering, and capturing value compared to our existing business model.

	OLD BUSINESS MODEL	LICENSING	AFISHA CARD EVENTS
Create Value	Editorial Content	Brand & Promotional Support	Promote Events
Deliver Value	Print and Web	Partnership	Leveraging Owned Assets
Capture Value	Ad Sales	Fees	Fees & Increased Subscription Sales

FIGURE 4.1   Afisha Business Model Transformation

So now we had two alternative business models to pursue, along with improving on our original one. We had no idea if either would work, so we gave the thankless job of testing them out to one of our most talented and promising executives, a young woman named Olga Sych.

Olga had come to our company through her brother, Vitaly, who was editor-in-chief of our flagship product, the *Korrespondent* newsmagazine. He was something of a growing celebrity, especially after the Orange Revolution had increased the visibility of political commentators. Olga, not one to live in the shadow of anyone and never lacking for ambition, was eager to make her mark and gladly took on the challenge.

Before we knew it, she outlined a licensing strategy and was contacting potential partners in every major city in Ukraine. A whirling dervish of energy, she traveled to each of them, researched each market, and soon had a list of promising candidates. In the months that followed, we built a national network of licensees and national coverage for the Afisha brand. It was more than we could have hoped for.

She also created an event calendar for the magazine to promote the Afisha card events. That was what created the issue that Olga came to me with a few weeks after our initial brainstorming meeting. "Grisha," she said, using the diminutive of my Russian name, "do you think we could hold two Afisha card events on the same night?" I didn't think it was a good idea to be competing with ourselves, so I asked her why we couldn't just move them to separate nights. "Because we have events booked for every night next week," she replied.

As it turned out, there was far more demand for Afisha branded events than we had realized. Within a few short months, instead of hustling to get one or two events per week, we were *limiting* events to seven per week. We were also getting requests for bigger promotions, and event agencies were calling and inquiring about partnerships. Subscriptions were up too, bringing in additional revenues.

Over the next few years, Olga built a thriving events business. When a French coffee brand came to us, we set up a partnership with a French film festival and created an art installation highlighting French film stars, with engaging blurbs about each written by our movie critic. It was a huge success! A travel company wanted us to drum up business, and we set up party trips in exotic locations, with discounts for Afisha cardholders (and a cut of the profits for us, of course). A beer company asked us to help launch a new brand, and we set up a six-city Frisbee tournament that went all summer long. It became the focal point of all of the company's promotional efforts for the brand launch.

Ironically, we never really made money off of the licensing idea that we had thought was a sure thing. The problem, which we didn't anticipate, was that the local markets were still not developed enough to support Afisha licenses. In the end, the licensees never created a sustainably profitable business, and neither did we. The events business, however, took off and became a major revenue stream. At the same time, it enhanced the Afisha brand and positioned it even better as the place to find something cool and fun to do with your free time. Best of all, it was a model that our multinational competitors, like *Cosmopolitan* and *Men's Health*, couldn't easily replicate. For all of their international prestige, they couldn't compete with us on edgy, authentic street-chic.

Although we didn't know it at the time, we had somehow stumbled and bumbled onto a genuine business model innovation.

That was a decade ago. If we faced the same situation today, we would have a clear framework to follow. It's called the Lean LaunchPad.

The Lean LaunchPad

The Lean LaunchPad is largely the brainchild of one man, Steve Blank, a child of immigrant parents who ran a grocery store in New York City.[2] After graduating high school, where he says he would have probably been chosen "least likely to succeed" if it had been put to a vote,[3] he attended Michigan State University for a semester before dropping out. From there, he made his way to Miami, where he worked at an airport and became fascinated with the electronics inside the planes. A friendly technician took him under his wing, and before long Steve found himself studying equipment manuals at home. Soon after, he enlisted in the Air Force to learn how to repair electronic equipment. He showed a remarkable aptitude and was managing a group of 40 technicians by the time he was 20 years old.[4]

When he got out of the Air Force in 1978, Blank went to Palo Alto. Silicon Valley was a mere shadow of what it is today, but there were a lot of military contractors looking for talented electrical technicians and a nascent start-up scene. Blank found himself very much in his element and eventually went on to work with eight start-up companies. Some were failures, but five of them went on to become public companies. In 1999, at the tender age of 45 but already a wealthy man, he retired.[5]

As he settled into his new life as a man of leisure, Blank began to reflect on his career. He started to write what he thought would be his memoirs, but as he did, he found that when he began to recount his experiences, he could see a clear and recurrent pattern. Every start-up begins with an idea, and that idea is always wrong in some way. What determined if the venture would succeed or fail had less to do with any particular quality of the initial vision, or even the market in which it sought to compete, than if the inevitable flaws were found and corrected faster than the company ran out of money.

Many find this notion startling. Why is the initial vision always wrong? Don't start-up founders have some understanding of the industry in which they seek to compete? Don't they do market research? Well, yes, but that's rarely sufficient. To understand why, think about planning a night out for your spouse or a close friend whom you know well. How likely are you to predict, with absolute precision, what they want to do on a particular evening? If you're anything like me, your hit rate will be fairly low. That's why most evening plans begin with the question, "What do you feel like doing tonight?" In essence, that's the problem that the Lean LaunchPad was designed to fix.

It occurred to Steve that start-ups were treated as if they were just a much younger version of an established company. But the truth is that they are totally different animals. While an existing enterprise has a clear model to follow, start-ups need to explore until they find one they can sustain. A successful business model cannot be simply conjured up or willed into existence, it is the result of exploration. What Blank noticed is that start-up founders were building the product first—and burning through most of their money—before the exploration began in earnest. So, not surprisingly, their first attempt almost always failed, which led to a mad scramble to correct their initial mistakes. With the benefit of hindsight, he saw that much better results could be achieved if start-ups merely accepted this simple truth and began their exploratory journey before they blew all their cash building out a full-blown version of a flawed product vision.[6]

His insight led him to develop a course called Customer Development that he taught at the Haas School of Business at the University of California at Berkeley and the School of Engineering at Stanford. That, in turn, led to a book, *The Four Steps to the Epiphany*. Later, one of Blank's students, Eric Ries, built on Blank's work and published *The Lean Startup*, which became a *New York Times* bestseller. Also, as we will see at the end of the chapter, Alexander Osterwalder created a tool called the Business Model Canvas that would help operationalize these concepts. Together, these ideas combine to form what is today known as the Lean Launchpad. In a nutshell, it boils down to three key concepts: Customer Development, the Minimum Viable Product, and the Pivot.

Customer Development

Remember that disruptive innovations are essentially solutions looking for problems. That's why they are so different from other kinds of innovations. When we pursue disruptive innovations, we are generally not trying to discover new technologies or improve on existing products, but rather to find a market for a technology that already exists. That's why disruptive innovations almost always require a new business model.

To see how this works, consider the story of Chester Carlson. Self-taught and brilliant, he worked for years tinkering with his invention even while holding down a day job and going to law school at night. When his wife got tired of the explosions he made mixing chemicals in the kitchen, he moved his work to a second-floor room in a house his mother-in-law owned.

After working on it for over a decade, Carlson finally had a working prototype and tried to interest the great companies of the day, such as Kodak, IBM, and GE, but all demurred. It wasn't that they weren't impressed with the machine, they just didn't see a market for it at the price they would have to charge to make a profit. Finally, Carlson teamed up with the Haloid Corporation, whose president, Joe Wilson, had a billion-dollar idea. Instead of selling the machines, why don't they lease them and charge per use? The idea took off, and the company we now know as the Xerox Corporation was born.[7]

The brilliance of Wilson's business model was that it couldn't possibly work for anyone but Xerox. The leases were priced so cheaply that there would only be a profit if customers made more than 2,000 copies per month. That seemed like a lot, but Wilson saw it basically as a chicken and egg type of problem. Companies weren't making copies because they didn't have a Xerox machine. Once they did, they would start seeing a need to make copies they never knew they had.

In 1959, Xerox launched its 914 copier, which became an instant hit. The technology made copying so much easier that before long their customers averaged 2,000 copies per day, instead of per month. Wilson's bet had paid off. Revenues grew at a 41 percent compound annual rate for over a decade, and the small firm soon became a titan of American business.

Notice that the technology breakthrough came 21 years before the business success—as we noted in Chapter 1, innovation is never a single event. During that time the central problem wasn't the lack of a breakthrough product, but the lack of customers and a business model that would allow Haloid to make money and finance further improvements. In this case, it only took a change in one element of the business model—how the firm chose to capture value—that made all the difference. Selling copiers was a bust, but leasing them turned out to be a once-in-a-lifetime opportunity!

Twenty-five years later, Canon and Ricoh would disrupt Xerox's business not by improving on the product, but by identifying a new market segment: small and medium-sized businesses that couldn't afford a top-of-the-line Xerox product. They started making copiers that didn't perform nearly as well, but were smaller and cheaper.[8] As the new products gained traction, the technology improved, and soon they began to compete for Xerox's big corporate customers, who now saw the benefits of buying smaller, cheaper desktop copiers that could sit on every floor rather than taking up an entire copy room like Xerox's products did.

In both cases, the essential insight could not be discovered in a lab or conjured up in some boardroom, but could only be arrived at through better understanding of the customer. That was the "repeatable pattern" that Blank noticed when he began to reflect on his career. Start-ups spend far too much time trying to develop products and not nearly enough to develop customers.

While Blank's ideas have become well established in recent years, initially they were seen as heresy. After all, how can you build a company without a product? But what he realized was that the product development process was ill suited to a company with no customers and no proven market. All too often, it leads you to produce the wrong product because all you have to go on are assumptions. If any of those assumptions turn out to be wrong, as is almost always the case, your product won't sell no matter how thoughtfully it is designed or to what specifications it is constructed. Even worse, by the time you find that out, you will have already burned up a significant chunk of cash, greatly reducing the likelihood that you will ever identify a viable business model before you go bankrupt.

So instead of starting with a clear product vision and then racing to a "ship" date, Blank suggests that first you start looking for customers. Notice, he doesn't say "a market," but simply "customers." That's no accident. As he writes, "you are going to develop a product for the few, not the many. . . . In a startup, the first product is not designed to satisfy a mainstream customer."[9] More specifically, he suggests that you find customers that have not only identified a problem, but have already either designated a budget to solve the problem or have already cobbled together a stopgap solution and are looking for something more permanent. He calls these types of customers "visionary customers."[10]

Yet merely asking customers what they want is not enough. You have to validate that they are actually willing to pay for your product or service. That's where the minimum viable product comes in.

The Minimum Viable Product

Consider the case of Webvan, a home delivery grocery service similar to those provided by Amazon Fresh, Tesco, and Whole Foods today. Founded in 1996, it was a promising idea and attracted enormous interest from investors, raising over $800 million over the next two years.[11] Wanting to build brand recognition and anticipation for its launch, it invested in an expensive marketing program to capture the maximum share of what promised to be a massive market.

But it wasn't all smoke and mirrors. The company also designed a great website and a highly advanced distribution system, with automated warehouses that were much more sophisticated than what the typical grocery chain had at the time. By 1999, it had 400 employees and launched its first regional web store. Soon after, it signed a billion-dollar deal with the construction company Bechtel to build 26 additional distribution centers and then hired another 500 employees to be sure that the company could continue to provide excellent service even as demand soared.

Webvan immediately found significant demand for its service and was delivering 2,500 orders per day, which was impressive. Unfortunately, it was not nearly impressive enough to support the massive infrastructure that the company had invested in. In fact, its distribution center was operating at a mere 30 percent of capacity. From that point on, Webvan was on a death march. It went bankrupt in 2001 and has been a cautionary tale ever since.[12]

Now consider the case of Nick Swinmurn. In 1999, at around the same time that Webvan was raising hundreds of millions of dollars to transform the grocery market, he believed that he could do something similar with shoe stores. Yet the similarities end there. Instead of raising money to invest in a sophisticated distribution platform, Swinmurn went to local shoe stores, took pictures of shoes, and posted them online. When a customer ordered a pair, he went to the store and purchased them for full price. He lost money on every sale.

But unlike Webvan, Swinmurn wasn't trying to run a business; he was running an experiment, and selling a few shoes at a loss was an incredibly cheap and efficient way to test his business idea. Instead of spending money on expensive marketing research to see what people said about their interest in buying shoes online, he was actually testing it with real paying customers. Once he saw that there was demand, he brought on investors and began to scale the operation. That business, called Zappos, had sales of more than $1 billion by 2008 and was sold to Amazon the next year for $1.2 billion.[13]

That, in essence, is the power of building a minimal viable product, and it was what we stumbled into when we created the events page in *Afisha*. Although we didn't know it at the time, we had found the perfect way to test a new business model: simply putting an announcement in our magazine and seeing what the response was. As it turned out, we immediately saw that the potential was far greater than we could have hoped for.

A minimum viable product is not a prototype. As Eric Ries writes, "Unlike a prototype or a concept test, an MVP is designed not to just answer product design or technical questions. Its goal is to test fundamental business hypotheses."[14] In Netflix's case founder Reed Hastings simply mailed a DVD to himself to see if it would work. It did, and he then knew that renting movies by mail was a realistic proposition.[15] Drew Houston of Dropbox created a three-minute demonstration video and put it on his company's website. The beta list went from 5,000 to 75,000 almost overnight, and he could be sure that there was real demand for the features Dropbox was working on. Manuel Rosso, the CEO of Food on the Table, a popular mobile app that provides easy-to-cook recipes, sale items, and grocery lists for weeknight diners, got his start by going to customers' homes. Each week, he would personally hand his customers a package containing shopping lists based on what was on sale at local markets and relevant recipes. His price for the service? Just $9.95 per week, not nearly enough to pay for his time and trouble. But he learned what customers wanted and what they were willing to pay for.[16] Once he knew that, all that was left was a set of fairly conventional engineering problems. Food on the Table was acquired by the Food Network in 2014.

A minimum viable product is absolutely essential to build a sustainable business model. It allows you to test your assumptions before you go off half-cocked on some ill-considered bet-the-company initiative. But it is also just the start. As noted above, at first you are just trying to find customers. Not just any customers, but as Steve Blank put it, *visionary customers*. These are the early adopters who are adventurous enough—or desperate enough—to take a flyer on a new and unproven product. As you scale your business, you'll find that the customers in the larger market have very different needs.

The Pivot

When we first envisioned the events business at Afisha, it wasn't really a business at all. It was merely a marketing scheme for magazine subscriptions. We felt that by adding value to the Afisha card, we could sell more subscriptions and cover more of our printing and distribution costs. It was a shot in the dark, but it worked. However, the results of our experiment were so impressive that we also saw the possibility that events could be a significant revenue driver. That required a serious reimagining of the initial vision.

At the beginning, we had a fairly simple plan. Local businesses would produce events, we would promote them, and our subscribers would get benefits through their Afisha card. However, to transform what was essentially a promotion into a serious revenue driver, we would have to make adjustments. The corporate clients that were willing to pay for events needed more than a simple announcement in our magazine. Olga had to beef up her team with people capable of designing, managing, and monitoring events. (We learned that the hard way. One of our early club launches attracted so many people that it nearly caused a riot.) We also needed to partner with event specialists, travel companies, and municipal authorities. Each of these new aspects required us to accept new challenges and learn new skills. It is a testament to Olga's talents that she pulled it all off.

Every initial vision is wrong. There is always some element of the business model that doesn't match reality. Whether it is the type of customer, the initial choice of partners, the distribution channel, or something else, as your business grows from the initial group of early adopters you will find that you have to change something significant to build a sustainable business model.

In *The Lean Startup*, Eric Ries tells the story of Votizen. It was the vision of David Binetti, who had created USA.gov, the first portal for the federal government. He saw an opportunity to build a social network for politics. The initial product took three months and $1,200 to produce. Initially, the sign-up rate was low, about 5 percent, but by tweaking the features, messaging, and design and split testing to evaluate the results, he was able to push that up to a much more viable 17 percent registration rate, with 90 percent of those actually activating their registrations and using their service. Still, less than 10 percent of users were coming back and inviting their friends to join, which was far from sufficient for achieving the kind of viral growth a social network would require.

So he changed his vision. Rather than merely just a place for users to discuss political issues, he gave them a mechanism to make an actual impact. He added a feature that allowed users to send printed letters and petitions to their public representatives. The thinking was that activists would be willing to pay to access engaged citizens who might be willing to support their cause. Results improved. Registrations rose to 42 percent, while retention and referrals grew to 21 percent and 54 percent, respectively. Still, the number of activists willing to pay was under 1 percent. Clearly, that could not support a viable business.

Finally, Binetti hit upon a model that worked. Rather than having activists pay for the ability to recruit supporters, he built a tool similar to Google's AdWords platform that let anybody who wanted to send messages to potential supporters. Now, 11 percent of users were willing to pay 20 cents per message. After 18 months and $120,000, he had finally found a sustainable business model that he could scale.[17] He soon raised $1.5 million in venture funding from Silicon Valley legend Peter Thiel, built a user base of 186 million, and in 2011 sold the company for an undisclosed amount.[18]

We tend to think of start-ups as a modern version of a Horatio Alger story. An unlikely underdog figures out how to make a better mousetrap and outsmarts its larger, better-financed rivals to prevail against all odds. Yet the work of people like Steve Blank and Eric Ries shows that's not really true. You don't start with a better mousetrap; you start out with a seriously flawed one. What makes the difference between success and failure is how willing you are to recognize that simple fact and work to identify a sustainable business model before you run out of money. The best way to do that is not to throw caution to the wind and charge forward with reckless abandon, but to explore, experiment, and iterate until you hit on the right combination of creating, delivering, and capturing value.

As it turns out, that's not just good advice for start-ups, but for any enterprise.

Applying Lean LaunchPad Principles to the Enterprise

At first glance, large enterprises don't have much in common with start-ups. They already have paying customers, a history of profits, and an abundance of resources. But, look a little closer and it becomes clear that there are important similarities. As history has shown, even smart, successful companies can see new product launches go horribly wrong. Remember New Coke? How about the Apple Newton? At the same time, as we saw with both Afisha and Xerox, even successful business models are often disrupted. That's why Lean LaunchPad techniques are as important for enterprises as they are for start-ups.

That's exactly what Eric Haller did when he returned to Experian. Although the company was not in crisis, he saw that there were far more opportunities in the marketplace than his company was able to pursue within its current organization structure. But rather than embark on an extensive—and expensive—product development program, he instead designed Experian DataLabs to co-create new business models with its customers.

A typical situation recently occurred at a meeting with a large bank, where one of the senior executives said, "You know we have a problem that's really giving us trouble. We have a lot of newer businesses that come to us for loans, and we need to do due diligence on them. It's an incredibly labor intensive process for us to verify whether they are a good credit risk."

Eric Haller just smiles when he hears things like that. "We regularly sit down with our clients and try and figure out what's causing them *agita*," he told me, "because we know that solving problems is what opens up enormous business opportunities for us."

From there his team of data scientists was able to put together a prototype and present it to the client within 90 days. It wasn't perfect—the system could only identify 20 percent of the bank's potential customers that had no discernable credit history, but that was enough to show the potential of their approach. Notice how much easier this process is for Experian than it would be for a start-up. Haller didn't need to work to get in the door; the bank was already a paying client. It also wasn't hard to identify a need as the bank executive was almost literally crying out for a solution. Within weeks of presenting the prototype, Experian had a preliminary contract.

Once the DataLabs team validates the client's interest—due to intellectual property considerations it almost always asks for a signed agreement before going beyond the minimum viable product stage—it begins to co-develop the product according to the client's specifications. This tends to be an iterative process, with a number of versions going back and forth. In the case of the credit verification product, over the next few months new features were added, such as a more helpful user interface, integration with other systems like auditing and workflow management, and customization options for the analysis. Many of these improvements would not have been possible without the client's input. Performance was also improved. Now the system was able to verify 50 percent of the "no hits" that were frustrating the bank.

It is at this stage that the new product is shown to at least one of the client advisory groups that Experian maintains in functional areas such as credit, fraud, and marketing services to see if there is more general interest. The additional consultation also makes it possible to pivot to different functionality, customer segments, or revenue models, if needed. Once the value proposition and the business model has been validated by Experian's current customers and further input is taken from Experian's client advisory groups and internal marketing staff, it is ready to be rolled out to the larger market. That's when the rest of the Experian organization gets involved.

Engineers scale up the technology to ensure that it can work in a larger environment. Product managers work on issues such as pricing, legal compliance, and positioning. The sales staff is trained to handle client questions, and a promotional campaign is designed and executed. Every aspect of the pilot project and the business model is refined and strengthened. This process can take anywhere from 3 to 12 months, depending on how much integration needs to be done with Experian's existing systems. That's not particularly fast by the standards of a start-up, but it's not altogether slow either, and it brings all the resources of a $4 billion company to bear, something that no start-up can match.

The credit verification product was formally rolled out in the summer of 2016 under the brand name BizVerify, about six months after the decision was made to move forward. That's about average for DataLabs projects. At the time of launch it already had three paying clients and an army of salespeople with established relationships supporting it.

What struck me when I spoke to the executives at Experian was how large firms can leverage their assets to make Lean LaunchPad techniques far more effective. Customer relationships are already developed and capabilities are already in place. Another factor is scale itself. Start-up firms usually only get to make one bet, but

Experian DataLabs has a dozen or more disruptive projects going on a regular basis.

Another application of the Lean LaunchPad is to help innovative new technologies cross the "valley of death," the notorious gap between the discovery of an innovative new technology and its commercialization. One way the U.S. government tries to close that gap is through Small Business Innovation Research (SBIR) commercialization grants, to help small firms with promising technology to advance their work to the point where it can attract funding from the private sector.

In 2013, Stanford University and the University of California at Berkeley, with funding from the National Science Foundation (NSF), set up the I-Corps program to teach Lean LaunchPad techniques to firms receiving SBIR grants. The results have been impressive. In the initial project, 19 out of 21 teams moved forward with commercializing their technology.[19] Considering that success rates for SBIR recipients often average around 20 percent,[20] that's an amazing success.

A similar Lean Launchpad program was started at Australia's Commonwealth Science and Industrial Research Organisation (CSIRO) with the help of Tim Kastelle, an innovation professor at the University of Queensland Business School. With its portfolio of 1,800 patents, CSIRO thought it could do a better job at commercializing its discoveries. The program there was so successful that CSIRO has initiated a $150 million fund to support start-up firms based on research developed there, even though the agency suffered a 20 percent budget cut in 2014.

"We used to think, 'build it and they will come,'" Peter Kambouris, director of business development and commercialization at CSIRO told me. "Now our researchers regularly go out to industry to understand where we can make the most impact, and that allows us to pivot and align our resources to meet those particular challenges. The Lean LaunchPad has also helped us create a much more collaborative relationship with industry to the point where we are now truly codeveloping exciting new products, rather than just attempting to sell what we had already invented."

So clearly, Lean Launchpad principles are not just for start-ups, but for any organization of any size, public or private. Business models can also work wonders when effectiveness is not just a matter of profit and loss, but social impact.

Designing New Business Models for Social Good

By any measure, Children's Health in Dallas is a world-class institution. It boasts a top-notch medical staff, is consistently ranked among the best children's hospitals in the country, and features a Level 1 trauma center. Yet by 2011, despite the accolades, its CEO, Chris Durovich, was beginning to have doubts about the center's impact on the community.

The problem was that although its patients were getting excellent care once they entered the facility, the health indicators in the community as a whole were getting worse, especially with regard to chronic conditions such as diabetes and asthma. Durovich was determined to fix the problem. So he brought in Peter Roberts, a longtime healthcare executive, to diagnose the problems in the community and design solutions that would make a positive impact. That's what led the two to bring in the Business Innovation Factory, a nonprofit organization set up by Saul Kaplan, a former executive director of the Rhode Island Economic Development Corporation, to explore, design, and test new business models for social enterprises. Eli Stefanski, a Parson's graduate who cut her teeth designing development projects in places like sub-Saharan Africa, was chosen to lead the project.

Traditionally, the way medical professionals seek to improve healthcare is by improving hospital operations through better training, procedures, and processes. But in this case, the Children's Medical Center was already considered one of the finest institutions in the country. So rather than look inside the hospital for answers, Stefanski and her team went out into the community.

Their first task was to diagnose the problem. "We wanted to understand why delivering world-class treatment wasn't having an impact," she told me. So her team sifted through hospital records and identified 32 families that had at least one member suffering from a chronic condition, about half of which used the emergency room for primary care.

Once the families agreed to take part in the study, the team interviewed and then observed them in the context of their daily life—going to the grocery store, playing with the kids at the park, and so on. They also had them do "projection activities," such as asking family members to create a collage about how they see the world and various situations within it.

What they found is that the families didn't think a lot about health specifically. What concerned them was general well-being, including how they felt both mentally and physically, how effectively they were able to respond to life situations, how they were connected or disconnected with knowledge that could help them navigate life's obstacles, and how much support they felt from other family members, friends, and members of the community.

The team also saw that the children, to a large extent, experienced the world through their family and that the healthcare system was largely undermining rather than supporting social levers of support. It seemed that there could be a great opportunity to empower "first generation changemakers" to help the families interact with the healthcare system in a more positive way.

After Stefanski and her team had spent six months researching the problem and developed a workable hypothesis, the way forward seemed clear. They set out to design a community outreach program through 16 primary care centers that would leverage rather than undermine community and family relationships to promote better well-being. Alas, while the idea seemed to be a no-brainer, much like the Afisha licensing scheme, it proved to be unworkable. The administrators of the primary care centers were reluctant to burden their already overworked medical staff with additional responsibilities. They were, in many ways, too invested in the traditional model. As they saw it, it was their job to provide care for the sick, not to do community work.

So the team set out to build the necessary infrastructure within the community itself. They designed an assessment tool, the "family well-being quotient," that identified a set of behaviors that determined well-being and evaluated the families every two weeks for three months. At the same time, they gave the families a set of design challenges to come up with programs that would improve their well-being. Two of these—a "pop-up food and nutrition experience" created for and by the families and a three-week educational camp with a hip-hop theme—were put into action. Over the next three months, well-being scores improved markedly.

Creating those first prototypes helped the team learn about the conditions for well-being, but they still needed to find a sustainable model. The hospital also learned from a study with asthma patients that using techniques similar to what Stefanski and her team had found effective in Dallas communities led to an almost 50 percent decrease in emergency room visits.[21] That has the potential to free up an enormous amount of resources that can be deployed more effectively elsewhere.

So now, Children's Health is pivoting to a new model: a community-based approach that is integrated into an HMO managed by the hospital, which is expected to enroll 15,000 children and their families in 2017. Navigators from Children's Health will be retrained and repurposed. Instead of just identifying symptoms and encouraging adherence to treatment, they will focus on empowering well-being in the families as a whole. To do so, they integrate with the Children's Health and Wellness Alliance, a nonprofit that weaves together more than 100 community resources such as schools, social service, and faith-based organizations.

For example, previously a navigator might visit a home of a child who suffered an acute event of diabetes or asthma and check for symptoms, such as glucose levels or the presence of allergens. The navigator might also bring along an extra inhaler or some pamphlets on diet. The goal was to transition that acute event into a manageable condition. Now, however, the goal will be customized goal setting related to well-being. For example, if the family is having problems with rodents in their building, they might be directed to a community housing advocate so that they can avoid a high-pressure situation with an indifferent landlord that would be bound to increase the stress level of the whole family.

The plan will be funded through the assumption of Medicaid liabilities for the children and will use a portion of those funds to finance navigators and other programs to support well-being among the HMO members. As Peter Roberts told me, "Through the work of Eli and her team, we have seen demonstrable proof that by increasing the scope of our care to encompass the social determinants of health—including the patients' families—we can significantly improve medical outcomes while reducing costs. It's critically important that we look beyond the care we deliver in the hospital; we have to engage people where they live and the communities that serve them."

Clearly, the patterns Steve Blank noticed among start-ups in Silicon Valley are far more pervasive and widely applicable than he first imagined. Whether it is an entertainment magazine in Ukraine, a children's hospital in Dallas, or a world-class research organization in Australia, the basic principles of the Lean LaunchPad—get out of the building, build a minimum viable product, learn, iterate, and pivot—apply equally well. Innovation requires far more than tinkering with test tubes and algorithms and pilot projects—it also requires us to identify a sustainable business model.

The Business Model Canvas: A Management System for Innovating New Business Models

Clearly, business model innovation is becoming an essential skill for all types of enterprises. However, merely learning the concepts is not enough. To be able to effectively innovate business models consistently, we need a management system, just as we do for other business processes, like marketing or accounting. That's exactly the problem a young doctoral student began working on in 2000.

Alexander Osterwalder's path to his PhD dissertation was unconventional, to say the least. As a first-year undergraduate student at the University of Lausanne in Switzerland, he was more interested in beach volleyball than his studies. With dreams of a professional career, he made it to class infrequently and failed out of the business program. Eventually, he got his academic career back on track and graduated with a degree in political science.

Osterwalder also found a field of academic study he could be passionate about. Inspired by his professor in management information science, Yves Pigneur, and rejected by McKinsey & Co., the only firm he applied to, Alex decided to undertake doctoral studies, and he jumped in with all the passion and fervor that he once directed at beach volleyball. "When I start something that I'm passionate about, I really want to be the best," he told me. And his professor had a particular project in mind for his new protégé.

At the time, with the Internet ascendant, there was a lot of discussion about business models in the air, but it was little more than a colloquial term. It seemed that there was vast potential in creating a management system for business models, but there was little in the way of established principles from which to build on. As Osterwalder would write, the term "business model" became a "buzzword and was used by managers, academics and journalists for everything and nothing related to the 'new economy.' "[22]

Over the next four years, Osterwalder rigorously scoured the academic literature for any discussion of business models he could find. As he read paper after paper, he found no shortage of wisdom, but very little continuity. There were different definitions of what a business model was, what business models were composed of, and what made them successful. Eventually, he managed to pull together the disparate threads into something resembling a coherent whole, distilling all he had read and seen into nine distinctive components that make up business models.

He published his dissertation, "The Business Model Ontology," in 2004 and posted it on his blog. To his great surprise, people began downloading it. First it was just a trickle, then dozens, and eventually thousands were flocking to his site to see what he had written. Almost overnight, he became a minor Internet sensation. Soon invitations to speak came rolling in.

In the years that followed, Osterwalder established his own consultancy and started working with companies looking to create, define, or innovate their business models. He also traveled to Silicon Valley and met Steve Blank, who invited Alex to visit him at his ranch for the weekend. The two became fast friends and spoke into the night about business models. As he continually worked with companies and traveled, it became increasingly clear that businesses needed more than just business model concepts; they needed a practical tool that they could work with every day.

It was with that idea in mind that Osterwalder created the Business Model Canvas* (shown at the end of the chapter in Figure 4.2), which he published in his 2010 book *Business Model Generation*. Today, the Business Model Canvas has come to be seen as such an essential tool for developing business models that it is increasingly difficult to get a start-up funded without it. In essence, it is a more refined and actionable version of his original PhD dissertation, incorporating the nine business model components, which he calls building blocks, into an easy-to-use tool that business executives all over the world use to develop new business models. "The essential power of the Business Model Canvas is that it makes business models clear and tangible by creating a tangible artifact. That's what facilitates better thinking and more strategic conversations around creating and iterating business models," Osterwalder told me.

When I think back to those days in 2006 when we began innovating the Afisha business model, what I remember is how much

---

* The Business Model Canvas can be downloaded from the Strategyzer website at http://www.businessmodelgeneration.com/canvas/bmc.

pressure we felt to come up with a viable plan. Although we had learned from operating our digital business many of the most important components of the Lean LaunchPad framework, such as prototyping, iterating, and the value of running experiments, we were still somehow under the impression that it was our job as managers to have all the answers. The events business seemed like nothing more than a happy accident.

It's clear now that we should have spent more time pursuing similar "accidents." All too often, managers see their jobs through two lenses: strategy and execution. That's a reasonable approach when you are operating in a stable market, with clearly defined industry boundaries, a stable customer base, and a predictable technological environment, but few businesses enjoy those luxuries anymore. They are largely relics of a dying age.

We can no longer assume that how we create, deliver, and capture value will continue to be relevant for any period of time. In all likelihood, at least one of those elements is already being disrupted or soon will be. We need to start treating business model innovation with the same discipline that we treat any other business function, like production, marketing, or finance.

* * * * *

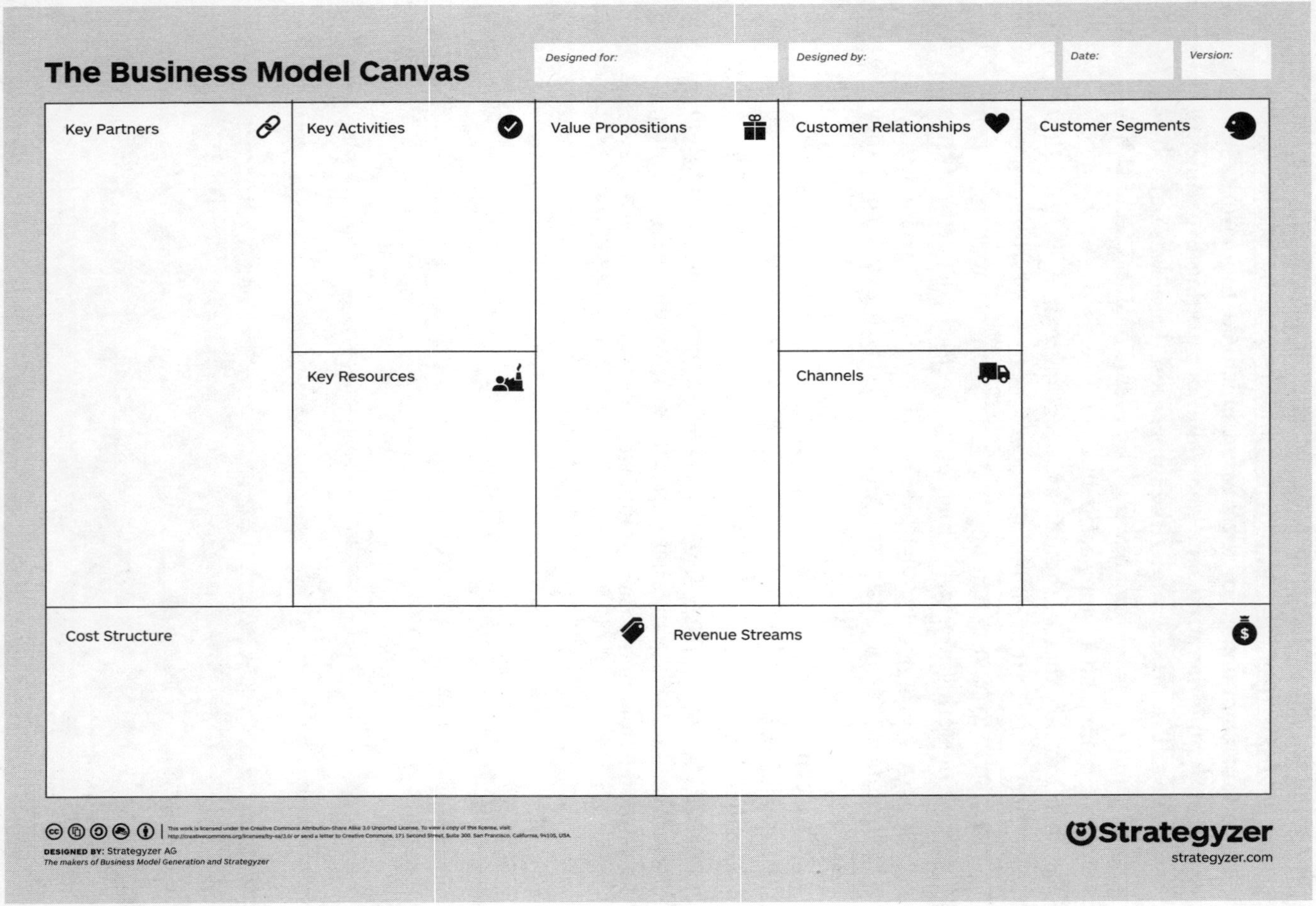
The Business Model Canvas
Designed for:
Designed by:
Date:
Version:
Key Partners
Key Activities
Key Resources
Value Propositions
Customer Relationships
Channels
Customer Segments
Cost Structure
Revenue Streams
This work is licensed under the Creative Commons Attribution-Share Alike 3.0 Unported License. To view a copy of this license, visit: http://creativecommons.org/licenses/by-sa/3.0/ or send a letter to Creative Commons, 171 Second Street, Suite 300, San Francisco, California, 94105, USA.
DESIGNED BY: Strategyzer AG
The makers of Business Model Generation and Strategyzer
Strategyzer
strategyzer.com

FIGURE 4.2 Business Model Canvas (http://www.businessmodelgeneration.com/canvas/bmc)

THE NINE BUSINESS MODEL BUILDING BLOCKS

1. **Key partners.** These are the key partners you will need to create, deliver, and capture value, including buyers, suppliers, strategic alliances, and joint venture partners.
2. **Key activities.** These are all the activities you will need to engage in to successfully execute your business model, including production, logistics, problem solving, maintaining platforms, and so on.
3. **Key resources.** These are the resources you will need to either acquire or gain access to, such as physical assets, intellectual property, human capital, and financial resources.
4. **Value proposition.** The value proposition describes the benefits that your business model will produce for your customers.
5. **Customer relationship.** This building block describes the relationship you will have with your customers, such as dedicated personal assistance, self-service, advisory service, and so on.
6. **Channels.** These are the ways you will interact with your customers, such as retail outlets, a website, distribution partners, and so on.
7. **Customer segments.** These are the particular types of customers that you believe will be willing to pay for your product or service (mass market, niche market, etc.).
8. **Cost structure.** Your cost structure is the total costs you will incur from acquiring and maintaining key resources, operating key activities, and costs related to key partnerships.
9. **Revenue streams.** These are the various ways you will capture value, such as through sales margins, service fees, subscription fees, and so on.

---- CHAPTER FIVE ----

Opening Up Innovation

Given enough eyeballs, all bugs are shallow.

—LINUS'S LAW

When Microsoft launched Kinect for the Xbox in 2010, it quickly became the hottest consumer device ever, selling 8 million units in just the first two months.[1] It was, not surprisingly, the product of millions of dollars of investment and years of hard work. The journey began in 2006, when Don Mattrick, the head of the software giant's thriving Xbox business, issued an inspired challenge to his team: find me a way of to get rid of the game controller.

A small incubation team was formed under a promising technology whiz named Alex Kipman, who would later go on to develop the HoloLens for Microsoft. The team quickly identified an Israeli company that had developed a key technology: a device that could shoot off infrared beams of light into a room and measure the changes in the patterns as they bounced off surfaces. From there, Microsoft researchers wrote sophisticated algorithms that would allow the system to track the body movements of a specific person without getting confused by rapid changes in position or appearance. Speech recognition, the product of longstanding research that had already been underway at the firm, was also added. The result was a truly revolutionary product.[2]

The device caught the attention of more than just technology journalists and adoring fans. Before long, hackers started breaking into Kinect and modifying its technology. Ordinarily, the software giant would have sprung its famously aggressive legal department into action, sending out "cease and desist" letters threatening grave consequences for meddling with its proprietary technology. But that never happened. In fact, Microsoft soon released a software development kit (SDK) to help the hackers along and would later release portions of the source code under an open source license. Just a few years earlier, even these relatively small steps would have been considered heresy at Microsoft, but there was still more to come. The company would soon announce the creation of an accelerator program that would invite developers to share their Kinect modifications and offered $20,000 and office space to the developers of the 10 most promising projects to develop their ideas further.

These developments were an absolute shock to many in the tech community. Microsoft, which had elevated its opposition to the open source movement to nearly the status of a religion—CEO Steve Ballmer had once referred to Linux as a "cancer"—now seemed to be embracing it fully.[3] What could account for such a dramatic about-face?

As it turns out, the forces driving open innovation by 2010 had become so powerful that not even Microsoft could deny them anymore.

The Erosion of Proprietary Advantage

In the nineteenth century, the industrial revolution fundamentally changed the way things were made. Production, rather than being dispersed among cottage industries and guilds, became centralized in large factories. Charismatic men like Vanderbilt, Carnegie, Rockefeller, and later Ford built enormously powerful enterprises that controlled all aspects of production, from the supply of raw materials and the capital stock to distribution and sales channels.

Yet the twentieth century saw the rise of a much different kind of organization. The combination of antitrust laws and the sheer scale of the type of enterprises that were emerging required a very different form of management. The hard-charging robber barons were replaced by professional managers such as Alfred Sloan at General Motors, Charles Schwab at U.S. Steel, and Owen Young at General Electric. Hardly household names, they were more akin to technocrats, engineering ever-greater efficiency to keep the productivity machine humming smoothly.

Microsoft was very much in line with this type of twentieth-century organization. Although it didn't depend on physical products for its revenue, its strategy was driven by its desire to dominate the entire value chain through its control of the operating system for computers. So it was natural for the company to see the open source movement as nothing less than a horde of barbarians at the gate. The initial assault on Microsoft's dominance was Linux, an open source operating system that competed directly with the tech giant in the corporate market. Even a mere mention of its name would induce scowls at Microsoft's Redmond headquarters.

Linux was the brainchild of a student at the University of Helsinki named Linus Torvalds. In 1991, Torvalds began developing a version of the Unix operating system that was used in high-powered workstations popular with large enterprises and scientific institutions at the time. Unlike Microsoft, he didn't seek to sell his work, but released it for free and invited other developers to improve it. He posted this message on Usenet with the source code:

> Hello netlanders,
>
> Do you pine for the nice days of minix-1.1, when men were men and wrote their own device drivers? Are you without a nice project and just dying to cut your teeth on an OS you can try to modify for your needs? . . . . :-)
>
> I'm doing a (free) operating system, just a hobby, won't be big and professional. . . . I'd like any feedback on things people like/dislike . . .
>
> This is a program for hackers by a hacker. I've enjoyed doing it, and somebody might enjoy looking at it and even modifying it for their own needs. . . . Drop me a line if you are willing to let me use your code.[4]

By 1993, Torvalds and his band of volunteers had developed a system that was just as stable and reliable as commercial versions of Unix. What's more, it was far more flexible. If you needed to run a piece of software that wasn't currently supported on Linux, you could just alter the program to fix your problem, and it would help everyone else who used the operating system too. As the community around Linux grew, it became an unbeatable proposition. As powerful as Microsoft was, it couldn't compete with thousands of highly skilled programmers willing to work for free.[5]

Linux wasn't an isolated event, either. Randy Terbush, today the CTO of medical technology start-up Lifeguard Health Networks, remembers starting to work with open software in the 1980s, when the AutoCAD software he was using at his job at an engineering firm wasn't doing what he needed it to. As a soils engineer, he had to determine if a particular environment was safe to build on and deliver precise documents laying out specifications. It wasn't the type of thing where you had much room for error. If the documents he created weren't perfectly understood, disaster could ensue.

So Terbush initially went on Usenet to get help modifying the AutoCAD software, but his time in the online discussion groups soon turned into something much more. He called it an "online university" because there were so many people who were so knowledgeable and also so willing to mentor him. Terbush was an enthusiastic pupil and within a few years became a top-notch programmer.

When the Internet was opened up to allow commercial applications in 1994, Terbush sensed opportunity. He quit his job and started a web hosting company. However, there was no commercial web server software you could simply buy off the shelf. At the time, many of his friends on Usenet were using a version developed by Rob McCool at the National Center for Supercomputing Applications at the University of Illinois at Urbana, but after McCool left the center to join entrepreneur Marc Andreessen at the soon-to-be blockbuster start-up Netscape, that no longer seemed like a reliable option.

By this point, Terbush's business was booming and he was serving high-profile clients such as Schoolhouse Rock and Sesame Street. The idea that their websites could go down because of unreliable web server software simply wasn't acceptable. So he and seven of his friends on Usenet formed the Apache group to develop an open standard. "We weren't anarchists," he remembers. "We were seeking to create some kind of order and protect our own businesses. At the time, AOL, Microsoft, and others wanted to create their own standards, which would have turned the web into a set of walled off islands instead of an open marketplace. That would have meant absolute chaos for everyone. The market was crying out for a reliable standard and the fact that we were open and free, and were offering a license so that other businesses could be protected, was a major spur to adoption."[6]

In 1999 the Apache Software Foundation—ironically the same entity under which Microsoft would open source the Kinect source code years later—was formally incorporated in Delaware. It was soon followed by PHP, an open source program for creating web applications and MySQL, an open source system to run relational databases. Taken together, they formed the LAMP stack (Linux, Apache, MySQL, and PHP) that ensured that Microsoft would never enjoy the dominance over the web that it had achieved over personal computing.

By 2010, when Microsoft launched Kinect, the strictly proprietary model of the twentieth century was clearly on its last legs. In addition to the LAMP stack, open source projects had already become standard in a number of other areas, such as the R Project in statistical software and Hadoop in data storage. Facebook had opened its platform to outside developers using application program interfaces (APIs) and soared past MySpace to become the world's most popular social network. Everywhere you looked, open models were trouncing closed ones.

It was, to be sure, an incredible turn of events. Up till that point, the path to success was clear: control what you can and leverage any advantage you might have to gain even more control. But now, *proprietary* was becoming a bad word and control didn't seem like it conferred much advantage at all. In *Open Innovation*, Henry Chesbrough identifies four factors that led to this erosion of proprietary advantage.[7]

The first factor was the rise of the venture capital market. Chesbrough notes that before 1980, there was little venture capital to speak of, which made it hard for entrepreneurs to attract talented staff and other resources. In fact, it wasn't until the late 1990s that large pools of venture capital became available for start-ups. By 2000, the amount of venture funds invested had risen to the stratospheric level of $80 billion in a single year. That changed the game entirely.

The second factor was the increasing availability and mobility of skilled workers. As education levels rose, more people with advanced technical skills populated the marketplace, especially those with skills in digital technology. Also, thanks to the proliferation of university computer science departments, a large pool of highly qualified people made their careers outside of large corporations. The rise of venture capital accelerated this trend as well-funded start-ups were able to hire top talent from established firms.

The third erosion factor came from the established firms themselves. As their internal research and development efforts produced more technology than they could successfully bring to market, they often found it profitable to license technologies to employees who thought they saw an opportunity. Chesbrough specifically points to Xerox PARC, which led to more than 20 spin-offs between 1979 and 1998. Some of these, like 3Com and Adobe, eventually would achieve multibillion-dollar valuations.[8]

The fourth and final erosion factor that Chesbrough pointed to came in the form of the increasing capability of suppliers. As venture capital, the explosion of technical talent and the increasing prevalence of successful spin-off companies converged, highly qualified suppliers often had far better capabilities than large-scale enterprises in technological niches. This often meant that even market leaders had to go outside their internal research and development capabilities to gain access to top-notch expertise in specialty fields.

A fifth factor that Chesbrough did not mention, probably because it wasn't yet apparent when he published his book in 2003, was that the Internet made remote collaboration extraordinarily feasible, even among people who didn't know each other. This is what accounted for the increasing viability of open source communities such as Linux and the Apache Foundation in the 1990s.

Clearly, Microsoft was late to get the memo. IBM, for example, began to embrace open source communities in the mid-1990s. But by 2010, when it launched Kinect, the writing was so clearly on the wall that not even Microsoft could ignore it anymore. Today, the company supports a variety of open source efforts, even Linux, which it once regarded as a "cancer."[9]

Yet not all large enterprises were so slow to catch on. In fact, in 1998 the pharmaceutical giant Eli Lilly was sowing the seeds for a project that would take the concept of open innovation far beyond where anyone thought it could go.

InnoCentive: Linux with a Bounty

When Alph Bingham was a graduate student in chemistry at Stanford in the 1970s, he was struck by how many ways there were to approach a tough research question. "The professor would present us with a problem, and 20 different people would have 20 different ideas about how to solve it," he told me. "It wasn't like when I was an undergraduate, where most test questions had a 'right' answer. These were really tough problems that nobody knew the answer for.

We would only know what the right answer was when it was implemented and actually led to a solution."[10]

After receiving his PhD in 1977, Bingham went to work as a researcher for the pharmaceutical firm Eli Lilly, where he was charged with solving problems similar to those he had encountered in graduate school. He would be handed a complex chemical structure and would have to figure out how to synthesize it. Yet while he might be able to think of dozens of ways to attack the problem, there were often millions of possibilities. Unlike in graduate school, though, there weren't 20 other people working on the same problem. It was often just him. "Several of us thought it would be great if other people were working on same problem," he says. "So we started a lunch group to discuss various approaches, and that helped, but it was still way inadequate."

By the late 1990s, Bingham had risen through the ranks and had become a vice president responsible for managing Eli Lilly's portfolio of research. It was his job to oversee the processes that would green-light new projects and then decide if they should be continued, ramped up, or killed. He often saw promising projects that ran into insurmountable barriers. Would more time have led to a game-changing solution or just consume more capital and resources? It was hard to know for sure. He wondered if there wasn't a better way of resolving these dilemmas. He was familiar with the Linux movement and its mantra, "Given enough eyeballs all bugs are shallow," and he thought that maybe it was possible that the same type of approach would work in the pharmaceutical industry.

It was around this time that Bingham was invited to a brainstorming session that one of the IT executives put together to stimulate new ideas for how the firm could leverage the Internet. They discussed many different possibilities, but it was then that Bingham and his colleague Aaron Schacht first became excited about the idea of creating something like Linux, but with a bounty to be paid for a useful solution, to attract more diverse approaches to the problems that Eli Lilly was working on.

Drug development is notoriously expensive. First, a "theory of the case" must be developed about how to solve a particular medical problem like, say, hypertension. Then research must be done to determine whether a compound with the desired properties can indeed be created. This usually takes one to five years and costs tens of millions of dollars when you include all the failed efforts. From there the drug candidate goes to a formal preclinical stage, followed by Phase I and Phase II trials, to determine whether the drug is safe and effective. That costs roughly another $40 to $100 million. Only a fifth of the drug candidates ever make it to Phase III testing, during which it must be proven that the treatment in question delivers a demonstrable benefit over existing therapies. Almost half of all drugs fail in late Phase III trials, and, when it's all said and done, only 15 percent of drugs that enter clinical testing ever get approved. Clearly, developing a new drug is an enormously expensive proposition.

As a portfolio manager, it was abundantly clear to Bingham that even a marginal improvement in Eli Lilly's success rate could mean a lot of money. In fact, he estimated that even a 10 percent increase in throughput could be worth hundreds of millions in revenue per year.

Over the next few years, as he and Schacht discussed these ideas among themselves and with several colleagues, an idea began to take shape. They thought it was possible to create a website—molecule .com was the name they envisioned—that would invite scientists to suggest approaches to problems that Eli Lilly's researchers hadn't considered. It would also offer cash prizes for problems solved. Even a relatively large prize of tens of thousands of dollars would pale in comparison to the cost of drug development. The two also suspected that the high failure rate of drug candidates was due, at least in part, to false negatives. In other words, it was possible that researchers often had the right idea, but just couldn't identify the right approach to make it work.

In 2000, Bingham was invited to take part in a new senior executive program for high potential executives within Eli Lilly to explore issues relevant to the company's future. Every three weeks, the group would travel somewhere, like a prestigious consultancy or a hot technology firm, where they could learn about the emerging Internet business, get ideas, and then make proposals to Eli Lilly's powerful operations committee.

One of the proposals the group presented was the formation of a new business unit called e.Lilly, which would incubate new ideas related to the Internet. It was approved and formed in May of 2000 and was to be made up of two divisions, one to support Eli Lilly's sales and marketing operations and another to support R&D operations. Bingham was tapped to lead the R&D division. Nine months later, in February 2001, Eli Lilly's chairman green-lighted the website idea, but the name was changed to InnoCentive.

From there, things moved very quickly. The business model and site, incubated by Darren Carroll, InnoCentive's first CEO and subsequent chairman, went operational 103 days later and was announced at a Price Waterhouse conference in Barcelona at 10 a.m.—or 4 a.m. on the east coast in the United States. Before Bingham had finished speaking, people were already visiting the site, and by the end of the day it had thousands of hits. Clearly, Bingham and his colleagues were onto something.

They were offering up to $25,000 in prizes, and people soon began sending in solutions in droves. However, Bingham noticed a curious fact. "Our intention was to get more chemists involved in chemistry problems and biologists involved in biology problems, but we quickly found out that the people who solved the problem had some type of lateral expertise," he told me. "For example, a drug doesn't work because it is binding to a specific molecule in the blood and that's preventing delivery to a specific site of action. This has a biochemist stumped. But a physicist might have been studying the electrical properties of covalent bonds and be able to figure a way of preventing the bonding to the blood molecule." By the end of the year, as many as a third of the first set of challenges—very difficult problems that had been around for a long time—had been solved.

By 2002, less than a year after the site was launched, the decision was made to recruit noncompetitive companies to post their problems onto the platform. It began with three firms, and the results were more than encouraging. In fact, it soon became clear that the more problems they posted, the better the solutions became.

"We saw that nothing increased the number of solvers better than the number of good problems," Bingham told me. Over time, Inno-Centive began recruiting even competitive pharmaceutical firms to post their challenges because the team realized that was the best way to attract highly qualified solvers in large numbers.

By 2005, it became clear that InnoCentive had potential far beyond Eli Lilly and it was spun out in a private placement. By 2007, some 400 problems posted by 50 firms—ones that their own researchers had failed to crack—had been solved by the InnoCentive community of more than 120,000 solvers. Each problem attracted the attention of about 200 people on average and about 10 of those submitted solutions. In all, about a third of the problems posted got solved.[11]

But even more impressive than the rate at which solutions are found is the way they were arrived at. For example, in 2007, due to the oil spill that resulted from the Exxon Valdez hitting an iceberg in 1989, the Prince William Sound in Alaska still had tens of thousands of gallons of crude oil trapped along its coastline. Part of the problem was that because of the low temperatures the oil would freeze and become too thick to pump. This type of problem, called "viscous shear," had been plaguing oil cleanup efforts in low-temperature environments for decades, but no one could figure out what to do about it.

A challenge was placed on InnoCentive to see if anybody could solve the problem. As it turned out, a man named John Davis, who had studied chemistry but had no experience in the petroleum industry, remembered a technique he had seen during a summer job working construction. To keep large amounts of cement from drying before it could be poured, it was common to use a device that employed high frequency sound waves to vibrate the cement and keep it from hardening. Davis thought it seemed like a similar type of problem, and he submitted the technique he remembered from the construction site as a solution. He won the challenge and received a $20,000 bounty, which, considering the importance of the recovery efforts, was a bargain.[12]

Amazing stories like that are more the rule than the exception when it comes to InnoCentive challenges. In one case, a plant biologist and a dermatologist applied a method used in the cosmetic industry to help solve a challenge related to a new diagnosis for Alzheimer's.[13] A Bulgarian, citing a Mexican publication, identified a new application for GlaxoSmithKline's new bioelectronics technology.[14] Bingham told me of one challenge that received a proposed solution in less than 24 hours from someone working in an oil field in Kazakhstan. Apparently it was something the man had thought up years before but never published. The scientist had no idea how it could be useful until he saw the challenge posted on InnoCentive.

Clearly, Bingham and his colleagues had hit on a powerful model. As we discussed in Chapter 3, well-defined problems often go unsolved because the relevant field is missing one small but crucial piece of information. Through applying an open innovation approach, it's possible to cast a net so wide that it literally covers the entire world. With enough eyeballs, all bugs do indeed become shallow!

As it turns out, the researchers at Eli Lilly weren't the only ones to notice how powerful open innovation could be. It was around the same time that some researchers at Procter & Gamble were about to embark on a very similar journey.

From Research & Develop to Connect & Develop

Procter & Gamble, like Eli Lilly, has a long history of innovation that stretches back over a century. In Procter & Gamble's case, its researchers did not seek to discover new cures but rather to develop products for ordinary consumers. Many have become household names. Head & Shoulders anti-dandruff shampoo, Crest toothpaste, and Pampers diapers—all firsts in their categories—sprang forth from the company's labs. Today, with over 8,000 scientists and technicians working in over 120 different scientific disciplines and an annual budget of more than $2 billion, top-notch research remains a major priority at Procter & Gamble.

It was against this backdrop that Nabil Sakkab took over as senior vice president of research and development at the Fabric Care division in 1996. Eager to excel at his new job, he started by charting out a strategy to produce superior results. Unfortunately, as he analyzed the data, he didn't see how he could even match past performance, much less improve on it. Historically, Procter & Gamble had doubled revenues every 10 years. Looking at what he had in the pipeline and what his resources were, he just didn't see how that was going to happen unless he figured out a profoundly different way of doing things.[15]

So he started by creating a list of the 10 most important problems that his division faced and began to think about strategies that could solve them within his research budget. That's when it occurred to him that the company's suppliers could play an important role. Procter & Gamble had developed deep working relationships with virtually all of the world's top chemical firms, but he realized that they were being underutilized. Up till that point, they were essentially acting as outsourced manufacturers, but they were also powerful scientific organizations in their own right. "Why just limit ourselves to buying their hands," Sakkab thought, "when we can rent the heads as well?"

So he took a problem from his list and prepared a technology brief to one of his top suppliers. "In the beginning it was a culture shock," remembers Chris Thoen, one of Sakkab's top lieutenants. "Will people start to think that we are unable to solve our own problems? So we needed to go to a supplier that we could really trust and that could trust us. We needed a comfortable environment with great confidentiality."[16]

Despite those reservations, that initial pilot program worked amazingly well. The compound they needed was developed on time and under budget. From there, Sakkab and his team started delivering technology briefs to other suppliers. Not long after that, Sakkab began collocating his researchers at suppliers' labs. Soon they were finding that they were developing new materials that they couldn't have identified themselves and shortening development cycles at the same time. "We took problems that had been sitting around for years and were able to solve them in months," Sakkab remembers.

They also began finding that they needed to develop new skills internally. "You need people of a different mindset for an open innovation," Thoen says. "You need people who have a PhD in generalism. They need to be more flexible than a typical research scientist, and they need to be able to ask questions across a wide range of disciplines."

Despite the initial success, Sakkab saw that he could take the idea much further. He had already seen examples of open innovation at work. For example, he had read a story about a struggling mining business named Goldcorp. With the business in jeopardy and frustrated by the lack of progress, CEO Rob McEwen decided to do something truly different. In what became known as the Goldcorp Challenge, he took 400 megabytes of proprietary data, put it online, and offered $575,000 in prizes for anybody who could locate promising seams. More than 1,400 contestants identified 110 new targets, 80 percent of which resulted in substantial new discoveries of gold.[17]

Sakkab soon found himself spending more time looking at what was going on outside his company's labs. "We had a small corporate innovation group that built a search engine," he told me. "It allowed us to search the world, and I became its number one internal client. We started to see things that we hadn't seen before, and that opened up a whole new world. That really created a culture change. We saw that we had to look outside our organization." He also went to visit Alph Bingham at Eli Lilly to see what the company was doing with InnoCentive.

By 2002, there was awareness among senior management that open innovation was a major opportunity, and the Connect & Develop program was initiated as a companywide program. It had three major components. First was the practice that Sakkab had pioneered in his division of integrating Procter & Gamble researchers with suppliers' labs. Second, a global network of innovation scouts—called technology entrepreneurs—was set up to catalyze Connect & Develop processes, such as writing technology briefs for suppliers and other potential partners, keeping up-to-date with technical literature, and meeting regularly with university and industry researchers. Third, the company became active on InnoCentive and helped to create two additional networks: NineSigma, which helps connect companies with problems to institutions such as private and academic labs that can solve them; and YourEncore, which built a network of retired scientists and engineers who solve problems in their spare time.

Today, it is clear that Connect & Develop has been a resounding success. Sakkab ended up meeting the goals he set out to achieve for his division, helping to grow his business by 50 percent while reducing R&D resources by 25 percent by the time he moved to a corporate role in 2005. It also led to the development of Swiffer and to the expansion of Febreze, both of which are now billion-dollar brands.[18]

Perhaps most important, it led to the creation of breakthrough new products that Procter & Gamble could never have come up with itself. For example, when Procter & Gamble identified a small French company, Sederma, that was working on a new chemical to repair wounds and burns, it formed a partnership that resulted in Olay Regenerist, which became a blockbuster wrinkle cream. Tide Pods, a revolutionary product that combined a detergent, stain remover, and brightener all in one easy-to-use product, was codeveloped with MonoSol, a firm with just 400 employees. Crest Whitestrips was created with the help of Corium, a pharmaceutical company. The list goes on.[19]

Clearly, open innovation has greatly enhanced Procter & Gamble's ability to compete. To understand the extent to which it has impacted the company, let's examine the company's innovation portfolio mapped out on the four quadrants of the Innovation Matrix (Figure 5.1).

P&G Innovation Matrix

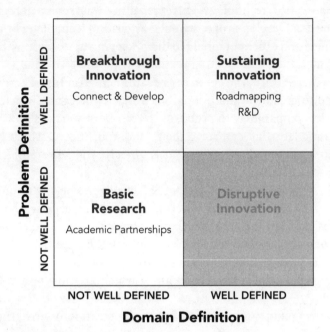

FIGURE 5.1 P&G Innovation Matrix

The Four Quadrants
BASIC RESEARCH

While the bulk of the company's research efforts are focused on solving specific problems related to its product lines, Procter & Gamble remains dedicated to scientific exploration in a variety of areas, such as genetic sequencing and understanding biochemistry on a molecular level. It actively participates in scientific conferences and encourages its researchers to publish in peer-reviewed journals. It also maintains a number of academic partnerships with a number of technical universities.

Such a heavy investment in basic science may seem surprising for a company that sells basic items such as paper towels and laundry detergent, but that is exactly the point. The bar for innovation in such basic and longstanding product categories is set much higher than in a start-up looking to come up with the next hot app. In order to make an impact, you often need to come up with something truly new. That means you need to alter the basic chemistry of products that have been around for decades.

BREAKTHROUGH INNOVATION

Even a vast organization with over 8,000 researchers is still limited. Procter & Gamble's Connect & Develop program allows it to leverage its internal capabilities and almost literally make the entire world its lab. From chemical companies to biotech firms to individual scientists on platforms like InnoCentive, it can put hundreds of thousands of eyeballs on a really tough problem.

Still, as Chris Thoen pointed out, it was an enormous cultural change to make this possible. It's not easy to admit that you can't solve every problem within your organization, but besides the pride of its internal scientists, there were also legal, organizational, and competitive issues to be considered. All of these had to be overcome before Connect & Develop could be made successful.

SUSTAINING INNOVATION

Like most large enterprises, Procter & Gamble has a well-established strategic roadmapping process that calls for continuous improvement, and the company has a long history of developing products that are "new and improved" products. Yet one interesting twist is that it embeds its consumer research organization inside its product research organization. So sociologists doing ethnographic studies in which they embed themselves inside consumers' lives to identify unmet needs work side-by-side with chemists and engineers who are charged with coming up with technical solutions.

DISRUPTIVE INNOVATION

As a company, Procter & Gamble has a history of pursuing disruptive opportunities, but has not been able to establish a consistent program of disruptive innovation. In 1999, then CEO Durk Jager set up an internal structure called the Innovation Leadership Team to fund and incubate disruptive innovations such as Febreze air freshener and ThermaCare bandages. It later worked with Clayton Christensen's consulting firm, Innosight, to help it uncover technologies that have disruptive potential. It also set up a fully owned subsidiary, FutureWorks, that was charged with testing and incubating new business models.[20]

One particularly interesting FutureWorks project is Tide Dry Cleaners. Through the Connect & Develop program, the company identified an ecologically safe and more effective waterless cleaning solvent, which opened the door to not only a new product, but an entirely new business model. It opened three test locations in Kansas City and, after they proved successful, opened a national franchise operation, which later launched a chain of Mr. Clean car washes.

The FutureWorks unit, however, was shut down in 2013, and there are no current companywide disruptive strategies in place. For the moment, the company seems to be focused on rejuvenating its conventional businesses.

Procter & Gamble has been in business since 1837, and its tradition of innovation certainly didn't start with Connect & Develop. It has long been a high-performing organization with world-class labs, legendary marketing capabilities, and top-notch manufacturing facilities. Yet today, it's clear that Connect & Develop has created a new engine to drive its innovation efforts. While before it was limited to the skills of its internal researchers, today Procter & Gamble can draw on a global network of partners to help it solve problems for its customers. That drives its ability to develop new products and create new business models.

CHAPTER SIX

Innovating the Core— the 70/20/10 Rule

> *You've got to think about big things while you're doing small things, so that all the small things go in the right direction.*
>
> **—ALVIN TOFFLER**

In August 1995, Netscape, a start-up company that marketed the first consumer web browser, had the most successful initial public offering in history. Although the stock was initially to be set at $14 a share, due to an excess of demand the price was doubled to $28 a share. Amazingly, it soared to $75 on the first day, making the barely one-year-old company with no profits worth $2.9 billion. In that instant, the web was transformed from an obscure set of protocols used exclusively by specialists into a mainstream phenomenon.

Nevertheless, being a very new technology, not much was known about the web at the time. So two young graduate students at Stanford, financed by a grant from the National Science Foundation (NSF), set out to study it mathematically. They built a small piece of software to crawl around the pages of the web, recording its links as it went. As they analyzed the data, using an algorithm they called BackRub, they were able to confirm their thesis that much like the system of "cites" in an academic journal, the pages with the most links were the most important. It was at that point that Larry Page and Sergey Brin realized that they had the makings of a revolutionary search engine and a great business, which they named Google.

In the ensuing years, Google became a juggernaut. First, it took a commanding lead in Internet search. From there, it grew to encompass a dizzying array of products. YouTube, which it acquired in 2006, is the world's most popular video hosting site. Android is the world's most popular mobile operating system. Google Docs offers customers a free alternative to Microsoft's Office Suite. Google Maps is a market-leading navigation service. Google Ventures (GV) invests in start-up companies, and the company's X division develops next generation projects, such as self-driving cars, drone powered product delivery, and other "moonshots."

To reflect the growing diversity of the business, Page and Brin recently decided to rename their company Alphabet so that web-related services could function as a standalone business and the other ventures would be grouped into a separate set of financial statements. In 2015, its "Google segment revenues" were $74.5 billion, while its "Other Bets" amounted to merely $448 million, the vast majority of that amount coming from just two sources, Nest and Google Fiber. So even after 20 years of innovation and product development, its core business still makes up for 99 percent of the company's revenues.

Many people think of innovation as discarding the old to make room for the new, but Google shows that even a highly successful, forward-looking technology company earns most of its money from the older products in its core businesses. Its "Other Bets," while growing fast, amount to just a drop in the bucket.

And Google is more the rule than the exception. As we will see, the most profitable opportunities almost always lie in strengthening your core business, or at least in something closely related to it. Still, as technology changes and culture shifts, businesses mature and industries sometimes run out of steam. That presents a dilemma: you need to innovate for the marketplace of today, while also preparing for an alternative future. Although still a young company, Google has already begun to prepare for a time when its core search business is no longer able to fuel the stellar growth the firm has come to enjoy.

That's smart and sensible, but it's still no guarantee. Remember, as we noted in Chapter 3, Clayton Christensen began his research on disruptive innovation because he noticed that many successful companies that fail do indeed prepare for the future. In fact, many of the failed companies he studied had excellent management, invested profits back into their companies' products, and sought out customer input in order to create products that customers wanted. They were disrupted not because they ignored threats to their business, but because they *didn't recognize threats to their business.*

That's what makes running an enterprise so difficult. You must make decisions in real time, with limited information and often under extreme time constraints. The case studies managers learn from in business school, on the other hand, are written with the benefit of hindsight, a process that tends to simplify the issues and often leads to platitudes, such as "you need to invest now and for the future." That may seem simple and straightforward enough, but unless you can predict the future with perfect foresight, it's not very useful advice. It tells you nothing about what to *actually invest in.*

The same goes for the need to innovate your core business. It may seem like an obvious point, but defining your core business is anything but easy.

The Longstanding Struggle to Define the Core

In 1960, Harvard professor Theodore Levitt published a landmark paper in *Harvard Business Review* that urged executives to adapt to the marketplace of the future by asking themselves, "What business are we really in?" He offered both the railroad industry and Hollywood studios as examples of industries that failed to adapt because they failed to define their business correctly. Railroads, he argued, merely saw themselves in the "railroad business," but if they saw themselves as being in the "transportation business," they could have competed in the auto, airline, and even telephone industries. In a similar vein, the Hollywood studios saw themselves as being in the "movie business," and missed opportunities that would have been obvious if they saw themselves as being in the "entertainment business."[1]

Defining what business you're in is one of the most important strategic decisions you can make. Bain consultants Chris Zook and James Allen expanded on Levitt's point in their book *Profit from the Core,*[2] in which they argue that firms that focus on their core business significantly outperform those who stray. "Most companies that sustain value creation possess only one or two strong cores," they wrote, and pointed out that diversification usually leads to worse performance. Zook and Allen further noted "acquisitions made for the purpose of expanding scale in a core business have a success rate that's at least twice that of acquisitions to diversify and expand scope."[3]

So how do you define your core business? Zook and Allen suggest that it is the "set of products, customer segments and technologies with which you can build the greatest competitive advantage,"[4] which can be determined by analyzing profitability, growth, and relative share of a particular market segment.

They also make the point that while opportunities outside your core industry often appear more attractive, focusing on your core business can help you earn superior loyalty from customers, dominate a particular sales channel, develop differentiation through innovation efforts, and increase access to capital through attaining market leadership. Meanwhile, companies that stray from their core often end up in businesses that they don't fully understand and in which they have little equity built up with customers, suppliers, and other partners in the new industry.

Often, a single industry can have multiple cores. For example, Zook and Allen explain that in the car rental industry, Hertz and Avis focus on the lucrative airport business, while Enterprise has built a commanding position in the market for insurance and repair replacement vehicles and Alamo found a profitable niche by focusing on leisure rentals in tourist areas. All can be defined as being in the "car rental industry," but each has built a very different business model catering to different customers, requiring different assets and capabilities.

The authors also recognize that businesses can profitably expand in areas adjacent to the core, based on core customers, core capabilities, and core sales channels. For example, Disney started out making short cartoon films, then expanded to feature length movies, television, theme parks, and licensing.[5] The diamond giant De Beers has expanded from its core in engagement rings to adjacencies such as diamond anniversary bands and diamond solitaire necklaces.[6]

The problem with all this is that there are so many ways you can define a core business and, therefore, what is adjacent to the core, that it's very hard to use the concept as a guide for strategy. Wasn't Xerox focusing on its core when it failed to market the Alto as a personal computer in favor of building a more elaborate system to automate offices? Or would personal computers have been adjacent to the core somehow? Didn't Steve Jobs stray from the core when he moved Apple into music players, smartphones, and retail stores?

What about Kodak, which focused on its core film developing business all the way to bankruptcy?

Even the experts themselves seem confused. Since Levitt first published his article, the railroad business, protected as it is from foreign competition, has thrived while the Detroit automakers have struggled. Union Pacific, the leading railroad company, has a market capitalization of over $70 billion, about 40 percent more than Ford or GM. Disney, the leading movie studio company, has a market capitalization of about $170 billion. That doesn't seem too shabby either. In fact, both the railroad companies and movie studios as a whole remain quite profitable even today, despite Levitt's misgivings in 1960. How many other industries have fared as well?

For their part, Zook and Allen praised Enron's ability to "shift the core to drive into new horizons" before it came crashing down,[7] but questioned the viability of Amazon's move to sell products other than books.[8] We can only wonder what they would have thought about Amazon's move into cloud services, but it is now a $10 billion business that is growing by more than 60 percent per year.[9] Does that mean it was "straying from the core," or was Amazon CEO Jeff Bezos simply "shifting the core to drive into new horizons" like Enron did? In fact, the authors themselves even recognize the confusion. "We are surprised at how often we find that members of management teams, when interviewed separately, differ in their opinions of the core customer set and products," they write.[10]

That's the problem with ambiguous concepts like "core" and "adjacencies." They are always relative terms, so it's easy to fall into the trap of calling anything successful a "core" or an "adjacency" and dismissing strategic moves that don't work out as unsuccessful "diversifications." To be fair, Zook and Allen do point out that every move into an adjacency is fraught with risk, but then again, so is sticking to the core. PC makers like Dell and Compaq stuck to their core in an eroding market, and it killed them. Many of the same forces are now putting pressure on Intel. Should it stick to its core business in microprocessors or move into some adjacency? It's really hard to tell.

The truth is that in any given business, the odds favor the core, but especially today, when technology shifts can disrupt your business in an instant, you need to constantly be looking for new opportunities, wherever they lie. However, you must also be careful to manage risk while you do so. Fortunately, there's a very sensible model that can help us do that.

Innovating in Three Horizons

Management is not an exact science. As management guru Henry Mintzberg explained, "The great myth is the manager as orchestra conductor. It's this idea of standing on a pedestal and you wave your baton and accounting comes in, and you wave it somewhere else and marketing chimes in with accounting, and they all sound very glorious. But management is more like orchestra conducting during rehearsals, when everything is going wrong."[11]

So as much as we might wish it were otherwise, much of what we do is guesswork and a lot of our bets are going to go wrong. There's no brilliant strategy that will help you avoid that—it's just part of the learning process. As Thomas Edison himself is said to have put it, "If I find 10,000 ways something won't work, I haven't failed. I am not discouraged, because every wrong attempt discarded is another step forward."

So the key to successfully managing your core and adjacencies is not to try to achieve perfect knowledge, but to manage risks by allocating resources according to your best guesses about what is core and what is adjacent to your business. A popular guide that has emerged for doing that is the three horizons model, a version of which you can see in Figure 6.1.

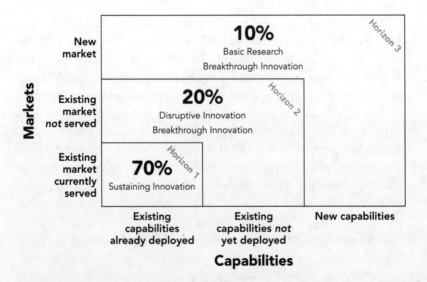

FIGURE 6.1 Three Horizons of Innovation

The three horizons framework originated with a popular book that three McKinsey consultants published in the late 1990s called *The Alchemy of Growth*.[12] The purpose of the book, in the authors' own words, was to "offer a way of thinking that balances the competing demands of running existing businesses and building new ones."[13] Although it was originally conceived as a general management framework, it has since been adopted by the innovation community and been given the proportions 70/20/10.

The idea behind the three horizons framework is not to eliminate uncertainty, but to take your level of uncertainty into account when allocating resources. Put simply, you invest the bulk of your resources in capabilities (e.g., skills and technologies) and markets you know well, a much smaller portion toward adjacencies, and an even smaller proportion to future opportunities that don't even exist yet. The proportions 70/20/10 are intended to be general guidelines and do not lend themselves to a strict accounting. The primary insight is that businesses need to pursue all three horizons at once, albeit in different proportions.

While the three horizons framework may seem simplistic, that's part of its strength. It offers a simple framework and a simple language to discuss the core business, adjacencies, and long-term bets. Let's look at each of the three horizons in turn.

Horizon 1: The Core Business

The first horizon is the most straightforward and can be considered as investment into the core business. However, the "core" is defined much more loosely than in Zook and Allen's book. It is simply businesses in existing markets that the company already serves and capabilities that are already deployed. For all intents and purposes, we can consider Horizon 1 to be synonymous with sustaining innovation.

However, Horizon 1 can also be a trap. Because it aligns so neatly with an organization's normal strategic roadmapping process and involves existing processes, such as traditional R&D, engineering, and acquisitions, it is easy for managers to use innovation in Horizon 1 as a crutch. All too often, they look at all the activity going on in Horizon 1 and think that innovation is taken care of. As we saw in the case of Xerox, just because you are coming out with "new and improved" products every year doesn't mean your business is safe. When Japanese competitors like Canon and Ricoh disrupted the market with copiers that were slower and of poorer quality, but also smaller and cheaper, Xerox continued to build products that were bigger, better, and faster, because that's what customers were asking for. It almost killed the company.

Horizon 2: Adjacent Markets and Capabilities

The second horizon involves moves into either new markets or new capabilities or, in the language of the innovation matrix presented in Chapter 3, situations where either the problem or domain is not fully defined. These are adjacencies.

Clearly, adjacencies are high risk, high reward investments. As the authors explain in *The Alchemy of Growth*, "Horizon 2 is about building new streams of revenue. That takes time and demands new skills. Without Horizon 2 businesses, a company's growth will slow and ultimately stall. A good growth company needs to have several of these emerging businesses 'on the boil,' working to convert promising ideas into future earnings generators."

That's what Eric Haller did when he returned to Experian after seven years working in the start-up world. By launching Experian DataLabs, he gave the company a vehicle to continually explore Horizon 2 opportunities in cooperation with its customers. Also, by putting together a highly skilled team of PhD level data scientists and encouraging them to actively engage with the scientific community, he also built a window into Horizon 3 opportunities as well.

But an even better example of the value of Horizon 2 is Intel's investment into microprocessors. Until the mid-1980s, the company's main business was in memory chips, where it did quite well. But by 1984, faced with fierce competition from low-cost Japanese competitors, it was clear that its competitive position was eroding rapidly. The management team spent a year trying to devise various strategies to compete in memory chips before Gordon Moore and Andy Grove decided to exit the businesses altogether in 1985. However, due to their continued investment in a Horizon 2 technology, microprocessors, they had an emerging business that they could move their attention to. The rest, as they say, is history. Intel went on to enjoy greater success in microprocessors than it ever had with memory chips.[14]

Horizon 3: Long-Term Bets

Horizon 3 is where no present business exists at all. These are new technologies and new markets where neither the problem nor the domain is well defined. For the most part, these are explorations that involve basic research. However, sometimes the problems involved are so difficult that they cannot realistically be resolved in a Horizon 2 time frame, and breakthrough innovation strategies, such as setting up a Skunk Works, can be applied as well.

As explained in Chapter 3, very few companies invest in basic research, but many are able to build a competitive advantage by becoming adept at identifying and accessing publicly funded research at academic institutions and government labs. Pharmaceutical companies, for example, focus their Horizon 3 efforts on tracking research performed at the NIH and other institutions, such as the Howard Hughes Medical Institute. In a similar vein, home appliance manufacturers mine discoveries funded by the Department of Energy to develop sustaining innovations, such as improved energy efficiency, in their Horizon 1 businesses.

* * * * *

Thinking in terms of the three horizons is a simple way to keep your organization firing on all cylinders. While the majority of our time needs to be spent focusing on the core business of today, we should never stop building for the future, and the 70/20/10 rule is a remarkably good framework for setting priorities and allocating resources.

One major advocate of the approach is Google's chairman, Eric Schmidt, who, along with Google senior executive Jonathan Rosenberg, wrote in *How Google Works*, "the 70/20/10 rule ensured that our core business would always get the bulk of the resources and that the promising, up-and-coming areas would also get investment, it also ensured that the crazy ideas got some support too, and were protected from the inevitable budget cuts. And 10 percent isn't a lot of resources, which is fine, because overinvesting in a new concept is just as problematic as underinvesting, since it can make it much harder to admit failure later on. Million-dollar ideas are a lot harder to kill than thousand-dollar ones."[15]

An interesting point to note is that it's not clear whether Google's management adopted the 70/20/10 approach directly from *The Alchemy of Growth*. Schmidt and Rosenberg credit it to a simple observation cofounder Sergey Brin made in 2002. At the time, the company managed resource allocation through maintaining a list of top 100 projects, but it was quickly becoming clear that that particular method would not scale. So Brin went down the list and noticed that 70 percent of the projects were directed at the core businesses of search and advertising, 20 percent to adjacencies that were emerging as promising businesses, and 10 percent involved completely new ideas.[16]

So maybe somebody at the meeting where Brin examined the list had read the book, or at least had heard of the three horizons approach from somewhere. Or maybe it was simply rediscovered at Google. This type of thing is surprisingly common. As we saw in Chapter 5, executives at Eli Lilly and the founders of the XPRIZE came up with similar ideas at around the same time in blissful ignorance of each other. Scientists who uncovered the rules of genetic inheritance in the early twentieth century found, undoubtedly to their chagrin, that an obscure Austrian monk named Gregor Mendel had discovered those same rules 50 years before!

Wherever the idea came from, the salient point here is that the 70/20/10 rule is at the heart of how Google innovates. However, like much in the company, the three horizons are so tightly integrated that they end up looking more like an ecosystem than three separate buckets, so we can learn little by examining them in isolation. Instead, let's see how they work together inside one of Google's most important projects, Google Brain.

Inside Google's Brain

Like anything Google does, its deep learning initiative is rooted in its fierce commitment to research. The spirit of discovery is deeply embedded in Google's DNA. After all, the company got its start from Sergey Brin and Larry Page's NSF funded research project to catalog the web. That serious commitment to discovery has continued and Google invests billions of dollars every year on research and development.

Yet even that enormous dollar figure doesn't tell the whole story. Google also routinely acquires early stage start-ups, many launched as a result of academic research, and invests in dozens of others through its venture capital arm. One of the start-ups Google acquired, DeepMind, made headlines by beating legendary Go world champion Lee Sedol.

And while the company doesn't directly invest in fundamental exploratory research like, as we will see in the next chapter, IBM does, Google maintains an active partnership with the scientific community through various programs. It funds over 250 academic research projects a year, maintains an active PhD fellowship program, publishes its research on public databases such as arXiv as well as on its own research website, and invites about 30 top scholars to spend sabbaticals at Google every year.

Sometimes these researchers stay for a while. Google offers scientists such a unique laboratory, with massive data sets, some of the best computing architecture in the world, and the opportunity to continue to publish openly, that the company is a big draw for top-notch scholars who want to augment their academic experience with some time devoted to working on real-world problems.

For example, early in Google's history, Dr. Mehran Sahami, one of the top computer science professors at Stanford, left the university to join Google Research, where he helped both to build the company's machine learning capabilities and design its university relations program. When he returned to Stanford, his time at Google led him to reimagine the computer science curriculum based on the needs he saw at Google and the industry as a whole. He is now associate chair of the department.

Another notable case involved Andrew Moore, a professor at Carnegie Mellon University. In 2006, he took a leave of absence to open a Google Research facility in Pittsburgh, where Carnegie Mellon is located. Over the next eight years, he grew the Pittsburgh operation from a start-up lab to one of the best-performing centers of excellence within Google, employing hundreds of top researchers. In 2014, he returned to Carnegie Mellon, where he now serves as dean at the School of Computer Science.

Another star from the academic world that came to Google was Andrew Ng, a legend in artificial intelligence circles, who arrived in 2010. Ng quickly bonded with two other researchers, Greg Corrado and Jeff Dean, who were also interested in a relatively new type of artificial intelligence called deep learning. Soon, the three were working together as part of their "20 percent time," the firm's legendary practice of encouraging employees to work on projects that interest them.

20 percent time is perhaps Google's best-known innovation practice, but it is frequently misunderstood. First, it did not originate with Google, but with 3M, which began the practice in 1948. Over the years, it has resulted in a number of hit products, such as Post-it Notes, Scotch Tape, and Scotchgard fabric protector.[17] Second, much

like the 70/20/10 rule, it shouldn't be taken absolutely literally. As Schmidt and Rosenberg put it in their book, "It's not about time, it's about freedom." The idea is to encourage people at Google to pursue projects that interest them, even—or maybe especially—if what interests them is completely unrelated to their day jobs, which is why many people refer to the practice as "120 percent time."

For example, in 2004 a Google engineer named Kevin Gibbs came up with the idea of having Google predict what a user is searching for after typing just a few characters. As he started working on it in his spare time, other engineers became interested in the project too and began to help him out with it. Their efforts eventually became Google Autocomplete, which offers a drop-down menu offering suggestions as soon as you begin typing in the search box. At this point, nearly every Internet user on the planet has most likely used it at one time or another. And it would probably never have happened if Gibbs had been required to get approval for it. Other important Google products, such as Google News and Gmail, began the same way.[18]

Another interesting aspect is that, while allowing employees to use company resources for their own pet projects may seem profligate to many efficiency-minded managers, it's actually an effective way to manage resources. For a 20 percent time project to get off the ground and become a product, it needs to get enough people excited about it to want to contribute their time and efforts rather than working on a project of their own. That's probably a much better indication of viability than the usually politics-driven process for funding projects that is endemic in most companies.

So Google Brain didn't start out as a result of any strategic process, but rather as three guys really interested in solving a very tough problem. To understand what they were after, it helps to know something about how the brain works.

When you see a friend across a crowded bar, it seems like a single event, but it isn't. Different regions of your brain process different aspects of the experience, such as colors and shapes, and integrate them into larger concepts, such as a human face, a hairstyle, or the signature style of a popular designer. Scientists call these different aspects "levels of abstraction." Ordinarily, computers tend to work in a linear fashion, so they have a hard time working with more than a few levels of abstraction. However, the trio thought they could do much better, expanding the hierarchy to 20 or 30 levels, which would allow for much deeper machine learning than had been previously achieved.

Before long, they were making progress. As Corrado told me, "For a network to learn, you need data, and Google has lots of it. The other element is really fast computing, and Google's expertise in distributed computing was also enormously helpful. So we were able to advance machine learning enormously quickly." In fact, their part-time project looked so promising that management decided to move it to the X division, the company's internal Skunk Works, which it calls a "moonshot factory," that is specifically set up to tackle Horizon 2 and Horizon 3 projects.[19]

Most of the projects at the X division are expected to fail. In fact, Astro Teller, who oversees the division, is adamant that its success is rooted in aggressively killing projects as soon as it becomes clear that they won't pay off. He feels so strongly about this particular point that he wrote an article on the site Backchannel.com[20] and gave a TED talk about it.[21] At the outset, Google Brain looked like it might very well be one of those failed projects. After all, its success depended on redefining the boundaries of what was thought possible.

Nevertheless, the "moonshots factory" had much to offer. There, they were not only able to work on deep learning full-time, but could also recruit a staff of five or six other top-notch scientists and engineers with PhDs in math, neuroscience, and computer science. "The time we spent incubating in the X division was really essential," Corrado told me. "We could advance the core technology without being tied to a particular product. We went from three people working part-time to eight or nine working full-time. That's the perfect size to move really fast. We were like a small start-up, but had the resources of this enormous enterprise."

The result of that incubation period was an actual product. Called DistBelief, it became their first-generation machine learning system. Before long, DistBelief was incorporated into a variety of Google products, such as Google Maps, Google Translate, and even YouTube (to help users find the videos they're looking for).

In 2012, the team graduated from the X division and has now became a full-fledged division within Google, which has grown to around a hundred researchers at any given time, including Geoffrey Hinton, a giant in the field of deep learning, who joined in 2013. It has also built a second-generation product, called TensorFlow, that's been open-sourced under an Apache license, which has allowed the team to innovate even faster. "Having this system open-sourced we're able to collaborate with many other researchers at universities and start-ups, which gives us new ideas on how we can advance our technology. Since we made the decision to open-source, the code runs faster, it can do more things, and it's more flexible and convenient," says Rajat Monga, who leads the TensorFlow team.[22]

Today, Google Brain has become an integral part of the innovation ecosystem that spawned it. The team works actively with its internal "customers" within Google product teams to put deep learning at the center of everything Google does. Just about anyone within Google can access TensorFlow to make their product smarter and more effective. These kind of deep learning techniques have made Google voice search faster and more accurate, reducing the error rate from around 23 percent to around 8 percent, while cutting the time to complete a search by nearly one-third of a second—considered to be a very significant improvement in the field. Errors in image search have also been reduced by two-thirds, and users can now search unlabeled photos for everything from sunsets to specific dog breeds.

It has also led to new features, such as Smart Reply on Gmail, which offers recommendations to respond to incoming messages. Google Translate has been expanded to 100 languages, covering 99 percent of the world's population. Google Brain will most likely lead to completely new products, but it's already showing enormous value in improving the firm's core capabilities.

In most organizations, innovation is treated as a fairly linear process of research, development, demonstration, and deployment, with each step acting as its own silo. But at Google, everything works as a tightly coupled feedback loop, with researchers and product teams working hand in hand to not only create new products, but also to identify fruitful research areas for further study. "Getting close to data and the real needs of users gives you the opportunity to innovate further," Corrado told me. He and the Brain team work actively with not only product groups, but also fellow Googlers working on 20 percent projects. Rather than a group of mad scientists working on Frankenstein monsters deep in the bowels of the organization, they are active collaborators.

That's how Google Brain filters throughout each of the three horizons. TensorFlow provides access to basic machine learning tools, which open up new possibilities for Google's engineers, who then reach out to the scientists within Google Brain to create new products and features. That creates a rich problem set that helps draw top-notch researchers to Google who, in turn, create even more exciting new technology.

What's interesting about how Google innovates is that it doesn't rely on any one innovation strategy. Product managers focus on customers' needs. Researchers go where the science takes them. Engineers working on 20 percent time projects explore their own passions. Each of these facets is tightly integrated with the others.

One of the reasons that Google has been so successful is the way it's been able to integrate an entire portfolio of innovation strategies into a seamless whole. That takes more than a management philosophy or a streamlined operation; it requires a true spirit of discovery deeply embedded into the organization's DNA. However, it is also a potential recipe for chaos. By applying an additional level of scrutiny in the form of the three horizons model, Google's leadership can ensure that all of the creative energy inside the company remains focused on short, medium, and long-term objectives in a reasonably balanced way.

In effect, rather than an innovation strategy, Google has built an innovation ecosystem in which the whole is vastly more than the sum of its parts. It is also the only organization I found in my research that is active in all four quadrants of the Innovation Matrix, which is probably one reason that the founders thought it was necessary to create the holding company Alphabet so that it could separate the largely Horizon 1 Google business from its active explorations into Horizon 2 and Horizon 3.

Alphabet's Innovation Portfolio

To get a better sense of how it works, let's see what it looks like when we overlay the entire Alphabet structure onto the Innovation Matrix (Figure 6.2).

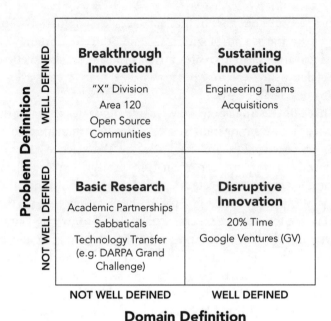

FIGURE 6.2 Alphabet's Innovation Portfolio

The Four Quadrants

BASIC RESEARCH

The company, for the most part, does not invest in exploratory research directly, but has built strong links to the academic community, even going as far as to invite about 30 top researchers annually to spend a sabbatical year at the company. This helps give it an insider's perspective on academic research, most of which is publicly funded, and invest in promising technology early on. For example, its self-driving car program arose from the government funded DARPA Grand Challenge, which invited teams to compete to build an autonomous vehicle for a $1 million prize. Google hired the winning team from the 2005 Grand Challenge to spearhead its own efforts.

Technology transfer is tougher than it sounds. Every year, research funded by programs like the National Science Foundation (NSF), the National Institutes of Health (NIH), and the Department of Energy (DOE) results in tens of thousands of scientific papers, and the practical applications stemming from those discoveries are often not clear, even to experts in the particular fields where they apply. However, by actively participating in the scientific community, Google can gain insights into which discoveries have the potential to become pathbreaking products.

BREAKTHROUGH INNOVATION

Before the Brain project arrived at the X division, the notion of building a practical deep learning system was just an idea. In fact, company executives told me that it was something that had been tried (and failed) twice before even within Google. But at the X division, they could assemble the right people with the right skills to transform a crazy idea into useful technology.

Many emergent technologies, such as self-driving cars, still have difficult problems to work out, and the multidisciplinary teams at the X division provide an excellent environment to solve them. This type of Skunk Works strategy has proven to be effective when confronted with well-defined problems but poorly defined domains. Both technology transfer and 20 percent time projects can feed into the X division when a technology looks promising but problems associated with it prove too complex to be solved with a more conventional team. More recently, the company has created a new unit, called Area 120—a play on the company's "20 percent time" practice—where new ideas can be incubated.

Another way that Google pursues breakthrough innovation is, as we saw with TensorFlow, to contribute its technology to open source communities. This allows its internal researchers and engineers to actively collaborate with a wide array of people, including academic researchers, start-ups, and anyone else who might have something to contribute.

SUSTAINING INNOVATION

Every day at Google, tens of thousands of engineers work to improve its existing businesses. Many of these are simple tweaks to the algorithm, but others are advances in highly complex technologies such as image and voice recognition. In many companies, sophisticated sustaining innovations like these would be pursued through a separate R&D program. At Google, however, the engineering focus and competency is so great that sustaining innovations are more of an everyday job.

DISRUPTIVE INNOVATION

Google pursues disruptive innovation primarily through the "20 percent time" that Google employees use to pursue passion projects. Google has been especially adept at turning 20 percent time projects into popular services. Gmail, Google News, and Google Maps all started out as 20 percent projects. It also identifies promising opportunities through Google Ventures (GV), its venture capital arm that invests in seed, venture, and growth stage funding. These are impressive technologies with no clear business model. They are, in effect, "solutions looking for a problem."

* * * * *

The salient point here is that even at a company as innovative and disruptive as Google, most of its efforts go toward supporting its core business. Even adjacencies, like Gmail and Google Maps, are used to drive search revenues. The other bets like self-driving cars and Google Fiber might get more attention, but they have so far had very little balance sheet impact. However, no business grows forever, and when search revenues eventually do slow down, hopefully one or more of the blue-sky initiatives will be ready to pick up slack.

Another thing to consider is that Google's 70/20/10 policy is fundamentally an admission that it has no crystal ball. In effect, it doesn't believe it is smart enough to predict the future, so instead of making any "bet the company" initiatives, it is content to continue making relatively small wagers and see what pays off. In a way, that's disappointing. We so often expect leaders to point the way forward, I'm sure that for many, Google's lack of a master plan must seem inadequate.

On the other hand, if the guys at Google can't come up with a sure-fire strategic plan for the future, who can? It is the small bets, compounded over time, that pave the path to the future.

CHAPTER SEVEN

Pursuing Innovation at Scale

Yesterday we pioneered for today; today,
we are pioneering for tomorrow.

—THOMAS J. WATSON, CHAIRMAN
AND CEO, IBM 1914–1956

When Apple came out with its iPhone in 2007, Steve Ballmer, Microsoft's CEO at the time, dismissed it out of hand, saying, "There's no chance that the iPhone is going to get any significant market share. No chance. It's a $500 subsidized item. They may make a lot of money. But if you actually take a look at the 1.3 billion phones that get sold, I'd prefer to have our software in 60% or 70% or 80% of them, than I would to have 2% or 3%, which is what Apple might get."[1]

He was, of course, gravely mistaken and, because of Ballmer's foolish arrogance, Microsoft missed out on the boom in mobile computing, while Apple rode it all the way to becoming the most valuable company on the planet. Other attempts to adapt to Apple's innovations, such as the Zune music player, didn't gain traction either. To many observers, especially the business press, it seemed that Microsoft, the Redmond giant that had dominated the technology industry for decades, was now in decline. Some even predicted that it would soon fail as a company altogether.

Yet somehow, none of that ever came to pass. In fact, Microsoft prospered. Over the next 10 years, it grew revenues at a compound annual rate of 11.4 percent and maintained margins of nearly 30 percent.[2] While Microsoft no longer wields the power it once did, it remains the third most valuable company in the world, with a market capitalization of over $400 billion.

So what happened? How did Microsoft, which had so obviously misread the market for mobile computing, manage to prosper?

The truth is that the reason Ballmer was so out of touch with the mobile business was probably because he was so focused on another area that was more suited to Microsoft's capabilities, strategy, and culture. While a resurgent Apple had focused its efforts around consumer electronics, Ballmer and his team had been embedding themselves deeper and deeper into enterprises, making sophisticated software that could run large networks efficiently. All of this was housed in a little-talked-about division, Servers and Tools, which had grown to $20 billion by 2013.[3]

Today, its Azure cloud services platform, which was developed in the Servers and Tools division,[4] is vying for leadership with Amazon Web Services and IBM's Bluemix platform. It is growing at rates that sometimes top 100 percent per year.[5] What's more, its strong position in cloud services gives it a gateway to sell an entire suite of exciting products to enterprises, like its popular SharePoint team collaboration software.

Now clearly, Microsoft is not a nimble company. It doesn't impress anybody with brilliant market launches or slick branding. What it has done is make substantial investments in the research division it set up in 1991. When you are building capacity in your business decades ahead of time, you really don't need to be that fast. So while it is easy to be impressed by start-ups that zoom their way from zero to billion-dollar valuations in a matter of months, we shouldn't forget that in its 30 years as a public company, Microsoft has never had an unprofitable quarter.

There's a substantial difference between hitting on the next big thing and developing a business consistently, generation after generation. Very few have been able to pull it off. In fact, nearly 90 percent of the original companies that made the Fortune 500 list in 1955 are no longer in business.[6] Yet some are able to continually innovate for decades or even longer. Procter & Gamble has been around since 1837 but still manages to come out with blockbuster new products like its Swiffer and Febreze air fresheners. GE was founded in 1892, and it retains market leadership in advanced industries such as jet engines and medical diagnostic machines. Nike is over 50 years old but consistently introduces exciting new innovations every year.[7]

While agility has become the mantra of the digital age, creating something fundamentally new is a slow, painstaking process, and although small start-ups can move fast, larger enterprises have the luxury of moving deliberately. They have loyal customers and an abundance of resources. They can see past a venture capitalist's horizon of three to five years and invest for the long term. It is only by taking that kind of long-term perspective that you can consistently innovate at scale.

There is no company that exemplifies this principle better than IBM, which has continually reinvented itself in its century-long history.

IBM's History of Reinvention

The First Crisis

The 1952 U.S. presidential election was historic in more ways than one. As a gimmick, CBS put Remington Rand's UNIVAC on air to project election results as early returns came in. About 8:30, the "electronic brain" predicted General Dwight Eisenhower would take 438 electoral votes to Adlai Stevenson's 93, a massive—and unlikely—landslide, and gave 100-to-1 odds that Eisenhower would win. The newsmen scoffed and refused to broadcast the result. To help the machine save face in the event that the Stevenson triumph that many human prognosticators had foreseen actually came to pass, they announced on air that UNIVAC had predicted only 8-to-7 odds in Eisenhower's favor.

Yet as it turned out, UNIVAC had been right all along, which meant an enormous coup for Remington Rand and a disaster for IBM. Information processing, an industry that IBM had created and dominated for decades, now belonged to its rival. It seemed to many that the company that had become an icon had already seen its best days and was now in a state of decline. It wouldn't be the last time.[8]

The company we now know as IBM started out as the Computing-Tabulating-Recording Company, or C-T-R, which made a wide array of scales, time clocks, and punch card tabulators. In 1914, its investors hired a former sales manager from the National Cash Register Company, Thomas J. Watson, to be its general manager.[9] He would run the company till one month before his death in 1956.

Watson immediately got to work improving operations at the debt-ridden company. A master salesman and motivator, he immediately began building the culture of integrity, work ethic, and engineering prowess the organization later became known for. Results steadily improved, and before long, C-T-R started showing black ink. By the 1920s it had become a strongly profitable company.

Yet it was Watson's vision that truly transformed the company. He saw that the time clock and scale businesses were just a distraction. The future lay in information processing, a term that Watson himself had coined. It was still a nascent technology, but Watson noticed that customers were fascinated by his machines' ability to process small cardboard cards that stored information in the form of holes punched in any one of 960 designated locations, neatly arranged in a pattern of 80 columns with 12 spaces each. He also recognized that the technology could be greatly improved by employing talented engineers to improve the product, creating a world-class sales force to help customers identify new applications for the machines, and honing manufacturing operations to boost reliability.[10]

Although we take the value of information technology for granted today, back then it was a radically new idea. The legendary management guru Peter Drucker said of his first meeting with Watson in the early 1930s, "He began talking about something called data processing, and it made absolutely no sense to me. I took it back and told my editor, and he said that Watson was a nut, and threw the interview away. . . . But if there had been a *Harvard Business Review* (during the 1930s), it would have run stories about him, and he would've been considered a nut or a crank."[11]

Nevertheless, Watson, a man who never lacked for confidence in himself or his company, forged ahead. He eventually divested the time clock and scale businesses to focus on the punch card tabulating machines and changed the name of the company to International Business Machines in 1926,[12] With laser-like focus on steadily improving his organization as well as the capability and performance of his products, Watson and IBM prospered. But it was actually two bet-the-company decisions Watson made in the depths of the Great Depression that would make both him and his company icons of American business.

The Making of an Icon

When business investment plummeted after the stock market crash of 1929, Watson saw an opportunity to make a grab for market share. Between 1929 and 1932, he actually increased production capacity by a third, even though sales had slowed and machines were piling up in the warehouse.[13] It was a daring bet and nearly killed the company. However, in 1934, with IBM deeply in the red and near-certain prospects of bankruptcy looming if things didn't change, President Franklin Roosevelt signed the Social Security Act.

As Kevin Maney wrote in his biography of Watson, *The Maverick and his Machine*, "No single flourish of a pen had ever created such a gigantic information processing problem." Almost overnight, every business in America, as well as the federal government, had an enormous demand for tabulating machines, and IBM had them in spades. The company's revenues jumped from $19 million in 1934 to $31 million in 1937—more than 60 percent growth in just four years.[14]

The second fateful decision came in 1932, when Watson announced that he would invest $1 million to create a new research division.[15] At the time, $1 million represented 6 percent of total revenues, a hefty bet in good times, but an unbelievable gamble in the middle of a depression. Nevertheless, Watson felt strongly that it would allow IBM to finally pull ahead of Remington Rand and other competitors. As it turned out, he was right, and his company would build a dominant position in punch card tabulators that it would never relinquish.

So by the election of 1952, IBM dominated the market for information processing, However, UNIVAC represented a new kind of threat. Digital computers were potentially millions of times more powerful than tabulating machines. Although IBM's research division had been making steady progress toward building a commercial version of its own, James Rand, the founder of Remington Rand, scored a coup when he enticed J. Presper Eckert and John Mauchly, the inventors of the ENIAC, long considered to be the first digital computer,[16] to join his company and develop the UNIVAC. Now, after spending decades at the head of the pack, IBM found itself racing to catch up.

Yet while Remington Rand had surged ahead for the moment, Watson's IBM still had an ace up its sleeve—the research division it had started two decades before. With consultation from the mathematical genius John von Neumann, its researchers and engineers had been working on their own digital computer, the 701, which they unveiled in April 1953. Within a very short time, IBM had pulled even. Before long, its storied sales organization and superior manufacturing capabilities gained favor with customers and the company slowly pulled ahead.

But IBM still wasn't finished. The firm continued to improve the speed and reliability of its computer design. It also invented a revolutionary (for the time) magnetic tape storage system, which it included in its next model, the 702, and also launched a smaller version, the 650, increasing its market share further. Throughout the 1950s, IBM steadily updated its products and continued to roll out important innovations, such as FORTRAN, the world's first programing language, invented by IBM engineer John Backus in 1957.

The final blow to Remington Rand and other competitors' hopes of becoming a significant rival to IBM came in 1964, with the arrival of the System 360. It cost $5 billion to develop in 1960, an enormous sum equivalent to about $30 billion in 2016.[17] One of its chief selling points, besides unmatched speed and reliability, was that it was a scalable system of computers and peripherals that customers could add to over time. The 360 was a system—and a level of investment—that nobody could match. It was largely on the strength of the 360 that IBM dominated the computer market for the next two decades.

Still the company continued to innovate. It developed the SABRE airline reservation system in 1962, still in use to this day. DRAM chips, the working memory that allows us to pull applications and data from hard drives effortlessly while we continue to work, was invented at IBM in 1966. NASA astronauts flew to the moon with the help of IBM computers in 1969, and the company introduced floppy disks and relational databases in the early 1970s. IBM's combination of technical, operational, and marketing prowess was unlike anything the world had ever seen. From 1965 to 1984, the firm's revenues grew at a compound rate of 14 percent, while consistently maintaining 60 percent gross profit margins.[18]

Darker Days Lead to the PC Revolution

By the late 1970s, much like in the 1950s, dark clouds were beginning to loom in the form of a new computing paradigm. One of the keys to the System 360's success was that it was vertically integrated. IBM's Research division continually fed the company's engineers with a constant stream of innovative new components, which allowed IBM to stay ahead of its competitors' capabilities.

However, much like we saw in Chapter 5, Henry Chesbrough's factors of erosion had diminished IBM's ability to dominate technology the way it once had. As information technology became increasingly important in business and society, computer science departments began to spring up around the country, churning out thousands of qualified engineers. At the same time, the rise of the venture capital industry made it much easier for entrepreneurs to finance new companies to compete with IBM. Finally, those new competitors aggressively recruited IBM's technical talent. To paraphrase Bill Joy, even for IBM, most of the smartest people now worked somewhere else.[19]

Another factor in IBM's decline was the rise of the UNIX operating system, developed at Bell Labs. Unlike IBM's strictly proprietary model, UNIX created an open computing environment, which allowed different players to create only part of the solution and, with the help of UNIX, integrate it into a seamless whole. At the same time, companies like Hewlett-Packard, Wang, and Control Data had introduced cheaper minicomputers, while upstarts like Apple, Commodore, and Tandy had introduced personal computers into the market.

Although IBM still dominated in mainframes, its share of the total computer market dwindled from 60 percent in 1970 to just 32 percent in 1980. Its stock fell by 22 percent as it became completely shut out of the burgeoning market for smaller, cheaper computers that was growing by 40 percent annually.[20] Once again, IBM found itself being caught flat-footed.

It wasn't that the company wasn't capable of making a personal computer—in fact, it had already built several prototypes. It was just that any personal computer built according to IBM's standard production processes would be far too expensive to succeed in the marketplace. If IBM were to build a computer for the masses, it would have to be done in another organization.

So that's what IBM did. In September 1980, IBM CEO Frank Cary and President John Opel authorized Don Estridge and Bill Lowe to set up a Skunk Works in Boca Raton, Florida, and begin work on what was to become the PC.[21] The original team of a dozen people quickly grew to 150, but Estridge and Lowe knew that simply adding people was not enough; they would also need to break all the rules by which IBM normally built products.

Rather than use IBM's proprietary technology, it created an open architecture and relied heavily on outside vendors, including, fatefully, Microsoft for the operating system and Intel for the microprocessor. The product would be sold in retail stores rather than through IBM's vaunted sales force, which was also a first. And, in a move that was nearly considered heresy at the time, it released a detailed technical guide[22] that would allow other companies to make similar machines and encouraged outside developers to create software for its computers.

The approach was an enormous success. In July 1981, just one year after development began, the company announced the introduction of the PC. It quickly became the market standard and the first choice for software developers to create applications for. The product seemed to almost literally fly off the shelves. Once again, the company proved that it could meet an enormous challenge, adapt to new realities of the marketplace, and prevail.

The Gerstner Years

Although the PC was an unqualified success, it would also sow the seeds of IBM's next crisis. As company CEO Louis Gerstner would later write in *Who Says Elephants Can't Dance*, "We surrendered control of the highest value components: the operating system to Microsoft and the microprocessor to Intel. By the time I arrived at IBM, those two companies had ridden this gift from IBM right to the top of the industry."[23]

In fact, when Gerstner was named CEO in 1993, the company was going through the worst time in its history. Although, as we have seen, its leadership in the industry had been challenged before, this was a truly existential crisis. The new open model based on client-server architecture had ravaged demand for its core product, mainframes, the sales of which dropped from $13 billion in 1990 to $7 billion in 1993. For the first time since the Great Depression, the dark specter of bankruptcy loomed over IBM.

It was also a very different crisis than IBM had faced before. The transition from punch card tabulators to digital computers and from mainframes to PCs were largely technical challenges, which the company could overcome through superior research, engineering, and sales organization. This time, however, the problem wasn't that IBM had lost its technical edge. In fact, the research division was enjoying somewhat of a heyday. It had just received back-to-back Nobel prizes in 1986 and 1987, for the scanning tunneling microscope and high temperature superconductivity, respectively. In 1989, it introduced silicon-germanium chips, which would soon become standard in wireless networks. So IBM retained many of the assets and capabilities that made it an industry leader. This was primarily a crisis of business model, rather than business process.

As a longtime IBM customer, Gerstner had experienced frustrations with how IBM did business firsthand. When he was at American Express, he remembered when an IBM representative had threatened to pull support from a massive processing center just because one of his division managers had installed a single competitive computer. American Express was not only a loyal, longstanding customer; it was one of IBM's largest accounts. Enraged, Gerstner placed a call straight to the chief executive's office to complain.[24]

Eventually, the matter got resolved, but the incident—and the arrogance it displayed—stuck with Gerstner. He saw how the proprietary mentality chafed customers and, now that they had no shortage of other options, he wasn't surprised they were leaving in droves. The idea that customers would accept a single IT supplier was a relic of the past. The model that had served the company so well for so many decades was broken; it just seemed like nobody at IBM was willing to accept that fact.

At the same time, Gerstner saw great opportunity. The new open architecture of the industry was also creating headaches for customers. At least with IBM the process was fairly simple. You would call up your salesperson, tell him or her what you needed, and the organization would deliver a solution. Now, customers had to deal with a dizzying array of suppliers and integrate everything themselves.

Gerstner saw that instead of trying to force a proprietary stack of technologies down customers' throats he could create a new business model aimed at the customers' "stack of business processes." So while the base technologies would be open and free, IBM would create value through proprietary systems, software, and applications to solve its customers' problems. As he would later write, "We bet that the historical preoccupations with chip speeds, proprietary systems, and the like would wane, and that over time the information technology industry would be services-led, not technology-led."[25]

What Gerstner recognized was that his firm had unique capabilities that no one else could match, such as a legendary research organization, world-class engineers, a top-notch sales force, and deep ties to customers, that could be leveraged to completely reshape the business—and the industry. That's how you innovate at scale.

Gerstner could not magically transform an 80-year-old company that employed thousands of people into a nimble start-up, but what he could do was transform the culture and direct the firm's unique capabilities in new directions.

To better understand what Gerstner did, let's look at IBM's business model transformation in terms of the "create, deliver, and capture value" framework we discussed in Chapter 5 (Figure 7.1).

	OLD BUSINESS MODEL	NEW BUSINESS MODEL
Create Value	Development of Hardware and Software	Developing and Integrating Solutions
Deliver Value	Sales Organization	Service Organization
Capture Value	Sales	Fees

FIGURE 7.1   IBM Business Model Transformation

The old model was based on developing, delivering, and capturing value through proprietary technology and a dedicated sales force. For a long time that model was very successful. However, as new technologies like UNIX and personal computers drove the market toward a more modular form of organization, customers no longer valued IBM's vertically integrated approach. In fact, they found it constricting and presumptuous. The notion that one company could dictate to the market what it needed was not only outdated, but also increasingly untenable.

The new business model was based on a profoundly different strategy. Rather than focus on selling products, IBM aimed at selling solutions. If, say, a major airline needed a reservation system that could track thousands of flights and passengers around the world, IBM would deliver it using the component technologies best fit to that task. Or if a major retailer needed a system that could track millions of pieces of inventory throughout the supply chain, IBM would deliver that, too, and it would incorporate the hardware and software best fit to the task no matter who made it.

In other words, IBM would no longer be a product business, but a knowledge business, whose main supply chain ran from the research organization straight through the engineers and consultants to the customer. It was an offer that no company on earth could match. No one else had a research organization like IBM's, with more Nobel prizes and Turing awards than most countries. No one else had decades of experience working closely with clients to devise solutions. It was a wrenching transformation to be sure, one that stretched the ability of even someone like Lou Gerstner to bend a company's culture to his will, but somehow IBM pulled it off.

As Irving Wladawsky-Berger, a key figure in IBM's resurgence, told me, "There were three reasons we didn't die. Number one was the world-class R&D labs. When the asteroid hit, we had the technology in place to make changes to our business. The second was that we had earned loyalty from our customers from years of strong service. Third, we were really lucky to get Lou Gerstner, who put together the strategy to chart a new course."[26]

e-Business

Once Gerstner had stabilized the business, it was time to get it moving forward again. "By early 1995, we were out of intensive care and into the recovery room," Wladawsky-Berger remembers. "At that point, the question was, how do we create a new course for the future. Then the gods sent us a gift in 1995: the Internet. That's when it shifted from being an obscure technology used by scientific labs and research institutions to a much more mainstream technology. Lou commissioned a major task force to figure out what to do about the Internet, which determined that IBM should fully embrace the Internet in every facet of its business."[27]

While many of its rivals felt threatened by the Internet, IBM immediately saw that it played right into the strengths of its new business model. Yes, the Internet would be disruptive, but that meant that IBM's customers needed its expertise more than ever! Who else had the knowledge to transform the legacy systems of traditional businesses to a new age of technology? As Wladawsky-Berger explained to me, "Our clients didn't want to hear that they would have to throw out the business processes they'd been developing for decades. We went to them and said, 'We can help you.' We were almost the only people who were telling them that they could leverage existing IT assets they'd worked so hard to build and integrate them with the Internet. By doing that, we were able to once again achieve a major leadership position."[28]

The Internet initiative, branded as "e-business," led to yet another transformative opportunity—Linux. Once again, where the company would have once seen a threat, it now saw opportunity. As its customers were increasingly looking to companies like Red Hat to move their systems over to Linux, IBM began offering them the option of mainframe computers and software applications already integrated with the open source software. That gave customers confidence that everything would work together seamlessly right out of the box. In time, it became a major selling point.

This time, however, the transformation wasn't so wrenching. "Once we went through the cultural transformation to embrace the open standards of the Internet, it was a much easier transition to embrace Linux. I've always felt that our success with Linux was a direct consequence of our shift to the Internet," Wladawsky-Berger told me. [29]

And that's the key thing to understand about innovating at scale. Start-ups begin with a blank page, with few assets and no investment in the status quo. It is in their nature to disrupt the marketplace. Established companies, with entrenched assets and obligations to existing customers, must eventually learn to disrupt themselves. They need to figure out which parts of their existing business model to keep and which to throw away. For IBM, its commitment to its core capabilities in world-class research, engineering. and sales has remained solid throughout its long history. Everything else, however, is negotiable.

If Thomas J. Watson were to return to the company he built today, he would find many elements that he would recognize. The commitment to research and engineering is still there, as is IBM's hardware and software businesses. What's different is how those assets are leveraged.

There are few, if any, organizations that can boast of a history of reinvention like IBM. It transcended the shift from tabulating machines to digital computers, then mainframes to PCs, and then, after a near-death experience, made the transition from products to services. Along the way it faced fierce competition from tough competitors like Remington Rand, DEC, Sun Microsystems, Compaq, and a host of others. All are now either greatly diminished or gone entirely.

At the core of the company's ability to consistently adapt to technology shifts is its ability to innovate at scale. Over the past several years, I've spoken to many of IBM's top executives, engineers, and scientists to understand how it pulls it all off.

How IBM Innovates Today

At the core of innovation at IBM is its longtime commitment to basic research. As Vannevar Bush described when he was designing the scientific architecture that would make the United States a technological superpower, fundamental and exploratory research is the seed corn that makes everything else possible.

In many ways IBM Research stands alone. For sure there have been many other excellent corporate research organizations, such as the legendary Bell Labs, Xerox PARC, and, more recently, Microsoft Research, but none can match IBM's consistent performance over such a long period. Xerox PARC had an astounding burst of creativity throughout the 1970s but did little work of significance beyond that. Microsoft Research has also done important work, but it has only been in operation since 1991. After the breakup of AT&T in 1996, Bell Labs lost much of the support that made it a world-class scientific institution. IBM research, which has been operating continuously since 1932—85 years and still going strong—is a unique innovation asset.

When I asked Bernie Meyerson, IBM's chief innovation officer, what accounted for the Research organization's unique track record of success, he told me, "First and foremost, I credit IBM's management, both Research and Corporate, for our success. To be blunt, we have had the incredible benefit of a long-term view of the world held by our founder, T. J. Watson Sr., that has set the tone for all the generations of management to come. There is a fundamental understanding at all levels of executive management that our Research Division is the engine that powers innovation, and that belief has enabled Research to remain a vital component of IBM's long term agenda, both in its shaping and execution."[30]

It is that level of commitment, in turn, that has made it a beacon for many of the world's top scientists. Unlike at an academic institution, IBM researchers are not bogged down with class schedules and publishing requirements. At the same time, they are given considerable freedom to explore areas that interest them.

Charlie Bennett, who many consider to be the "father of quantum information theory," told me, "I came to IBM Research because it was one of the few places where one could do research in the interdisciplinary subject I was interested in, the physics of information processing. I've had the freedom to think about what I wanted, and to visit and collaborate with scientists at universities and laboratories all over the world."[31] The legendary, if iconoclastic, Benoit Mandelbrot, who invented the field of fractal geometry, put it more simply, "I stayed because nobody offered a better fit, and quickly thrived."[32]

It is hard to convey how unusual this commitment to open exploration is. There are probably only a handful of companies in American history that have truly supported basic research—today IBM and Microsoft are rare exceptions—and the ones who have are rarely able to sustain their commitment for very long. The work done at IBM Research often doesn't find a useful application for a decade or two—and sometimes longer—but it provides a continual stream of new knowledge that its engineers can transform into pathbreaking products.

"You're never certain as to what's going to be commercially fantastic," says, IBM's Meyerson, whose own work on silicon-germanium chips revolutionized the ability for chips to facilitate communication in wireless networks such as Wi-Fi. "That's why we take an unconstrained approach to research and innovation. We want to know about everything that can help us solve a problem."[33]

Another facet of how IBM innovates is that it continually meets with customers to understand their needs. Steve Jobs famously said, "People don't know what they want until you show it to them," but Meyerson counters, "Our customers can't tell us about a future that doesn't exist yet, but they can tell us about unresolved problems and we can get to work on them. Addressing a really grand challenge like Watson can begin 5 or 10 years before the result is seen in public. It was a science project, but with business problems in mind."[34]

IBM also maintains its longstanding commitment to open technology that began with Linux, both through the direct participation of its engineers and through the contribution of its patents, which helps it leverage its own efforts. For example, Rob Thomas, vice president of information management at IBM, told me, "Open sourcing our machine learning engine allows us to expand the number of people improving its capabilities from thousands of internal engineers to tens of thousands—and eventually to hundreds of thousands—in the open source community."[35]

Simply put, IBM's innovation efforts focus on solving really big problems that few, if anyone, else can effectively take on. Today, the company is in the midst of reinventing itself again as the technology industry is rapidly moving from the installed solutions that have powered the company for the last 25 years to much cheaper and more efficient cloud-based solutions. The transition has, at the time of this writing, led to 17 straight quarterly declines in revenue. While IBM does not face an existential crisis like it did in the 1990s—it had an operating profit of over $15 billion in 2015—the challenges ahead will be formidable, and the company must continue to innovate at a very high level.

IBM's New Era of Innovation

Lou Gerstner's turnaround at IBM is legendary. He took a deeply ingrained culture, hardwired into the organization over eight decades, and transformed it to go in a completely different direction. What had been a proprietary enterprise aimed at selling products became an open enterprise focused on solving its customers' problems. As Irving Wladawsky-Berger put it to me, "It was imperative that IBM became a much more market-centric company. Instead of expecting to create new markets, we had to find our place in the marketplace."[36]

Yet much like in the past, IBM's success sowed the seeds for problems later on. For the past quarter century, the company's profitability has depended on its customers buying big systems. That's what's driven demand for both its consulting services and its technology. However, as companies have begun rapidly shifting from installed solutions to cloud platforms, IBM's once thriving business in high-end computer hardware, such as servers and mainframes, as well as the operating systems that run them, has been in a tailspin, dropping by more than 20 percent per year. As I noted above, that doesn't threaten IBM's existence, it's still a very profitable company, but since 2010 about $20 billion has been shaved off of its annual revenue.[37] That's a pretty big hole to fill if current CEO Ginni Rometty is going to get the company growing again.

At the same time, there is an even bigger problem on the horizon. For the past 50 years, computer technology has primarily advanced through engineers figuring out how to squeeze more transistors onto silicon chips. This phenomenon, commonly known as Moore's law, has led to a doubling of computing power every 18 months, making computers today millions of times more powerful than they were a half century ago. Put simply, that is what has made our modern world possible.

Still, the laws of physics impose limits. Eventually, transistors become so small that the subatomic forces known as quantum effects start interfering with their function. We will hit that point sometime around the year 2020. After that, no more progress will be possible through conventional means.

So IBM has to innovate on three horizons. First, it must create solutions so powerful that it can create enough value to replace the revenues it is losing from hardware sales. Second, it must learn how to apply those solutions to adjacent areas. Third, it must come up with completely new computing architectures that can drive technological advancement beyond Moore's Law.

IBM Research is an enormous enterprise, encompassing thousands of scientists across 12 labs on six continents, and there is far more work going on than I can summarize here. So I would like to focus on four areas that I think are particularly important: data and analytics, cognitive computing, neuromorphic chips, and quantum computing.

Data and Analytics

Achieving a leadership position in data and analytics is one of CEO Ginni Rometty's five "strategic imperatives" for IBM[38] because of intense enterprise demand for powerful solutions that can make sense of the mountains of data that corporations generate every year from customer interactions, suppliers, and other partners. As the Internet of Things becomes increasingly embedded through sensors on everything from vehicles to ordinary household appliances, the amount of data that organizations need to digest is expected to increase exponentially in the years to come.

Another data challenge comes from data systems themselves. Most enterprises have a wide variety of different systems within various functional and organizational boundaries. For example, a retailer may have separate systems for purchasing, inventory, point-of-sale, and e-commerce, while a large bank may have separate systems for commercial lending, mortgages, and trading. Some of these are legacy systems developed and installed decades ago, while others are more recent. The result is that most organizations have large amounts of data stored in different places using different protocols that don't work together well.

IBM is tackling the data challenge in two ways. First, it maintains an active investment in open source communities like Hadoop and

Spark, tasking thousands of engineers and contributing hundreds of patents to help these technologies advance. At first glance, this may seem overly altruistic if not just downright foolish. However, the work that IBM engineers contributes to these communities is multiplied a hundredfold by the tens of thousands of other active members in those communities.

The second way IBM is innovating in the data and analytics space is through the work its engineers and consultants do to solve customer problems. In effect, collaborating with open source communities relieves the company of the burden of maintaining basic technologies, freeing up a lot of resources to build unique solutions on top of them. For example, the company has recently created a new platform for data, called the Data Science Experience, that allows its customers to gather information from all of those disparate systems and protocols within their organizations and work with it as if it were just one huge database. It also helps integrate data trapped in outdated proprietary systems with data now available on open protocols, such as economic and population statistics on Data.gov.

Cognitive Computing
IBM has been working on artificial intelligence for decades and over the years has actively researched many different techniques, such as natural language processing, machine learning, and decision-making algorithms. All of this came to a head one night when an IBM researcher named Charles Lickel was sitting in a bar and noticed that everything went quiet when the patrons stopped to watch Ken Jennings's historic run on the game show *Jeopardy!*.

Fascinated, he came up with the idea of building a system that could compete with human contestants on the show. He got the backing of Paul Horn, at the time executive director at IBM Research, and the Jeopardy Grand Challenge was launched.[39] Eight years later, on Valentines Day in 2011, IBM's Watson system first squared off against Jennings and another *Jeopardy!* champion, Brad Rutter. The machine thoroughly trounced the human players over three rounds. For his final response, Jennings wrote in, "I, for one, welcome our new computer overlords."

Today, IBM is working with customers such as MD Anderson Cancer Center and Geico Insurance Company to create cognitive systems that can augment human decision making.[40] At the same time, it offers training in cognitive systems and APIs in its developerWorks platform so that even start-up companies can access its technology to build cognitive solutions.

Neuromorphic Chips

Today's computers were designed to calculate, a task that they do extremely well. A typical computer chip can process billions of calculations per second, which allows them to perform logical functions very efficiently. However, they are poorly designed to perform tasks that humans do with ease, such as recognizing a face or catching a ball. Our brains can do those things well because they are, in technological parlance, massively parallel. Each one of our billions of neurons can, potentially at least, communicate directly with every other one.

When IBM scientist Dharmendra Modha simulated a human brain with a supercomputer, he found that our brains are, in fact, a billion times more efficient than today's computer architectures. He realized that if he could close just a small part of that gap, he could produce something truly revolutionary—a neuromorphic chip that can vastly outperform, in terms of both speed and power consumption, conventional chips for cognitive tasks like Watson does.

First funded by a DARPA grant in 2008, Modha and his team have been working for eight years to make good on that vision. Today, there are more than 100 IBM TrueNorth neuromorphic chips in circulation being tested by academic and governmental institutions as well as other partners to create next-generation products in areas like robotics, medical imaging, and autonomous cars.[41]

Quantum Computing

Potentially the most powerful idea in technology today is that of a quantum computer. To understand why, we first have to think about how a classical computer functions. In essence, today's computers transform long series of ones and zeros—called bits—into logical statements and functions according to a set of rules called Boolean logic. So, for instance, to represent a character, we need eight bits to generate 2^8, or 256, possible combinations, which is plenty of space to accommodate letters, numbers, punctuation, and other symbols. With processors able to handle billions of those bits per second, we can get a lot done even with basic, everyday machines.

The math of quantum computers works in a somewhat similar way, except because of superposition and entanglement, instead of combinations, it produces "states." These states do not conform to any physical reality we would be familiar with, but roughly represent separate dimensions in which a quantum calculation may take place. So an eight quantum bit (or qubit) computer can be in a superposition of 256 different states (or dimensions), while a 300 qubit computer can be simultaneously doing more calculations than there are atoms in the universe.

There are, however, some problems. First, nobody knows how to build or use a large-scale universal quantum computer. Second, quantum calculations work much differently than classical ones, so it's not quite clear how we can harness the potential power of quantum computers for the types of tasks that traditional computers are really good at. Still, for some applications, like cryptography and certain types of simulations, the vast potential of quantum computers is already clear.[42]

IBM has recently made a five-qubit computer available on the cloud,[43] where academics and students can work on problems and learn how to create programs in a quantum environment. It hopes to have a 50- to 100-qubit version within the next decade.

So IBM is clearly active in all three horizons we discussed in Chapter 6, although unlike Google, IBM doesn't set concrete goals for each horizon. Its engineers and consultants work closely with customers to develop solutions for Horizon 1 in areas like data and analytics. At the same time, it runs pilot programs with organizations like MD Anderson and Geico to find new areas to apply advanced technologies like Watson. It also offers those technologies, through APIs, to anybody who believes they can develop a profitable application. Both of these activities help IBM identify adjacent business markets, it can enter in Horizon 2. Finally, IBM Research continually explores the far reaches of scientific possibility in Horizon 3. In the case of quantum computing, this effort has been ongoing since at least 1993.

IBM's Innovation Portfolio

IBM's innovation activity is indeed so vast it's hard to take it all in. Unlike Google, which offers a large but limited number of products to consumers, IBM, through its corporate and government customers, is active in just about every human endeavor you can think of, from manufacturing and retailing to healthcare and space exploration.

Still, when we overlay IBM's innovation portfolio onto the innovation matrix, we can begin to make sense of it (Figure 7.2).

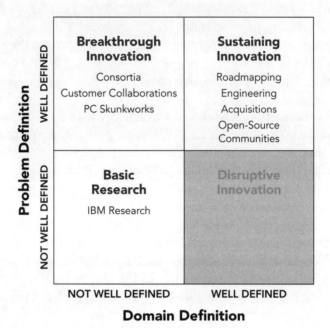

FIGURE 7.2   IBM Innovation Matrix

The Four Quadrants
BASIC RESEARCH

IBM's Research division has been the driving force behind the company's success for the better part of the last century. It is a world-class institution by any standard, but as a corporate lab it stands alone. As we have seen, it has played a major role in IBM's history of reinvention. For all the problems the company has faced in the last 100 years, a lack of advanced technology has not been one of them.

Another aspect of IBM Research, which is often overlooked, is the value it generates through collaboration with its customers. Scientists at IBM meet often with customers to get a sense of where the really thorny problems lie. This is often what inspires them to do their best work. Benoit Mandelbrot, for example, came up with the ideas that led to his creation of fractal geometry though his work trying to reduce static in communication lines. They also help provide consultation, which is a genuine sales asset. Very few companies in the world can send out a Nobel laureate or a Turing Award winner to work on a customer's problem.

BREAKTHROUGH INNOVATION

IBM uses a variety of strategies to solve well-defined problems that defy easy solutions. It participates in a number of research consortia that pool the resources of other organizations, brings multidisciplinary teams of consultants, engineers, and research scientists to work with domain experts in the various industries it serves, and, on occasion, creates special task forces like the one set up to design the PC.

Yet what sets IBM apart is just the sheer volume of expertise it has within its organization. When you get an MRI at a hospital, IBM invented the technology that made that possible. Book a flight on a plane, and IBM designed the reservation system. Stream a movie on your tablet computer, and IBM created the chip technology the wireless network runs on. It's that breadth and depth of expertise, plus an extremely collaborative culture forged over decades, that makes the company an incredibly effective problem solver.

SUSTAINING INNOVATION

Like most tech companies, IBM continually works to improve its products. It recruits the best engineering talent it can find and listens to its customers. When it sees a hole in its portfolio, it acquires a company with the capabilities it needs, as it did with SoftLayer in cloud services. These are all pretty standard sustaining innovation strategies.

One thing that IBM does differently in this quadrant is its commitment to open source communities. In most cases, open innovation is a breakthrough innovation strategy because open source communities bring a greater variety of talents to a problem than any one organization could alone. Their mantra, after all, is "With enough eyeballs, all bugs are shallow." In IBM's case, however, that's not really a concern. It could easily build its own version of Linux, Hadoop, or Spark if it wanted to. However, by supporting these communities the company can greatly reduce the resources it would have to invest to maintain platforms, and those resources can be focused on building proprietary technologies on top of them.

DISRUPTIVE INNOVATION

IBM does not pursue disruptive innovation strategies as a core strategy, although it has demonstrated that it is perfectly capable of understanding the skill set. It's a global leader in agile development methodologies and even runs a program called Bluemix Garage that teaches other companies how to implement Lean LaunchPad and Design Thinking techniques. It also routinely engages in the kind of customer development processes that we saw in Chapter 4.

The difference is that when IBM meets with customers, it is often looking 5, 10, or even 20 years out and is willing to work that long to bring truly pathbreaking technologies to market. Its focus is not disrupting the marketplace, but solving problems for its enterprise clients.

The key thing to understand about IBM's innovation portfolio is that it wouldn't work for any other company. IBM is not agile like a start-up, nor does it have the design sensibilities of Apple or the entrepreneurial energy of Amazon. Rather, it leverages its own unique capabilities in research, engineering, and sales. That's how you innovate at scale.

PART THREE

INNOVATION FOR THE DIGITAL AGE

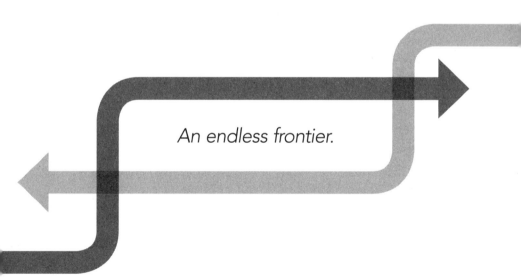

An endless frontier.

CHAPTER EIGHT

Leveraging Platforms to Access Ecosystems

No matter who you are, most of the smartest people work for someone else.

BILL JOY

In 1904, the great German sociologist Max Weber visited the United States on a three-month lecture tour. Expecting to see a backwater lagging far behind industrial Europe, he instead found a thoroughly modern society with thriving factories and great metropolises filled with soaring skyscrapers. Yet he was also struck by the almost unbelievable lack of organization, with little in place to regulate and organize all the activity.

He would later draw on his experiences in the United States when he wrote *Economy and Society*, in which he argued that traditional forms of authority would no longer suffice in an industrialized society. In its place, he saw the need for a new more rational form of authority, with specified job requirements, training in order to fulfill those requirements, consistent and comprehensive rules to govern operations, and extensive record keeping in the form of written documents and communication. In essence, Weber was advocating for a new form of organization he called *bureaucracy*.

The term has since taken on a pejorative meaning, but it's important to note that a century ago bureaucracy was an important innovation. In an industrial age, productivity no longer depended on the skill of artisans, but the efficiencies of organizations. Those organizations, in turn, could not plausibly be run solely through the personal authority of leaders, but needed systems in place in order to operate with any measure of competence. No one person, no matter how smart or charismatic, could effectively coordinate the work of thousands. Bureaucracy performed that function reasonably well.[1]

While Weber described the form of modern organizations, a young economist named Ronald Coase was interested in their function. In his 1937 paper "The Nature of the Firm," Coase argued that firms exist to minimize transaction costs, especially informational costs. He wrote:

> The main reason why it is profitable to establish a firm would seem to be that there is a cost of using the price mechanism. The most obvious cost of "organizing" production through the price mechanism is that of discovering what the relevant prices are. This cost may be reduced but it will not be eliminated by the emergence of specialists who will sell this information. The costs of negotiating and concluding a separate contract for each exchange transaction which takes place on a market must also be taken into account.[2]

He further suggested that as successful firms grew larger in scale, they would be able to reduce transaction costs through greater access to capital and specialized talent. However, Coase also pointed out that organizational costs posed a limit on the size of a firm, effectively arguing that an organization would continue to grow until the costs of organizing resources became so large that they would cancel out the reduction in search costs.

In 1985, a professor at Harvard Business School named Michael Porter built on Coase's ideas in his book *Competitive Advantage*, which quickly became the standard reference for business strategy. At the heart of his framework was the value chain (Figure 8.1). Porter argued, "The value chain is not a collection of independent activities, but a system of interdependent activities."[3] In other words, to gain competitive advantage, you need to manage the transaction and informational costs that exist all along the path from the acquisition of resources to the point of sale. Any weakness in that chain of control could cause a firm to lose its ability to leverage its assets and achieve sustainable competitive advantage.

FIGURE 8.1 Porter's Value Chain

That's essentially how the great enterprises of the twentieth century were built. Firms like General Motors under Alfred Sloan as well as IBM under Thomas J. Watson and, later, his son Thomas Watson Jr. so thoroughly dominated the value chains in their respective industries, from procurement to production to sales, that they were able to achieve efficiencies that their rivals couldn't hope to match.

So Microsoft's institutional suspicion of open source communities that we discussed in Chapter 5 was entirely rational. As a matter of fact, it was key to the company's enormous success. After all, there were many great technology companies that emerged in the 1970s and 1980s, but only one came to dominate as Microsoft did. Its ability to exert control over the value chain of an entire industry has had no equal since the days of the nineteenth-century robber barons.

What's most notable about the Kinect story we discussed in Chapter 5 isn't that Microsoft took so long to embrace open technology, but how it was finally able to break free of the principles that Coase and Porter set down and switch course. Many other companies did not and are no longer in business, while Microsoft remains a powerful force in technology even today.

How Search Costs Drive the Viability of Business Models

To really understand why Microsoft eventually embraced open platforms we need to look beyond Coase and Porter and look to the work of Peter Diamond, Dale Mortensen, and Christopher Pissarides, who won the 2010 Nobel Prize "for their analysis of markets with search frictions." Essentially, they found that much of what Coase said about firms applied to markets as well. Search costs drive our decisions in many ways that nobody had realized before. For example, we've all had the experience of overpaying for an item at a store because we simply don't feel like spending the time and effort to find it somewhere else, but few had suspected how search costs affect market behavior as a whole. And while many of us have put up with a boss we don't like rather than undergo the onerous hassle of a job search, few had thought seriously about how search costs affect labor markets in general.[4]

As we have seen in this book, digital technology has altered search costs in unexpected ways. For example, when Randy Terbush needed to find solutions to the problems he was having with his AutoCAD software, he quickly and easily found them from friendly computer programmers on Usenet. Later, he was able to work with the people he met online to create the Apache web server software that became the market standard, as have later projects of the Apache Foundation that followed, such as Hadoop and Spark. Today, tens of thousands of the world's most talented developers contribute to Apache software. That wouldn't be possible without the massive reduction in search costs that the Internet has made possible.

We have also seen how search costs often left important problems unsolved because the people with the right expertise were so difficult to find. InnoCentive brought those search costs crashing down, and pretty soon organizations were able to find answers to problems that had left them stumped for years. Procter & Gamble found this reduction in search costs so compelling that it created the Connect + Develop program, which led to billion-dollar product lines. It was these same forces that IBM took note of in the 1990s when it embraced Linux, as did Microsoft when it supported the Kinect hackers in 2010.

As Stephen Shapiro, formerly chief evangelist at InnoCentive, explained it to me, every organization faces a set of challenges that represent a bell curve. At one end of the bell curve, you have a set of problems where there are either established solutions or the skills to solve them are known and accessible, such as when choosing a supplier for basic components or services. In those cases, you only incur search costs in terms of price, reliability, level of service, and so on. On the other end of the bell curve are the really tough problems that have no clear solutions. In those cases, you incur search costs related to finding the talent, skills, and information you need to solve the problem. In the middle are opportunities to differentiate your business by leveraging internal assets and capabilities to solve problems.[5]

That, in a nutshell, is the effect that digital technology has had on markets and competitive strategy. It has lowered search costs outside of firms much more efficiently than it has lowered organizational costs inside of firms (Figure 8.2). So today, organizations must make very different decisions about what capabilities they will build and leverage internally and what will be cheaper and more effective to access externally.

Standard Problems	Zone of Differentiation	Unique Problems
Search for best price, reliability, level of service, etc.	Build and leverage capabilities within the firm	Search for unique talent, skills and information
Search Costs	Organizational Costs	Search Costs

FIGURE 8.2 Search Costs Inside and Outside of Firms

Irving Wladawsky-Berger understood this concept very early and actively incorporated open technologies like Linux into IBM's e-business strategy. He recognized that the Internet had diminished search costs to such an extent that some activities within his company would no longer differentiate it in the marketplace. So he was able to shift internal resources to solve problems that still required proprietary solutions, which was a major factor in reviving IBM's fortunes. Microsoft, on the other hand, continued to see open software communities as a threat and, until Kinect, failed to leverage their capabilities, which led it to miss significant opportunities.

Today, every organization must adapt to this shift in search costs. While we still need to build capabilities internally that lead to differentiation and competitive advantage, we also need to leverage platforms to access ecosystems of talent, technology, and information to help us solve standard problems at lower cost and also to identify unique assets that can help us solve really tough problems.

Today, power has shifted from corporations and other institutions to platforms because, as Bill Joy put it, "No matter who you are, most of the smartest people work for someone else." The same goes for resources like technology and information. No matter who you are, most of the best technology and important information resides somewhere else as well. Now that digital technology has reduced the costs of accessing resources so significantly, we need to rethink how we compete in the marketplace.

Clearly, a crucial skill for innovating in the digital age is the ability to utilize platforms to access ecosystems of talent, technology, and information that reside outside our organizations. Let's look at each in turn.

Ecosystems of Talent

In 2001, Fabio Rosati had his first midlife crisis. Although he was only in his midthirties at the time, he had already achieved an enormous amount of success. After graduating with a degree in finance and accounting from Georgetown University in 1987, he joined Gemini Consulting and quickly rose through the ranks to become president and CEO of the firm's operations in his native Italy. Later, he became COO of the firm's U.S. operations and then global chair of strategic consulting for Capgemini. In just 13 years, he had climbed to the very top of his profession.

But after reaching such lofty heights, Rosati realized he didn't want to be a consultant for the rest of his life. It was then that a call came in from a headhunter asking if he would like to take over as CEO of a start-up in transition. The company, Elance, had started out as an online platform for freelancers, but its investors had decided to switch the company's focus to enterprise software. They felt they needed someone with Rosati's expertise to manage the transition. Excited at the prospect of actually managing a company, rather than merely just advising managers, Rosati took the offer.

Once he relocated from Capgemini's New York office to San Francisco, he jumped into the task with gusto. The company had developed a new class of software now known as a "vendor management system," which allowed large enterprises to manage their ecosystems of external suppliers. For example, a company like General Electric, which had thousands of external service providers, could load all of its relevant information, including statements of work, rates, and other specifications, into the system. They could then use that centralized store of data to help them award, track, manage, and evaluate projects. It would help companies to ensure that the agreed rates were applied and best practices were implemented across the entire enterprise.

The business grew and began making money, but Rosati saw darker days ahead. The vendor management sector had gotten hot and was beginning to attract competition from the big enterprise software firms. It became clear that Elance would not have the resources to compete. So he and the investors agreed to sell the software business in 2006.

The company, however, still retained its name, a staff of about a dozen people, and enough capital to start over again. Over the previous six years Rosati and his team had learned a great deal about how enterprises work with outside contractors, and it seemed that there was a great opportunity to revisit the company's original idea—a platform for hiring freelance contractors.

In particular, they saw that the midlevel staffing industry was ripe for disintermediation. When Rosati looked at how firms hired contractors, he saw a process that was almost Kafkaesque. A company would send a brief to staffing firms, and a period of consultancy would ensue. Then the staffing firms would search for people in their databases who met the client's requirements, vet the candidates, and present them to the client. The whole process would typically take three to four weeks, and the staffing firms would charge a 40 percent markup. Almost to add insult to injury, the same candidate was often presented by several agencies, each at a different rate.

In Elance's original vision, a platform would simply replace these staffing firms, acquiring databases similar to what the staffing firms used and offering them to clients online. However, the six years of experience selling vendor management software had showed Rosati and his team that they could do a lot more. They could combine the search function of the platform with some of the tracking and management functionality that their enterprise software had provided. Rather than just facilitating a match between firms and contractors, Elance could widen and deepen connections between business and talent.

They started out with a system that fulfilled the search function of a typical platform—freelance contractors could post their skills and businesses could post the jobs they needed done—but they also would track and manage the work. Each job would have milestones, and money would be held in escrow till they were achieved, giving assurance to both sides of the transaction that obligations would be met. At the end of the engagement, both the business and the contractor would rate each other's performance.

As the platform grew, Elance learned from its most successful freelance contractors and business clients about what made engagements successful. It used these insights to improve its algorithms to include things like timeliness, responsiveness, and communication effectiveness in addition to the more conventional parameters of skills and experience. It quickly became clear that tracking engagements and outcomes allowed Elance to better match contractors to businesses.

Soon, the company took the next step and started offering companies private talent clouds. As it turned out, many firms already had preferred networks of freelance contractors that met their compliance requirements. These were people who had certified skills, had been vetted with background checks, and had signed nondisclosure agreements. They wanted to put these networks into the system, but keep them private so other firms couldn't poach their preferred contractors. For instance, if Nike often worked with a talented freelance designer, it certainly didn't want Adidas or Reebok to know about it!

This move also provided a benefit to the freelance contractors themselves because, in a sense, they could maintain both public and private identities on the platform. Although—and Rosati stressed this point to me—Elance went to great measures to ensure that nobody could maintain more than one identity on the platform, users could keep certain aspects of their company relationships confidential in private clouds. So, if that talented designer was getting steady work at Nike, she could offer a lower rate to it and a higher rate to businesses that only occasionally contracted her services.

At the same time, the private clouds helped the companies manage their external workforce more effectively. If a software engineer had done a great job for a project with one hiring manager, then her colleague in another department or in another office would see that in the private cloud and hire him for the next project. Once a freelance contractor joined a private talent cloud, she gained access to the entire ecosystem of the organization.

On the other hand, if a manager found that a contractor wasn't responsive or timely, then her colleague would see that too and hire someone else. In fact, all of this information was fed into algorithms to create better matches between businesses and contractors. Elance wasn't just creating efficiencies through disintermediation; it was actually improving the quality of relationships.

Eventually, the company saw an opportunity to go even a step further. It started to develop partnerships with companies that could train and certify contractors. So a firm looking for someone to do English to Russian translations, build a website in Python, or set up a Hadoop cluster for data analysis could be sure that a particular contractor was indeed proficient in the skills needed to do the job. At the same time, because Elance had visibility to both supply and demand on its platform, it could suggest to freelance contractors which skills could make them more marketable. So if work was drying up for PHP developers but companies were crying out for those that could build websites in Ruby on Rails, Elance could notify contractors that they could earn more money by getting certified in a computer language that was in more demand.

In 2008, Elance saw another opportunity when Apple announced it was going to be opening up its iPhone platform to outside developers. Rosati and his colleagues contacted Apple and were able to create resources to train freelance contractors how to develop for the iPhone's operating system, iOS. Within a few months of the software development kit (SDK) being released, there were 200 jobs on Elance for iOS developers. A year later, there were over 20,000.

Soon companies started coming to Elance with training programs. Microsoft needed more Azure and SharePoint specialists and sponsored training and certification. IBM did the same when it launched its developer cloud for Watson. Companies were able to populate ecosystems with the qualified specialists they needed, while contractors were able to gain greater access to the ecosystems of hiring companies.

In December 2013, Elance announced a merger with its chief competitor, oDesk, to create the dominant platform for freelance contractors. Eighteen months later, the combined firm was rebranded as Upwork, which today generates over a billion dollars' worth of jobs annually. Ninety percent of clients who use the service rehire there.[6]

Rosati no longer has an operational role at the company, but looking back he told me that he saw his company's mission as minimizing "friction" and search costs and specifically referred to the work of the 2010 Nobel Prize winners in helping him to shape its strategy. His company's mission was to drive search costs down at every step in the process, both within firms and throughout markets.

What made Elance so extraordinarily successful is that it went far beyond simple disintermediation; it sought to widen *and deepen* connections. Firms were not only able to connect to freelance contractors, they could also better evaluate their performance. Through private clouds, the contractors would be connected to the entire ecosystem of the hiring firm rather than just a hiring manager or a particular team. It also connected the ecosystems of training firms and qualified contractors looking to upgrade their skills. In effect, it made markets thicker, more efficient, and more transparent.

As we saw in Chapter 5, InnoCentive played a similar role, stepping in when search costs were so enormous that matches were never made. By creating a platform for companies to post problems, it created a new ecosystem of solvers that so dramatically lowered search frictions that it has been able to resolve about a third of the problems that had previously seemed unsolvable.

In effect, the ecosystem of solvers on the platform served as a human-powered search engine that enabled people with tough problems to access important personal knowledge that machine-driven search engines would find difficult—if not impossible—to index. Eli Lilly found this ecosystem so incredibly useful that it spun InnoCentive out as an independent entity because it saw that only the most complete ecosystem of problems could attract and grow that ecosystem of solvers.

In terms of Porter's formula for competitive advantage, where the idea was to optimize value chains, Eli Lilly's action doesn't make a whole lot of sense. The site Crunchbase shows that the spin-off only attracted $30 million in equity (and that includes Eli Lilly's contribution),[7] which is not a material event for a company that counts its revenues in the billions. Clearly, having access to an ecosystem of talent that could solve problems was worth far more.

Ecosystems of Technology

Let's think back to Apple's famous launch of the Macintosh in 1984. It was the first time the general public had seen the vision that Douglas Engelbart presented in 1968 at the "Mother of All Demos" come alive. Still, as we saw in Chapter 1, it had relatively little impact on society as a whole. Computers didn't start showing up in the productivity numbers until the late 1990s, more than a decade later.

From today's perspective, that shouldn't be all that surprising. The original Macintosh couldn't do very much. Besides the relatively weak processor and miniscule amount of storage, there was very little software for it. And even if there had been, who would have used it? Executives who depended on their secretaries to prepare correspondence and on the accounting department to crunch numbers weren't going to immediately start using word processors and spreadsheets.

In fact, when the scientists at PARC showed off the Alto, the precursor to the Macintosh, at the Xerox World Conference in Boca Raton, Florida, in 1977, the senior executives weren't particularly impressed. They simply didn't see how the machine was relevant to their jobs. Their wives, however—many of whom had previously been secretaries—were transfixed. They were the ones who could see how revolutionary computers would become.[8] If that seems unbelievable, I encountered the exact same attitude on a consulting project in Russia in 2003, when I recommended that the sales team send and receive their own e-mails rather than rely on an assistant to do it. "That's a job for secretaries!" the company's president growled at me.

Yet the problem wasn't only the power of the technology or the attitudes toward work at the time. The original Macintosh was cut off from the outside world. The commercial Internet wasn't widely available until the mid-1990s, so it couldn't send e-mails or search for information either.

Now look at Figure 8.3. It shows IBM scientist Jay Gambetta working on a tablet computer that is hundreds of times more powerful than the original Macintosh and costs about 15 percent as much in 1984 dollars. It also has access to millions of applications that can do everything from order a car to managing your finances.

But here's the kicker: Gambetta is using the tablet to access a quantum computer, something that wasn't even truly theoretically possible until 1993, when Charlie Bennett and his colleagues

FIGURE 8.3   IBM Quantum Computing Scientist Jay Gambetta uses a tablet to interact with the IBM Quantum Experience, the world's first quantum computing platform delivered via Cloud.
(Image courtesy of IBM)

performed their famous "quantum teleportation experiment."[9] There's more. Through its Quantum Experience program, IBM lets anybody in the world do the same.[10]

Think about that for a moment. Today, anybody in the world with an Internet connection can access technology that until a few years ago even top scientists in the field could not. They can do this not by virtue of position, privilege, or capability, but simply because they have access to a platform through the Internet.

Yet platforms do more than simply give us access, they also vastly reduce complexity. Angel Diaz, IBM's vice president of cloud architecture and technology, compares today's cloud platforms to computer languages. Just as early languages like FORTRAN encoded the highly complex commands of machine language into something much more manageable, today's higher-level computer languages encode earlier ones like FORTRAN, to the point that high school kids today can learn languages like Python and Ruby that can easily perform functions that would've taken a PhD to program in earlier days.

Today, cloud platforms like IBM's Bluemix are doing something similar for entire technologies. For example, if you wanted to build a website 20 years ago, you would need to hire a specialist to run the web server and another one to code the site. If you wanted to actually sell anything you would need an entire team to build the database, put in security systems to protect transactions, and manage customer relationships. Now, anyone who wants to can get on Bluemix and access dozens of services, including things that would have been out of reach for even the world's top computer scientists as recently as a decade ago, such as advanced analytics and predictive algorithms, visual recognition, language translation, and even applications that can interpret users' mood and personality traits.

Yet Bluemix is not a strictly proprietary platform. As we saw in the last chapter, IBM learned long ago that it does not make sense to compete with open ecosystems, so open source software makes up a big part of the Bluemix platform. Much like how Eli Lilly allowed other pharmaceutical companies to post problems on InnoCentive, its customers will see competitors' products available right next to IBM's offerings. As Diaz put it to me, "We benefit from having the most complete ecosystem on Bluemix, because that's what attracts the best customers, the best developers, and the best resources. It also gives us new opportunities to innovate and create new applications because it gives us new problems to solve."

To understand just how much power has shifted from proprietary models to open platforms, I talked to Christian Gheorghe, formerly chief technology officer of SAP, and now founder and CEO of Tidemark, an open enterprise platform that directly competes with his previous employer. Always a bit of a rebel, growing up in communist Romania he learned English by listening to Pink Floyd albums. After getting a master's degree in engineering, Gheorghe escaped to the West and kept going till he reached the United States, where he became a limousine driver and eventually a successful technology entrepreneur. His first business, which he started with a man he met driving limos, was sold to Experian for $32 million. Later, he created a new company that eventually became the predictive analytics powerhouse OutlookSoft. In 2007, it was sold to SAP for several hundred million dollars and Gheorghe joined the enterprise software firm as CTO.

Yet although he was now firmly ensconced in the technology establishment, he felt like it was time for a change. Much like in his native Romania, he felt that the old guard was pushing a defunct model long after it remained viable. "In the old model," he told me, "you had the power of the few. Large, powerful companies like SAP and Oracle were masters of their own ecosystem. They created the proprietary standards within that ecosystem, chose a small amount of partners that were beholden to them, and ensured that they controlled the most valuable aspects, such as customer relationships, architecture, and pricing."[11]

At enterprise software companies, the ecosystem was based on control of the proprietary database, much like Microsoft controlled its ecosystem through the operating software. Large companies would buy SAP or Oracle products and then hire one of its partners, like Accenture or Deloitte, to install it and build the business logic to integrate the database with the customer's business processes and the applications it wanted to run. This was often a multiyear, grueling process, and once it was completed, the customer was, to a great extent, locked in to the proprietary platform and the ecosystem.

Gheorghe saw two problems with that model. First, it inhibited innovation. Outside developers could only do what their proprietary partner allowed. Second, with more powerful open technology like the Apache Foundation's Hadoop and Spark, proprietary database solutions were no longer necessary. "We built Tidemark on top of open technologies from the start," he says, "because we believed that it offered much greater functionality and flexibility."[12]

To understand how today's open platforms give greater access to technology ecosystems and drive innovation, let's look at a retail example MIT professor Zeynep Ton described in her book *The Good Jobs Strategy*. Most retailers work hard to control labor costs. They want to have enough employees in the stores to service customers, but not so many that they are just standing around with nothing to do. One common solution is to build a predictive model of store traffic and staff the stores accordingly.*

---

* To be clear, Ton doesn't recommend optimizing costs in this way and points out that some successful retailers cross-train their staff so that they always have something to do during downtimes. She argues that offering employees stable schedules helps to improve productivity, not to mention the quality of life for the workers themselves.

This is exactly the type of job that enterprise software consultants thrive on. They encode the business logic in the database to record how much traffic each store gets each day and then use statistical models to predict what store traffic will be like at each location on future days. That information is then integrated with the scheduling software and produces staff schedules for each store manager.

On the surface, that seems like a very rational way to control costs and maintain service. But what happens if there is an unforeseen event like rainy weather or an accident creates a traffic jam that reduces sales at a store on a particular day? Unless the consultants accounted for those factors when they set up the system, it will result in understaffing on future days. Then, when the sun comes back out or the road gets cleared and customers return to the store, there are not enough people to service them effectively, which reduces sales again and results in staff levels being diminished further. Before long, a vicious cycle ensues, where understaffing leads to lower sales, which leads to more understaffing.[13]

Now let's suppose the retail company CEO recognizes the problem and demands that it be fixed. The consultants come back in and reconfigure the database to integrate with weather, road congestion, and other factors, which is another long and expensive process. Some time after that's completed, the CEO decides to begin a diversity program to ensure that her employees are not being discriminated against because of their race, gender, or sexual orientation when determining staff schedules. Once again, the database wasn't set up to take into account those particular data points, so the consultants return. Later, an ingredient in products the company sells is discovered to be toxic and those items need to be pulled from the shelves, but nobody knew there might be a problem with that ingredient when the system was set up. Back come the consultants!

Notice that these are all basic operational issues. What if the CEO wanted to truly reimagine her business? As we saw in Chapter 4, that would take no small amount of experimenting, iterating, and pivoting, and the systems would likely have to be reconfigured for each experiment.

Now you can see why Gheorghe built Tidemark on top of open rather than proprietary platforms. Open software can seamlessly integrate with any other application or data set through standard APIs. For example, if a customer is set up on IBM's Bluemix platform, it can install open technologies like Hadoop and Spark with a few clicks. It can also pull in other resources, like weather data from the Weather Company, the same way. Even without a platform like Bluemix, APIs can often be set up easily and quickly by a qualified professional—and even by many talented amateurs.

Tidemark's software is designed to accommodate large enterprises that have the resources to hire expensive consultants. Small businesses do not have the same luxury, so the rise of platforms is even more important for them. As digital technology becomes ever more pervasive, small independent firms need to be able to access powerful software in order to compete. Nowhere is this more true than with independent medical practices.

It used to be that a doctor could simply hang out a shingle, hire an assistant or two to handle appointments and billing, establish an affiliation with a local hospital, and thrive. Yet over the past few decades the burdens on medical practices have increased dramatically. First came the rise of managed care, which turned billing from a simple matter to a highly labor intensive and complex process of dealing with insurance companies. Obamacare and the rise of electronic health records (EHR) have only added to that burden. Doctors also must meet increasingly strict standards for privacy and security, and medicine itself has become more complex over the years, with far more specialties, tests, and procedures than a generation ago.

There are also opportunities to improve care through technology. Searchable databases have long replaced bookshelves of physician's reference books. Digital patient charts often include vastly more than notes taken during or immediately after patients' visits, but full histories complete with tests, radiology images, and years of basic data such as pulse, blood pressure, weight, and blood levels. These can be shared among physicians to provide better care and reduce medical errors.

Yet independent medical practices can scarcely afford to bring in teams of expensive consultants to build sophisticated systems for them. With that in mind, Kareo, a company founded by longtime technology entrepreneur Dan Rodrigues, built a cloud-based platform specifically to handle the needs of independent doctors. Today, Kareo serves over 35,000 independent medical providers in all 50 U.S. states.

Much like Tidemark, Kareo allows doctors to access ecosystems of technology designed to run their operations. Also, because it's based on open standards, it seamlessly integrates with hundreds of specialty applications—many of which are developed and sold by independent developers—through standard APIs. So, for example, a cardiologist may use Kareo for most of its back office and marketing functions, but may need electronic healthcare record software specifically designed for heart conditions, while a general practitioner may want to use Zocdoc, a mobile app that lets patients find doctors that have open appointments. On an old-school proprietary platform, that level of integration was often difficult, but now it just takes a few clicks.

So it's easy to see how open platforms are becoming essential to innovation. When we were locked in to proprietary models, we were very limited in what we could do because systems were set up to perform specific tasks. The moment we wanted to do something different, we were limited by cost, inconvenience, and the vision of whoever controlled the proprietary platform. Now that's changing. As IBM's Diaz put it to me, "Today, open platforms are removing all those barriers and giving us access to the world."

Ecosystems of Information

Clearly, Amazon is the 800-pound gorilla of e-commerce. In 2015, it accounted for a full 60 percent of U.S. online sales growth.[14] It gets a leg up on traditional retailers through leveraging three key assets. First, as a technology-driven company it has invested heavily into building a highly sophisticated platform since its founding in 1994, long before most traditional retailers even had a website. Second, as the biggest platform, it attracts thousands of third party merchants to offer the widest selection of goods at the best prices. Third, as the largest e-commerce company in the world, it has more data on consumer behavior than any company on the planet.

As e-commerce grew and Amazon became more dominant, Raj De Datta, CEO and cofounder of BloomReach, saw an opportunity. He asked himself, "How do we deliver a system that could deliver better consumer experiences online for retailers that are not Amazon?" He and Ashutosh Garg, formerly a top computer scientist at IBM and Google, set out to create a platform that would deliver a deep understanding of products that merchants were offering as well as of demand on the web. In essence, the company would create a platform for retailers with the data processing intelligence of Amazon.

The two were confident that they could build a platform just as technologically sophisticated as Amazon, but what they couldn't create was the data to feed into the algorithms. However—and this was a key insight—the retailers themselves already had it collectively. While the retailers would not be willing to share all personalized data on their customers, by including a wide range of traditional retailers onto the BloomReach platform, they could pool their non-personally identifiable data such as search results. BloomReach didn't need to know who these people were—their purchase intent would be enough.

So, for example, suppose that a customer was looking for a cocktail dress. That's a highly ambiguous term that may refer to a set of colors, length, style, and brands that change every season and sometimes even faster than that. Because of the ecosystem of data BloomReach has built through its ecosystem of clients—it currently powers a full 20 percent of U.S. commerce on the web—it can parse the various meanings of "cocktail dress" and place the most preferred option in front of the customer for each of its clients' landing pages. So all BloomReach clients can benefit collectively from insights derived from each other's websites.

BloomReach clients can use its data technology in a number of ways. Wayfair, a furniture retailer, might use the BloomReach platform to discover that customers interested in mattresses are also highly interested in pillows, creating the opportunity to cross-sell. Toys "R" Us, which earns 50 percent of its revenue in the holiday period, uses BloomReach systems to ensure that its search results include demand signals from across the web and not just from its own website.

Perhaps even more importantly, the retailers on the BloomReach platform—which includes brands ranging from Neiman Marcus and Williams Sonoma to Men's Wearhouse and The Container Store—can be confident that they have access to both the most cutting edge technology and a vast pool of data. That allows them to focus on the more human aspects of merchandising, such as working with vendors to codevelop specialized products, creating a superior in-store experience (offline sales still account for over 90 percent of retail in the United States)[15] and developing meaningful relationships with their customers.

A Fundamental Change in the Basis of Competition

Let's return to Michael Porter's theory of competitive advantage. We've already seen how his concept of the value chain became essential to driving corporate strategy in the latter part of the twentieth century, but a second key element was his five forces analysis (Figure 8.4):

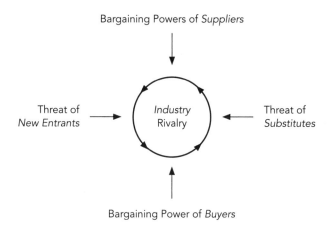

Bargaining Powers of *Suppliers*

Threat of *New Entrants* → *Industry Rivalry* ← Threat of *Substitutes*

Bargaining Power of *Buyers*

FIGURE 8.4   Porter's Five Forces Analysis

In a nutshell, Porter suggested that to achieve sustainable competitive advantage, businesses needed to minimize threats of substitutes and new entrants, while at the same time maximize bargaining power with buyers and suppliers. That, combined with a highly efficient value chain, would make for an unbeatable proposition. This is sometimes called the "positioning school" of strategy because it held that by making the right strategic moves, firms could build an unassailable strategic position. In effect, it saw business strategy as a game of chess.

This was the game that Microsoft played so well for so long. By identifying which parts on the board would be the most important, in its case the operating system and productivity software, it was able to achieve immense power over both its customers and suppliers, while at the same time minimizing the threat of entrants or substitutes. That's why it was so aggressive toward open source communities. Even a minor incursion threatened its strategic viability. Microsoft was, in that context, behaving rationally, if at times somewhat heavy-handedly.

However, clearly something fundamental has changed because it was only a matter of time before Microsoft found its once unassailable position absolutely indefensible and had to retreat. When platforms can connect us to massive ecosystems of talent, technology, and information—at minimal cost—control of those assets has become an illusion. Strategy, therefore, is no longer a game of chess but a process of widening and deepening networks of connections.[16]

And that's what we've seen throughout this book. Procter & Gamble boosted its innovation game and improved its competitive position not by increasing bargaining power with its suppliers, but by closely integrating with them to solve problems. Google saw that by open-sourcing its TensorFlow machine learning system it could gain access to ecosystems of talent and innovate faster and more effectively. IBM learned that by encouraging outside developers to build applications on top of its Watson cognitive computing system through APIs, Bluemix Garage sessions, and, at times, extending financing, it could build a much more expansive business than it ever could on its own. Even Microsoft has come full circle. At an event in 2014, CEO Satya Nadella proudly stated for the crowd, "Microsoft loves Linux."[17] To make it official, a few months later the message was reiterated on the company's official blog.[18]

So clearly, we need to give up the illusion of control and learn to use platforms in order to access ecosystems of talent, technology, and information. In a world connected by digital technology, power no longer resides at the top of value chains, but at the center of networks, and the best way to become a dominant player is to become an indispensable partner.

As we will see in the next chapter, leveraging platforms to access ecosystems will be even more important in the years to come. We are entering a new era of innovation in which the problems we need to solve will be bigger, more complex, and, increasingly, will require collective solutions.

CHAPTER NINE

A New Era of Innovation

We teach people that everything that matters
happens between your ears, when in fact
it actually happens between people.

—SANDY PENTLAND

As we near the end of this book, let's revisit the story about the discovery of penicillin that we first saw in Chapter 1. If you recall, Alexander Fleming first discovered the antibacterial effects of the mold at St. Mary's Hospital in London in 1928. As a skilled laboratory scientist with a medical degree, he had exactly the qualifications someone would need to discover an obscure mold with the potential to cure disease. However, he had very few of the skills one would need to transform that discovery into a cure.

In fact, what Fleming discovered couldn't cure anyone. It wasn't a drug but rather, as he called it, "mold juice." He had no way to make it stable so it could be stored or to administer it to patients. Even if there was, there was no way to make penicillin in anything near the quantities required to have therapeutic value. These weren't trivial problems but substantial obstacles that had no easy answers. It wasn't until a decade later, when Howard Florey and Ernst Chain happened upon Fleming's article in a scientific journal, that anybody made any real progress toward solving them.

Florey and his team had many capabilities that Fleming lacked. Ernst Chain was a world-class biochemist who was an expert at solving problems exactly like those needed to transform Fleming's "mold juice" into a storable powder. Norman Heatley, another member of Florey's team, was a whiz at scraping together useful apparatus from odds and ends he found around the lab. It was he who first figured out a way to build a system that could ferment the penicillin in quantities large enough to test on mice. There was also a wide array of technicians with other relevant skills who could contribute to the project.

Still, even the additional resources available at Florey's lab at Oxford were not enough to meet the challenge. It was only when Florey and Heatley travelled to the United States and began working with other labs that they were able to identify a more powerful strain of the penicillin mold and learned about corn steep liquor, a significantly more effective fermentation medium for penicillin. After that, they needed additional help from American pharmaceutical companies to scale up production.

So while the story of the discovery of penicillin is often portrayed as "accidental," it was clearly the result of a massive collaboration. None of those involved could have hoped to create the miracle drug by themselves, because no one person—or even entire labs—had the knowledge and skills to solve the all of the problems associated with the production of penicillin.

Yet besides the importance of collaboration, there are two other aspects we should note. First, that luck played an enormous role in how events played out. What if Chain had not happened upon Fleming's 10-year-old paper in a scientific journal? What if Florey, as a young Australian on a Rhodes scholarship, hadn't received the Rockefeller Foundation fellowship to study in America in 1926? It was through that fellowship that he formed a friendship with Dr. Alfred Newton Richards, who would later champion Florey's work in his role as chairman of the U.S. Committee on Medical Research and Development. It was later said that, "Without Richards, Americans would have never taken over production of penicillin."[1]

The second aspect of the story we should note is that, in many ways, the conditions were ideal for collaboration. Florey's lab in Oxford was only 60 miles from where Fleming worked in London, and Florey even served as an editor of the journal in which Fleming published his now famous—but then obscure—paper. Also, not inconsequentially, all the major players spoke the same language. Great Britain and the United States were close allies, so there were no political barriers to the cross-Atlantic collaboration. The Rhodes

Scholarship and Rockefeller Fellowship that Florey had won were established to foster exactly the types of connections that proved to be so important in the development of penicillin. So, what if all of these favorable conditions had not been in place?

Well, we don't have to look too hard for an answer. Remember in Chapter 2, when we discussed the importance of combinations in giving rise to innovation breakthroughs, we found that Darwin credited reading an essay on population growth by Thomas Malthus with giving him the final piece to the evolution puzzle. "Here, then I had at last got a theory from which to work," he would later write. Yet till the end of his life, Darwin never came across Gregor Mendel's work on genetics, which would finally put his theory of natural selection on solid ground. Like Fleming's discovery of the antibacterial effects of the penicillium mold, Mendel's work went unnoticed in a scientific journal, but in this case, it took another 50 years for it to be rediscovered.

The reasons for the disparity are not hard to surmise. Darwin and Malthus were both Englishmen, and Malthus's paper was well known in Great Britain at the time. The only curious thing about the episode is that it took until 1838 for Darwin to read it (Malthus wrote the essay in 1798). Mendel, on the other hand, was a German-speaking Austrian monk. It's not at all surprising that his and Darwin's paths never crossed.

Today, however, such things would be almost unthinkable. Even papers in obscure journals are immediately available online across the world. If Ernst Chain were alive today, you wouldn't catch him spending countless hours going through hundreds of old scientific journals to find studies relevant to his work—a few well-placed key words on Google would suffice. If Fleming couldn't figure out how to make penicillin into a storable powder, he could post the problem on InnoCentive. Corn steep liquor was an obscure fermentation medium in England, but it was very common in the United States, especially in the Midwest where Florey and Heatley came across it. Today, it is almost impossible to imagine that they would have to cross an ocean to learn about it. The fact is that a teenager with a mobile phone today has more access to information than any of these men ever did.

So it's not surprising that we saw the nature of collaboration change in the 1990s. Randy Terbush went online and not only found help with the problems he was having with his AutoCAD software, he found a community he could learn from and work with. That's what led to the Apache Foundation, which today supports dozens of open source software projects in addition to its initial web server, some of which, like Hadoop, Spark, and CloudStack have become critical standards for large-scale computing and data analysis. It was these types of open source projects that inspired Alph Bingham to create the InnoCentive platform at Eli Lilly and for Nabil Sakkab to conceive the Connect + Develop program at Procter & Gamble. It became clear that even companies with thousands of highly qualified researchers could greatly increase their effectiveness by collaborating far and wide.

These are interesting developments in their own right, but what's even more important is how these trends have changed the basis of competition. Even a company as powerful as Microsoft eventually had to succumb and begin to collaborate with the hackers who were altering its Kinect device. Today, companies like Tesla, Google, and many others open-source their technology and no one blinks an eye. IBM, as we have seen, regularly contributes hundreds of patents in order to protect open source communities from frivolous lawsuits.

Today, collaboration is no longer an option, but an absolute necessity. As Henry Chesbrough has pointed out, a wide array of forces, including the rise of venture capital, the proliferation of technical skills, and the increasing complexity of today's technology have greatly diminished the viability of the proprietary model. The Internet has only accelerated and strengthened these forces through the platforms, as discussed in the last chapter.

So while history clearly holds many useful and important lessons, that should not blind us to the fact that the future will look very different from the past. As knowledge continues to democratize and the ability to connect to ecosystems of talent, technology, and information through platforms accelerates, we have to treat collaboration as a competitive advantage.

The Future of Work and the Dynamics of Teams

Consider for a moment what work was like back in 1968 when Douglas Engelbart gave his famous "Mother of All Demos" presentation. Executives largely communicated by phone, and memos were typed up by secretaries. Data analysis was something you did with a pencil, paper, and maybe a slide rule. If you needed information you didn't have on hand, you would go to the library, or possibly a file cabinet in a storage room somewhere. If you needed to talk to somebody, you would have to catch the person at his or her office, either in person or by phone (there was no voice mail in 1968, and answering machines were not widely in use yet).

Now, consider how we work today. Our modes of communication have metastasized. We have e-mail, instant messaging, and mobile phones, which we can use to send information between meetings, sitting in airport lounges, or even while waiting for an elevator. If we need to pull up information from our files, we have gigabytes of mobile storage in the cloud that travels with us. We can also access the world's knowledge through an Internet search. We don't even need to type our queries into a search box anymore, we can just tell our phones what we're looking for and the information will come up in seconds. Compared to Engelbart's day, we have almost godlike power over information.

Clearly the nature of work has changed. MIT economist David Autor has argued that the important dividing line among jobs is no longer between manual and cognitive tasks as much as it is between routine and nonroutine work. So clerical workers like bookkeepers and travel agents have suffered, but financial analysts and wedding planners have done well.[2] In fact, a report by the McKinsey Global Institute notes that from 2000 to 2009, nearly all net new jobs were "interaction jobs" that require complex problem solving and personal skills. They calculate that nearly 5 million of these jobs were created over that period, while at the same time 3 million production jobs (factory worker, farmer, etc.) and transaction jobs (bank clerk, cashier, etc.) were lost.[3]

Even for high-level work, the skills required have changed. It used to be that having a great facility for numbers or an ability to retain large amounts of information were highly sought-after abilities. Yet today, when everybody has Excel at their fingertips and access to Wikipedia, those types of cognitive skills aren't nearly as valuable. One study of the U.S. labor market even found that the demand for jobs that require a high degree of cognitive ability, which had been rising for years, began to decline around the year 2000.[4] Put another way, as the amount of information available online has increased, the need for people who can carry around a lot of data in their heads has declined.

While the need for cognitive skills has diminished, we're also increasingly working in teams. The journal *Nature* recently noted that although up until the 1920s sole authorship of scientific papers was the rule, that custom had virtually disappeared by the 1950s, and today the average paper has four times as many authors as it did then. In fact, it is no longer unusual for papers to have as many as 100 authors![5] The makeup of those teams is also far more interdisciplinary, with researchers regularly collaborating with others outside their fields.[6]

What accounts for these trends? One factor is certainly that the problems researchers tackle today are much more complex than in past generations, involving not only petri dishes and Bunsen burners but genetic sequencing, computer modeling, spectroscopy, and literally thousands of other highly specialized techniques. Not surprisingly, solo researchers can simply no longer compete.

One study that analyzed 19.9 million papers over five decades, as well as two million patents over 30 years, found that teams markedly outperform individuals. "Teams typically produce more highly cited research than individuals do, and this advantage is increasing over time," the authors write. They also note that the pattern holds true across every discipline that they looked at, including hard sciences and engineering, social sciences, and arts and humanities. The effect is even more pronounced for the highest quality work, with team-authored papers in science and engineering 6.3 times more likely than a solo authored paper to receive at least 1,000 citations.[7]

My own research for this book reflected these same trends. I heard over and over again from top executives at major corporations and researchers at some of the world's leading scientific institutions about the importance of effective collaboration today. Although many of these organizations have multibillion-dollar budgets, not one person I talked to thought that he or she had enough resources to go it alone.

Angel Diaz, IBM's VP of cloud technology and architecture, probably summed it up best when he told me, "The ever-increasing capabilities of digital technology have empowered individuals like never before in history. That process will continue, but to truly change the world today we need more than just clever code. We need computer scientists working with cancer scientists, with climate scientists, and with experts in many other fields to tackle grand challenges and make large impacts on the world."

Taking note of these trends, longtime *Fortune* editor Geoff Colvin argues in *Humans Are Underrated* that the most critical twenty-first-century skill is empathy and calls for a shift in emphasis from "knowledge workers" to "relationship workers."[8] In a world of exponentially increasing complexity, no one person or firm can do it all, so those that can work well with others have a distinct advantage. That has major implications for how we educate, train, and manage people. It is no longer enough to simply offer extravagant compensation packages to hire the "best and the brightest" people. To innovate in this new environment, we don't need the best people—we need the best teams.

As it turns out, working in a team requires very different skills than the ones that make somebody a great solo performer. In the aftermath of 9/11, the CIA commissioned a study to determine what attributes made for the most effective analyst teams. What they found was surprising. As it turned out, what made for the most effective teams was not the individual attributes of their members, or even the coaching they got from their leaders, but the makeup of the group and interactions between them. Teams that worked interdependently, meaning that they were jointly responsible to fulfill a larger task, performed significantly better than "co-acting" teams that broke the task up into smaller jobs and worked in parallel, with each team member responsible for his or her share of the task.

The authors of the study concluded, "A large team task often requires that the team be composed of individuals with different expertise and specialties, which can foster the kinds of cross-functional exchanges that, occasionally, result in unanticipated insights and syntheses."[9] Their point about diversity was also found in another study, which suggests that diverse teams outperform homogenous ones even if the more diverse teams are less capable individually.[10]

So clearly, if we are going to innovate effectively in the digital age, we need to learn a lot more about what makes a great team. Certainly, like individuals, all teams do not perform with the same effectiveness. A team of researchers from MIT, Carnegie Mellon, and Union College has even found evidence for a "collective intelligence factor," similar to individual IQ, that determines how teams will perform on a wide range of tasks, such as brainstorming, negotiating over limited resources, solving visual puzzles, and making collective moral judgments. After examining the results, they found three traits that determined group performance.

The most important factor was social sensitivity, measured by a test that asks subjects to accurately read what others are thinking or feeling by looking at pictures of their eyes. Groups with members that scored high on social sensitivity performed markedly better than groups with members that performed poorly on the test. Second, groups that took turns speaking and spoke in roughly equivalent amounts performed better than ones in which one or two members dominated the conversation. Finally, the presence of women in the group also boosted performance, although it was noted that this last factor might be related to the fact that women often score higher on social sensitivity tests then men.[11]

Let's stop and think for a minute about how different this picture is from the traditional "brash and brilliant" stereotypes of innovators we see in Hollywood movies and in the business press. As it turns out, more often than not, the best innovators aren't hard-charging "type A" personalities who command our attention, but rather empathetic team players who are good listeners and are genuinely interested in what others have to say.

My own research bore this out as well. In the dozens of interviews I did for this book I found that the vast majority, with few exceptions, were not only helpful in providing me with their formidable expertise and experiences, but showed a genuine interest in my project. When I sent them excerpts to fact-check, in almost all cases they pushed me to give more credit to others and less to themselves. In some cases they agreed to look over early versions of chapters. You can imagine my surprise when, more than once, the early drafts came back not only with helpful suggestions, but also with my typos corrected. I couldn't help thinking what an inefficient use of resources it was to have some of the world's best scientists working for me as copy editors—*pro bono*, no less! Then I realized that's what made them such great innovators. They are simply the type of people who are happy to pitch in wherever they can be of help.

Bernie Meyerson was especially emphatic about the role that collaboration and personality attributes play in innovation. When I asked him what he thought accounted for IBM Research's remarkable track record as an organization, he told me. "We mercilessly squash the Ivory Tower syndrome that had led to the demise of other labs, as thinking of oneself as inherently the better of your peers in development, for example, leads to nothing ever making it out of the labs into the real world. Basically, many organizations have had superbly talented individuals, but few have created a collaborative culture in which those individual contributors would rally around a grand challenge and blow the field away, and then take it to market with the same enthusiasm."

He then continued in this vein in response to another question. He told me, "I have met many scientists who simply were in their fields for their own glory, and they do not do well and frankly are ill tolerated in our culture, as they fail in the long term given that you can always do better with more pairs of brilliant eyes on the problem being tackled."

Another aspect of innovation in the digital age is that it's not just humans we need to collaborate with, but machines as well. That was the idea behind the Oncology Expert Adviser that MD Anderson Cancer Center developed with IBM, using IBM's Watson system as its technological core. "Physicians, necessarily, spend most of their time treating common conditions," Dr. Lynda Chin, who helped lead the project, told me. "For example, in cancer, the vast majority of cases are breast, lung, and prostate. So oncologists are pretty familiar with those cancer types. But every so often, they will see a patient with acute leukemia, which is much more rare."

When that happens, they often need to spend countless hours referring to old textbooks, online references, and searching out specialists in narrow fields. This is all terribly inefficient. "If you go to Google or PubMed and look for a piece of information on a topic that you're interested in, you get back too many hits and they're not always helpful," Dr. Chin observes. Doctors can waste hours muddling through what can be a fruitless search.

There is, in effect, a wide gap between scientists generating knowledge and the people who are supposed to put those insights into practice. So when IBM came and showed her the capabilities of its Watson system, she saw an opportunity to close that gap and put all of the world's collective knowledge to work in the practice of everyday medicine.

Dr. Chin says that Watson allowed her to "imagine a system that isn't just to optimize a particular decision making point, but to really change how we think about medicine." The Oncology Expert Advisor allows doctors to delegate many time-consuming tasks to technology.

Even before the patient enters the room, the system can analyze his or her personal medical history, which often runs to hundreds of pages. Then, it can compare the case history with thousands of academic papers published every year as well as potentially millions of other patient records. It can also suggest innovative new treatments, such as Jim Allison's revolutionary cancer immunotherapy, that a practicing physician might not be completely familiar with.

All of this is, of course, beyond the capabilities of human doctors, who typically only get a limited time to prepare to see each patient. So being able to consult with Watson is enormously helpful. At the same time, as doctors provide feedback as to which of Watson's recommendations are helpful, the system continues to learn. In a sense, the doctors are also collaborating with others on the system and the algorithms encode their experiences.

All of this automation will also allow doctors to do the things that machines can't, such as listening to patients with empathy, answering questions thoughtfully, and taking the time to understand their how family and personal situations may affect care. In effect, by outsourcing many cognitive tasks to technology, doctors can focus on becoming healers again.

We've already seen that there is great potential for this type of human-machine interaction. Consider the fact that before 1997, when IBM's Deep Blue computer beat reigning World Chess Champion Garry Kasparov, it was thought that a computer could never beat a human grand master. Just a few years after that, even a $50 chess program could compete with the best human players. So it seemed that even for a high-level cognitive task like chess, machines were taking over.

However, in 2005 the online chess-playing site Playchess.com sponsored a "freestyle" chess tournament that allowed any combination of humans and computers to compete. Now humans armed with everyday laptops were dominating the supercomputers. As it turned out, however, the winner was neither a grand master nor a supercomputer, but two amateurs using three computers at the same time. It wasn't any one skill that proved to be decisive, but rather the successful integration of a diversity of skills that won the day.[12]

That is the promise of this new era of innovation. As barriers such as time and space—and increasingly ones related to language, culture, and occupational field—fall away, solving really tough problems is increasingly a matter of organizational and platform design rather than skill or cognitive ability. This is an important point to consider, as the challenges ahead will be more difficult and complex than anything mankind has faced before.

Moving from Disruption to Grand Challenges

The 1950s and '60s saw an enormous amount of fundamental innovations, many, but not all of which were driven by Cold War spending. Nuclear power, the space race, the discovery of the structure of DNA, the invention of the transistor and, later, the microchip all completely revolutionized major fields. If it is true, as the philosopher Martin Heidegger argued in his essay *A Question Concerning Technology*, that technology is an "uncovering," then it was in the early postwar years that the modern world was first discovered.[13] Much of the progress since that time has been merely exploring the rough outlines laid down by those early pioneers.

Yet today, we've largely reached the technological version of the manifest destiny. For the past 50 years, a large part of technological progress has been driven by our ability to double the number of transistors we put on a silicon wafer every 18 months or so, otherwise known as Moore's law. At some point the transistors become so small that subatomic quantum effects render them inoperable. That point is expected to be reached around the year 2020. Another key technology over the past 30 years has been lithium-ion batteries, which power our mobile phones, laptops, and, increasingly, electric cars. It will reach its theoretical limits in 10 years or so.

These are just two examples, but they point to a larger problem: for the past few decades we've largely been improving on and building new applications for technological paradigms that were uncovered a half century ago.

Clearly, that can't last forever. In fact, economist Robert Gordon argues that innovation in the United States has already begun to decline, and many of his points apply to all advanced economies. He argues, correctly, that productivity growth has diminished since the 1970s, with almost all of the innovation happening in the relatively narrow sector of digital technology, which he compares unfavorably to a century ago, when a wide range of technologies, such as the internal combustion engine, electricity, indoor plumbing, and household appliances such as air conditioners, washing machines, and refrigerators fundamentally changed the human condition.

Gordon sees even darker days ahead. In fact, he sees four primary headwinds, including income inequality, education, demographics, and government debt, that will depress productivity growth for decades to come. Income inequality has not only the direct effect of lower disposable income for the bottom 90 percent, it also leads to what economist and former Treasury secretary Larry Summers calls "secular stagnation," a glut of savings combined with depressed levels of consumption and investment.[14]

The education headwind arises from two factors. First, growing income inequality makes it hard for people with middle class incomes to finance a college education, and many are saddled with student debt long after they've graduated. This diminishes the ability of many to start new businesses. The second factor is that while high school graduation rates increased from 10 percent in 1900 to 80 percent by 1970, it is unlikely to go much higher and, in fact, dropped to 74 percent in 2000.

The third headwind is the aging of the population in the United States and other advanced economies. As the median age of the population rises, the ratio of workers to retirees lowers, making it harder to raise the productivity of society as a whole. It also increases healthcare costs, putting further burdens on the economy. This situation is exacerbated by the fourth headwind, rising debt, which will make it harder to finance productive investments.

In addition to these, Gordon also cites globalization, which intensifies income inequality, as well as global warming and environmental pollution, which will increase costs and further diminish our ability to invest in the future. Put it all together and the picture is pretty grim.[15]

However, there are some other factors that Gordon does not take into account. While it is true that most of the innovations of the past four decades have been focused on digital technology, those advances are now powering entirely new fields, such as genomics, nanotechnology, and robotics, which have the potential to significantly increase our prosperity and well-being.

Genomics is revolutionizing healthcare and making it possible to develop new cures to diseases, such as many forms of cancer, that were previously mostly untreatable. Advances in nanotechnology, to take just one example, are making it possible to rapidly increase the viability of solar energy, which may not only help to moderate the effects of climate change, but is also likely to significantly reduce energy costs in the decades to come. Robotics, including not only physical robots but also algorithms powered by artificial intelligence, can make human workers exponentially more productive.

We can also look at some of the recent innovations covered in this book. IBM's Watson cognitive computing system is being deployed at medical institutions like MD Anderson to make doctors more effective. Jim Allison's development of cancer immunotherapy allows people who would have once had only months to live to lead healthy and productive lives. New computer architectures like quantum computing and neuromorphic chips have the potential to increase the power of our current technology thousands of times over.

So we are at a crossroad. One path leads to the dystopian vision Gordon describes: diminished levels of productivity, leading to lower incomes and social strife. The other leads to advances that lead to higher productivity, more prosperity, and better lives for everyone. That seems like an easy choice to make, but to achieve a more favorable outcome than what Gordon predicts, we will need to renew our commitment to fundamental innovation.

That starts with investing in basic science, which, as Vannevar Bush rightly pointed out, "provides scientific capital" and "creates the fund from which the practical applications of knowledge must be drawn."[16] Many commentators have argued that this is due to "quarterly capitalism," which they attribute to the pressure that short-term investors put on corporate executives. However, even a cursory examination of the data shows that it is the government that is underinvesting in both infrastructure and research.[17]

Restoring funding to programs at agencies like the National Science Foundation, the National Institutes of Health, and the Department of Energy to at least their historical levels would be a good first step. However, it will not be enough. We will also have to innovate how we innovate, which will involve increasing collaboration between government agencies, academic institutions, and private institutions.

Fortunately, we already have a proven model for how to do that.

A New Breed of Innovation

In the mid-1980s, the American semiconductor industry seemed like it was doomed. Although U.S. firms had pioneered and dominated the technology for decades, they were now getting pummeled by cheaper Japanese imports. Much like cars and electronics, microchips seemed destined to become another symbol of American decline.

The dire outlook had serious ramifications for both U.S. competitiveness and national security. So, in 1986, the American government created SEMATECH, a consortium of government agencies, research institutions, and private industry. By the mid-1990s, the United States was once again dominating semiconductors.

Today, SEMATECH is a wholly private enterprise, funded by its members, but its original model is being widely deployed to solve new problems, such as creating next generation batteries, curing cancer, and reviving American manufacturing. The truth is that many of the problems we face today are simply too big and complex to be solved by any one organization or even any one type of organization.

As we have seen repeatedly in this book, there is a wide chasm that separates an initial discovery and a viable product idea. Every year, tens of thousands of papers are published in scientific journals, and any one of them, potentially, could hold the key to the next big thing. But for a private firm to invest millions of dollars in a new idea, there has to be more to go on. Another problem is that the research institutions themselves—government labs and research driven universities—have become so large that they've become notoriously hard to navigate. At the same time, the marketplace has become so fiercely competitive—and investors so demanding—that few are willing to take a flyer on an unproven technology.

To bridge that gap, new organizations have risen up that build on the original SEMATECH model to solve our toughest problems. The Joint Center for Energy Storage Research (JCESR) has a five-year mandate to develop next generation battery technologies. The Institute for Applied Cancer Science at MD Anderson (IACS) is exploring revolutionary new cures, and the National Network for Manufacturing Innovation (NNMI) is working to revive U.S. production capacity.

The key to making these organizations work is integrating the work of discovery-driven researchers, applied scientists, and engineers in the private sector. "Usually discovery propagates at the speed of publication," George Crabtree, director at JCESR, told me. "But here, we can operate within the time frame of the next coffee break."

That's essential, because the different players often have widely divergent incentives. Giulio Draetta, the director of IACS who formerly headed up global basic research at Merck, points out that for academic researchers, publication is the coin of the realm, so they are focused on uncovering results that are new and exciting, not on the marketability of their work. Profit-driven companies, on the other hand, feel so much pressure to go to market that they often pass on ideas with vast potential. "Venture capitalists are looking for rapid exits, and researchers are pretty much stuck with the idea that they came to the party with. That means it's very hard to cull bad ideas and lots of time, effort, and money are wasted," Draetta told me. Yet he has also found that when you put people together, they tend to widen their perspectives.

"Once you have everybody sitting around the table, it's much easier to come up with new ideas and to discard others that will not work," he notes. He has also found that, over time, academic researchers realize that there is a great opportunity to put out better publications and win more funding from closer collaboration with industry, while drug developers learn to build relationships, offer input, and be more flexible about exploring new directions.

One of the major advantages of this more integrated approach is that product developers can steer discovery-driven researchers in more fruitful directions. In battery research, for example, scientists have long focused on finding materials with greater energy density. Manufacturers, on the other hand, value safety just as much as performance so that they don't have to add extra shielding to the battery that increases weight and diminishes overall efficiency.

Draetta of IACS has found many of the same issues arise in pharmaceutical research. "That's exactly what we face all the time," he told me. "Often there are factors related to manufacturing costs, potential drug interactions, and other things that research scientists aren't aware of." Armed with that knowledge, work can be directed toward paths that offer greater viability.

This is absolutely crucial to accelerating innovation because once a scientist embarks on a particular direction, years can be spent performing the necessary research, verifying the results, and preparing it for publication. If that work turns out not to be useful, enormous amounts of time and effort are essentially wasted. However, if nonviable research can be pruned at the next coffee break, resources can be focused on areas that are more likely to lead to a true breakthrough.

Simply put, integrating efforts earlier in the process can save tremendous amounts of time, money, and other resources, while at the same time producing better results.

Getting input from manufacturers may seem like a no-brainer, but the truth is that it's difficult for scientists to do so in a systematic manner. An academic doing exploratory research in, say, genetics or materials science can't simply pick up the phone and ring up a manufacturer's hotline to see what engineers are thinking. Often, that information is considered proprietary.

Yet former President Obama's Advanced Manufacturing Partnership is working to change that. In 2011, he commissioned a report that called for an "innovation policy" rather than an "industrial policy."[18] The result of that report has been to set up a network of institutes that act as hubs for innovation in areas like 3D printing and integrated photonics.

So far, the program has exceeded the expectations of the initial plan. While it was intended to receive matching funds for the initial setup period of five to seven years, manufacturers have exceeded that goal by roughly 50 percent. Firms have also invested additional money to build facilities near the hubs to better integrate their operations with them. Congress has since passed legislation to expand the program and ensure its continuity.

Manufacturers are excited about the program as well. Dr. Mukesh V. Khare, IBM's VP of semiconductor research, told me, "We found in our previous involvement with SEMATECH that these types of consortia help us adapt investment, supply chain, and retooling for the future. So for photonics, which is a really crucial area for us, it made all the sense in the world to join the manufacturing hub." The company has organized its own Research Frontiers Institute along similar lines.

America has lost 5 million manufacturing jobs since 2000, so integrating scientists into the production process is just as important as integrating manufacturers into the discovery process.

* * * * *

The innovation architecture set up after World War II has served America extremely well. Publicly funded research, paired with a vigorous private sector, has made the United States a leader in virtually every area of advanced technology. Other nations may challenge that leadership in one industry or another, but nobody can match the breadth and depth of the United States.

However, the problems we need to solve today are far more complex than ever before. So it is imperative that we build a more complete ecosystem on top of the postwar architecture. "In the 1980s and before there was a continental divide that separated basic and applied science," Ron DePinho, president of MD Anderson Cancer Center, told me. "Since then, the idea of translational research has taken hold, but we still have an inefficient organizational infrastructure to pursue conversion of discovery into new therapies in any systematic way.

"As one example, there are 8,000 early cancer detection candidate biomarkers in literature. Yet only two have progressed to where they can be clinically effective. At MD Anderson, we've tried to change that by reaching out to all areas of the ecosystem, including academic institutions, venture capitalists, and industrial players ranging from big pharma to start-up biotechnology firms, because we believe that the best science happens when we get everybody's perspective," he says.

Many innovative enterprises have learned the value of instilling this type of iterative process across integrated, multidisciplinary teams within their organizations. As it turns out, if we are to solve our biggest and toughest problems and avoid the very real possibility of Robert Gordon's dystopian vision coming to pass, we need to learn how to implement that same level of collaboration across our entire society.

We are truly entering a new era of innovation in which things will look more like the 1950s and '60s rather than the 1990s or the aughts. It is no longer enough to disrupt and disintermediate industrial-era institutions; we must forge a new path with a renewed commitment to fundamental innovations. We need new moonshots for the twenty-first century.

Building Your Innovation Playbook

*We always overestimate the change that will
occur in the next two years and underestimate
the change that will occur in the next ten.
Don't let yourself be lulled into inaction.*

—BILL GATES

As we have seen throughout this book, innovation is far more complex than most people give it credit for. It is never the result of a single event but arises from a confluence of factors and often involves dozens of people—and sometimes many more than that—to bring an idea from its initial discovery to the point where it can actually make an impact on the world. It does not require a singular skill set or personality type, but in fact usually arises out of combinations of those things. There is no "silver bullet" that will enable you to magically begin innovating more effectively; rather it is a process of matching the right kinds of problems with the right kinds of strategies that will allow you to succeed.

Clearly, simple slogans like "innovate or die" are not enough. Everybody wants to innovate, and many think they can, but the number of organizations that are able to do it consistently, year after year and decade after decade, is exceedingly small. We need to start treating innovation as seriously as we do other organizational disciplines, such as finance, accounting, marketing, manufacturing, or logistics.

Also, as I noted in the last chapter, we are entering a new era of innovation in which we can no longer rely on trusty old paradigms like Moore's law to help us predict what the future will look like. We've advanced to the point where we're approaching theoretical limits in several key technologies, such as microprocessors and energy storage. New computing architectures are now being developed that nobody quite knows how to work with yet. We are also in desperate need of a new generation of battery technologies that nobody knows the specifications of yet. We also need to continually create new business models to make innovations such as these financially viable and sustainable. These are the types of fundamental breakthroughs we so desperately need to grow productivity in future decades if we are to avoid Robert Gordon's version of the future coming to pass.

At the same time, new fields such as genomics, nanotechnology, and robotics are moving so fast that we have to continually recalibrate our notions of what's possible. Clearly, it's no longer enough to move fast, iterate, adapt, and pivot—we must move forward with a deeper understanding of technology, the marketplace, and our role within it.

To do so, every organization—and every individual—must chart their own path. What may have worked fabulously for Steve Jobs or Elon Musk may not be right for you and your business. Rather, we must take a clear-eyed look at our own capabilities, challenges, and opportunities and develop our own innovation playbook. Here are six principles that will help you do that.

Six Principles to Develop Your Own Innovation Playbook

1. Actively Seek Out Good Problems

The Apache Foundation is truly a marvel of our age. As a collective, it outperforms even the most highly capable proprietary firms. Yet, as we saw in Chapter 5, it didn't start out with any grand ambitions, just as a group of eight guys with a problem they needed to solve—reliable software to run their web servers. As it turned out, many other people had the same problem and were willing to contribute their talents to the project. Today, it supports dozens of software projects in just about every conceivable domain. WordPress, the software that powers roughly 20 percent of the sites on the web, including CNN, Forbes.com, and millions of personal blogs, began the same way. Much like the Apache Group, WordPress founders

Matt Mullenweg and Mike Little, were simply looking for good software to use for their own websites.[1]

So to innovate, you don't need a brilliant idea, just a good problem that needs solving. As we noted in the very beginning of this book, innovations are "novel solutions to important problems." Important to whom? Well, that depends on who you are trying to serve. Businesses solve problems for their customers. Nonprofits focus on problems of particular communities. Scientists solve problems that other scientists believe are important. The problem Jim Allison devoted the bulk of his life to was simply to understand how the immune system worked, but as we have seen, solving that particular problem resulted in cancer immunotherapy, a revolutionary new cure that is giving new hope to thousands of terminal cancer patients who previously would have faced a death sentence.

Of course, the way people and organizations seek out problems can vary widely. Steve Blank urges entrepreneurs to "get out of the building," and Experian DataLabs regularly meets with customers to "see what's giving them agita." The world-class scientists at IBM Research set up "grand challenges," like beating a world champion at chess or the best human players at *Jeopardy!*. It was the latter challenge that led to the creation of the Watson cognitive computing system that is now so important to IBM's future. Google's practice of "20 percent time" is, essentially, a human-powered search engine for good problems.

What all these organizations have in common is that they continually seek out problems to solve. They are not merely looking to grow their top line, to make a customer happy, or to come up with some flashy feature that will get them noticed in the business press. If you want to be a great innovator, the first step is to find a great problem.

2. Choose Problems That Suit Your Organization's Capabilities, Culture, and Strategy

In his delightful memoir *Surely You're Joking, Dr. Feynman!*, legendary physicist Richard Feynman devoted the final chapter to what he called "cargo cult science."[2] He took the name from a peculiar phenomenon that emerged in islands of the South Pacific after World War II. Many natives on the islands observed soldiers build airstrips and soon after saw planes appear with valuable cargo. After the soldiers left, they built their own improvised airfields, with makeshift antennas protruding out of coconut helmets, improvised head-phones, and guys waving sticks to signal airplanes in the hopes that valuable cargo would drop from the sky for them, too. Anthropologists called the islanders who did this "cargo cults."

Of course, it never worked. Indeed, it seems more than a little bit silly. Simply setting up an airstrip is not what causes cargo planes to fly across the world to a particular location. Anyone who would believe such a thing is missing some very basic principles of how air travel functions. It is patently absurd.

Yet at the same time, many executives in business today believe that it's perfectly normal to adopt the externally visible practices of successful innovators in the hopes of getting the same results. Want to innovate like Steve Jobs? Some say that all you have to do is learn how to combine technology with ease of use and compelling design.[3] Want to know what makes Elon Musk such an amazing innovator? Read an article about his "five habits."[4] Want to be like Google founders Sergey Brin and Larry Page? Start a "20 percent time" program. Or wait, maybe you should simply just drop out of Harvard like Bill Gates and Mark Zuckerberg did. It seemed to work pretty well for them.

Clearly, none of these things are likely to lead to a billion-dollar company. Combining technology with design is a very good idea, but it doesn't mean you are solving an important problem. I don't know Elon Musk personally, and he seems like a fine person, but how many other billionaires share all of his habits? And clearly, very few people have succeeded through "20 percent time" programs or by dropping out of school.

The truth is that expecting to get the same results by emulating the actions of innovative people and organizations is essentially cargo cult thinking.[5] It isn't much more likely to lead you to success than building a makeshift runway and waving your arms will make planes appear out of the sky.

The most important drivers of success are the things that we can't see, like capabilities, culture, and strategy. Fusing technology and design was Steve Jobs's passion, which is why he built a company around it. "20 percent time" works for Google because it reflects the values and the culture that Larry Page and Sergey Brin instilled throughout their organization. Bill Gates and Mark Zuckerberg didn't build great companies because they dropped out of college; they dropped out of college because they were building great companies.

We've seen a lot of innovative organizations in this book, and they all do things very differently. Experian identifies problems its customers are having and will deliver a prototype solution in 90 days. IBM searches for "grand challenges" that it will spend years—and sometimes decades—on. Google deftly integrates its ability to push the boundaries of computer science into the day-to-day work of its engineers. These approaches work because they suit the capabilities, strategy, and culture of the companies that employ them. They are unlikely to work the same way for anyone else.

So if you want to innovate effectively, you need to choose problems that play to your own strengths, that will help your organization achieve its strategic objectives, and that will be meaningful to your culture.

3. Ask the Right Questions to Map the Innovation Space

As a manager, I always felt incredible pressure to innovate, but found very little to guide me. I read some very smart books that had some very good ideas, but the advice was often contradictory. Clayton Christensen's *The Innovator's Dilemma*, for example, showed that sometimes a product or service gets to the point that improving along conventional metrics will confer no additional advantage, and that opens the door for a disruptive innovator to change the basis of competition. But what if your industry hasn't yet reached that point? Well, in that case, Christensen's ideas aren't very helpful.

Another really smart book is Jim Collins's *Good to Great*, which advocates the "hedgehog principle" and suggests that the key to success is to figure out what you're really good at and do more of it. But according to Christensen, that's exactly how great businesses fail!

The same goes for Henry Chesbrough's ideas about open innovation. Clearly, as we've seen with InnoCentive, the Apache Foundation, and Procter & Gamble's Connect + Develop program, finding ideas outside your organization can be incredibly useful. But if that's the key to innovation, how do we explain Apple's incredible success over the last 15 years? After all, Apple is one of the most obsessively secretive companies on the planet.

As a matter of fact, show me any successful innovator, and I can show you another that is just as successful that does things very differently. Once again, there's no "silver bullet" for innovation. You have to start by defining problems, not preordaining solutions.

That's why if you remember one thing from this book, it should be these two questions:

1. How well is the problem defined?
2. How well is the domain defined?

Once you've asked those framing questions, you can start to define a sensible way to approach the problem using the Innovation Matrix (Figure EM.1). Notice that even within the different quadrants, there are still a variety of strategies that can be pursued. Both IBM and Google tackle fundamental problems that push the boundaries of science, but while IBM has a full-fledged research division, Google chooses to focus its efforts on academic partnerships and to invite top researchers to spend a year on sabbatical at the company. While Eli Lilly built an online platform to pursue open innovation and then spun it off, Procter & Gamble created Connect + Develop as an internal program. While many large technology companies employ a VC approach to experiment with new business models, Experian created its DataLabs.

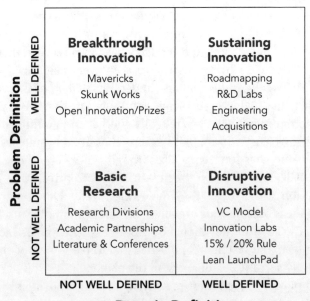

FIGURE EM.1 Innovation Matrix

So the key to innovating effectively is not the objective merits of any particular strategy, but whether that strategy addresses the problem you are trying to solve.

4. Leverage Platforms to Access Ecosystems of Talent, Technology, and Information

In Michael Porter's model, strategy is very much like a game of chess. He advised managers to drive efficiency by optimizing their firm's value chain, taking measures to minimize threats from new market entrants and substitute goods, and at the same time working to maximize their bargaining power with buyers and suppliers. By developing the right sequence of strategic moves, enterprises could position themselves to exert power and dominate their respective industries.

Clearly, much has changed since Porter formulated his theory of competitive advantage more than 35 years ago. Today, we live in a networked world, and competitive advantage is no longer the sum of all efficiencies, but the sum of all connections. Strategy, and by extension innovation, must focus on widening and deepening connections to talent, technology, and information.

So we increasingly need to use platforms to access those ecosystems. Even the internal capabilities of corporate giants like Procter & Gamble, Eli Lilly, and Microsoft pale in comparison to those that can be found outside the boundaries of an organization. As Bill Joy put it, "No matter who you are, most of the smartest people work for someone else."

Few retailers can match Amazon's scale and data competencies, but BloomReach allows firms like Neiman Marcus to access similar capabilities, partly by pooling their data with other online retailers so that its algorithms can spot trends faster. Upwork provides a fluid workforce of trained and certified specialists to organizations. IBM is highly dependent on the multitudes of software engineers in open source communities to innovate at a scale that it could never match. Procter & Gamble finds solutions to seemingly intractable problems from its Connect + Develop program. Experian codevelops innovative new products with its customers, who know far more about their needs than it ever could. Microsoft, which fought open source platforms for more than a decade, now embraces them, even going so far as to publicly proclaim, "Microsoft Loves Linux."

Power, therefore, no longer resides at the top of the value chain, but at the center of networks. That's why collaboration is becoming a new source of competitive advantage. Today, the best way to become a dominant player is to become an indispensable partner. Nobody, no matter what assets they control, can afford to go it alone anymore. So this new era of platforms offers great opportunities, but also great challenges. We now need to design our organizations for agility, empathy, and interconnectedness, rather than for scale, dominance, and efficiency.

5. Build a Collaborative Culture

It took a decade for Florey and Chain to uncover Fleming's discovery of penicillin because the challenges of time and space were significant at the time. There was no e-mail in the 1930s, and, in fact, even travel and telephones were relatively expensive and cumbersome. You did not simply ring somebody up or jump on a plane to go to a conference back then. There was also no Internet search, so to find Fleming's paper they had to go through an untold number of old scientific journals in order to come across it.

Today, those barriers have largely disappeared, but others still remain. Lynda Chin, who helped create the Institute for Applied Cancer Science at MD Anderson, told me about the challenges of integrating researchers, physicians, and drug developers, "Basic science is a long-term proposition" she said. "You need to be single-minded and stick with it until your hypothesis is disproved. Applied science, however, requires execution by a cross-disciplinary team, and you need to constantly make decisions about time and resources, taking into account not only probability of success, but also opportunity cost. Often, projects need to be delayed or killed outright if they are not feasible in an actionable time frame. This means two different cultures, and it is a challenge to integrate them effectively. We need to build a culture of understanding between the two disciplines."

To innovate these days, you not only need smart, creative people, but also empathetic ones who can listen, build relationships, and form mutual bonds of understanding. One brilliant but abrasive team member can poison the culture and bring collaboration to a screeching halt.

6. Understand That Innovation Is a Messy Business

All of the innovation strategies presented in this book have been proven successful, but the truth is that they have probably failed just as often. Innovation is messy business. While the term may conjure up visions of Steve Jobs wowing the crowds at Macworld, the reality is confusion, late nights, and petty squabbles over minutiae. We expect innovations to be well dressed, smooth talking, and brilliantly executed, but the reality is that the innovation process is anything but those things. It is not smooth or shiny. It stutters. It is often overweight and poorly groomed, with dark circles under its eyes from overwork. It comes into the world stumbling and falling, only later to gain Olympic level prowess. We glamourize the 1 percent inspiration but forget about the 99 percent perspiration. After all, perspiration stinks.

Many famous innovators failed horribly. Alexander Fleming published his paper and no one noticed. Yet still, he went back to work at his lab the next day. After Steve Jobs's failed Lisa project, he was hounded out of the company he helped found. It was more than a decade before he returned to create an even greater success. After IBM turned the computing world on its head with the launch of the PC, it soon found itself in near bankruptcy, but rose once again to become a giant in technology services.

That's why so few companies can innovate well. It is such hard, heartbreaking work. It is not for heroes like Hercules who, through great strength and prowess, win every battle. It is more like the myth of Sisyphus, that poor sap in Greek mythology who was doomed to push a boulder up a hill for all of eternity, only to have it roll back down just as he neared the top.

Still, as Albert Camus pointed out, the trick is to take joy in the boulder pushing, knowing it is likely to roll back down and give us another shot.[6] We can choose another direction, a different technique, or even a new mountain, confident that the top is waiting for us and, in time, we will get there.

NOTES

INTRODUCTION

1. http://www.theatlantic.com/magazine/archive/1945/07/as-we-may -think/303881/.
2. Robert Solow, "We'd Better Watch Out," *New York Times* Book Review, July 12, 1987, 36.
3. Scott Anthony, *The Little Black Book of Innovation* (Harvard Business Press, 2012), 16.
4. Ibid., 17.
5. Abraham Flexner, "The Usefulness of Useless Knowledge," *Harper's Magazine*, August 1939, http://harpers.org/archive/1939/10/the -usefulness-of-useless-knowledge/.

CHAPTER 1

1. Douglas Engelbart, "Augmenting Human Intellect: A Conceptual Framework," 1962, SRI Summary Report AFOSR-3223. Prepared for Director of Information Sciences, Air Force Office of Scientific Research.
2. Robert Solow, "We'd Better Watch Out," *New York Times* Book Review, July 12, 1987, 36.
3. A full account of the discovery of bacteria can be found in Eric Lax, *The Mold in Dr. Florey's Coat: The Story of the Penicillin Miracle* (Holt Paperbacks, 2005).
4. Ibid., 122–23.
5. Ibid., 154–56.
6. Ibid., 184–85.
7. Ibid., 204.
8. Eve Curie Labouisse, *Madame Curie: A Biography*, trans. Vincent Sheean (1937), 341.
9. A full discussion of the origins of the iPhone's technology can be found in Mariana Mazzucato, *The Entrepreneurial State* (PublicAffairs, 2015), 93–119.
10. https://www.nsf.gov/od/lpa/nsf50/vbush1945.htm.
11. Jennifer Couzin-Frankel, "Cancer Immunotherapy," *Science* 342, no. 6165 (December 20, 2013): 1432–33.
12. A full list can be found on the FDA website: http://www.fda.gov/Drugs /DevelopmentApprovalProcess/DrugInnovation/ucm430302.htm.

13. Hemant Ahlawat, Giulia Chierchia, and Paul van Arkel, "The Secret of Successful Drug Launches, *McKinsey Quarterly*, April 2014.

14. Sharon Belvin's story can be found here: http://www.cancerresearch .org/our-strategy-impact/people-behind-the-progress/patients/sharon -belvin. Others can be found here: http://www.wsj.com/articles/cancers -super-survivors-how-immunotherapy-is-transforming-oncology -1417714379.

15. http://www.nytimes.com/2015/10/03/opinion/the-folly-of-big-science -awards.html.

16. The segment can be seen here: http://www.cbsnews.com/news/ promising-duke-university-polio-brain-cancer-trial-given -breakthrough-status-60-minutes/.

17. Scott Berkun, *The Myths of Innovation* (O'Reilly, 2010), 8.

18. Paul A. David, "The Dynamo and the Computer: An Historical Perspective on Modern Productivity Paradox," *American Economic Review Papers and Proceedings* 80, no. 2 (May 1990): 355–61.

19. For a fascinating look at the "war of the currents," see Jill Jonnes's excellent book, *Empires of Light: Edison, Tesla, Westinghouse and the Race to Electrify the World*.

20. Robert Gordon, *The Rise and Fall of American Growth* (Princeton University Press, 2016).

CHAPTER 2

1. For the full story on Ignaz Semmelweis, see Sherwin B. Nuland, *The Doctors' Plague: Germs, Childbed Fever, and the Strange Story of Ignác Semmelweis*, Great Discoveries (New York: Norton, 2003).

2. Thomas Kuhn, *The Structure of Scientific Revolutions* (University of Chicago Press, 1962).

3. Ibid., 19, 24.

4. Ibid., 68.

5. Robert W. Weisberg, *Creativity: Beyond the Myth of Genius* (W. H. Freeman and Company, New York, 1993), 169.

6. Much of the biographical information given here is taken from Walter Isaacson's *Einstein: His Life and Universe* (Simon and Schuster, 2007).

7. Ibid., 82.

8. Ibid., 39

9. Michio Kaku, *Physics of the Impossible* (Anchor Books, 2008), 201.

10. Mario Livio, *Brilliant Blunders: From Darwin to Einstein—Colossal Mistakes by Great Scientists That Changed Our Understanding of Life and the Universe* (Simon and Schuster, 2013), 122.

11. Ibid., 103–14.

12. Francis Crick, *What Mad Pursuit: A Personal View of Scientific Discovery* (Basic Books, 1990), 60.

13. A complete list of DNA codes for amino acids can be found at https:// en.wikipedia.org/wiki/DNA_codon_table.

14. Solomon E. Asch, "Studies of Independence and Conformity: I. A Minority of One Against a Unanimous Majority," *Psychological Monographs: General and Applied* 70, no. 9 (1956): 1–70, http://dx.doi.org/10.1037/h0093718.

CHAPTER 3

1. http://www.bloomberg.com/news/articles/2012-12-06/tim-cooks-freshman-year-the-apple-ceo-speaks#p.
2. Walter Isaacson, *Steve Jobs* (Simon & Schuster, 2011), 385.
3. http://www.sjsu.edu/people/fred.prochaska/courses/ScWk170/s0/Basic-vs.-Applied-Research.pd.
4. Interview with author.
5. For anyone interested in learning more about how discoveries become technologies, I recommend W. Brian Arthur's excellent book, *The Nature of Technology: What It Is and How It Evolves* (Free Press, 2009).
6. Brian Uzzi, Satyam Mukherjee, Michael Stringer, and Ben Jones, "Atypical Combinations and Scientific Impact," *Science* 342, no. 6157 (October 25, 2013): 468–72, http://science.sciencemag.org/content/342/6157/468. Further discussion on this topic can be found in, Charles Duhigg, *Smarter Faster Better* (Random House, 2016), 209–15.
7. Steve Jons, Stanford Commencement Address, June 12, 2005. A full text and video of the speech can be found at http://news.stanford.edu/2005/06/14/jobs-061505/.
8. Interview with author (article).
9. Peter Diamandis, *Abundance* (Free Press, 2012), 221.
10. A full list of XPRIZES can be found on its website: http://www.xprize.org/prizes.
11. http://www.digitaltonto.com/2016/why-energy-storage-may-be-the-most-important-technology-in-the-world-right-now/.
12. Bernard Meyerson, Turing Lecture 2014. Confirmed by e-mail. A video of the lecture can be found at https://tv.theiet.org/?videoid=5012.
13. http://www.forbes.com/innovative-companies/list/2/#tab:rank.
14. Experian Annual Report, 2016

CHAPTER 4

1. These actually were dollars. At the time, because Ukraine's currency, the hryvnia, was not considered stable, prices in many industries were dollar denominated.
2. https://techcrunch.com/2012/04/15/steve-blank-teaches-entrepreneurs-how-to-fail-less/.
3. https://steveblank.com/about/.
4. Steve Blank commencement address, Philadelphia University, http://www2.philau.edu/commencement/address/SteveBlank051511commencement.pdf.

5. Ibid.
6. Ibid.
7. http://www.ideafinder.com/history/inventors/carlson.htm.
8. http://timkastelle.org/blog/2010/09/expand-the-market-for-innovation
   -success/.
9. Steve Blank, *The Four Steps to the Epiphany*, 33.
10. Ibid., 34–35.
11. Ibid., 2–3.
12. Ibid., 3–12.
13. Eric Ries, *The Lean Startup* (Crown Business, 2011), 57–58.
14. Ibid., 93–94.
15. Gina Keating, *Netflixed* (Penguin Portfolio, 2012), 1–2.
16. Ries, 99–102.
17. Ibid., 150–59.
18. https://techcrunch.com/2013/01/10/causes-acquires-votizen/.
19. A summary of the pilot project can be found at https://steveblank
    .com/2011/12/20/the-government-starts-an-incubator-the-national
    -science-foundation-innovation-corps/.
20. Full statistics for the SBIR program can be found on its website:
    https://sbir.nih.gov/statistics/award-data.
21. http://www.beckershospitalreview.com/population-health/population
    -health-strategy-cuts-asthma-related-ed-visits-in-half.html.
22. Alex Osterwalder, "The Business Model Ontology: A Proposition in a
    Design Science Approach" (PhD dissertation), 1.

CHAPTER 5

1. http://www.bbc.com/news/business-12697975.
2. A full history can be found at http://www.businessinsider.com/the
   -story-behind-microsofts-hot-selling-kinect-2011-1?op=1.
3. A more complete history of Microsoft's opposition to open source can
   be found at http://www.cnet.com/news/microsofts-long-history-of
   -open-source-acrimony/.
4. Karim R. Lakhani and Jill A. Panetta, "The Principles of Distributed
   Innovation," *Innovations: Technology, Governance, Globalization* 2,
   no. 3 (Summer 2007), The Berkman Center for Internet and Society Research Paper No. 2007-7. Available at SSRN: http://ssrn.com/
   abstract=1021034.
5. Eric S. Raymond, *The Cathedral & The Bazaar* (O'Reilly Media Inc.,
   1999), 15–16.
6. Interview with author.
7. Henry Chesbrough, *Open Innovation* (Harvard Business Review
   Press, 2006), 34–41.
8. Ibid., 4–11.
9. http://www.zdnet.com/article/why-microsoft-is-turning-into-an-open
   -source-company/.

10. Interview with author.

11. Lakhani and Panetta, "The Principles of Distributed Innovation."

12. https://www.innocentive.com/innocentive-solver-develops-solution-to -help-clean-up-remaining-oil-from-the-1989-exxon-valdez-disaster; https://www.innocentive.com/files/node/casestudy/case-study-prince -william-sound-osri-challenge.pdf.

13. https://www.innocentive.com/prize4life-awards-1-million-prize-for -major-milestone-in-als-research/.

14. https://www.innocentive.com/files/node/casestudy/challenge-snap -shot-gsk-electroceutical-ideation-challenge.pdf.

15. Interview with author.

16. Interview with author.

17. http://www.fastcompany.com/44917/he-struck-gold-net-really.

18. Interview with author and Nabil Sakkab.

19. An overview can be found on the Connect + Develop website: http:// www.pgconnectdevelop.com/home/stories.html.

20. A useful history of P&G's innovation efforts can be found in Bill James and Nabil Sakkab, "Can P&G Reinvent Itself?," *Center for Innovation Management Studies (CIMS) Newsletter*, July/August 2015, https://cims.ncsu.edu/cims_newsletter/julyaugust-2015/can-pg -reinvent-itself/.

CHAPTER 6

1. Theodore Levitt, "Marketing Myopia," *Harvard Business Review*, July– August 1960, 45, https://hbr.org/2004/07/marketing-myopia

2. Chris Zook and James Allen, *Profit from the Core* (Harvard Business School Press, 2001).

3. Ibid., 24.

4. Ibid., 34.

5. Ibid., 83.

6. Ibid., 81.

7. Ibid., 116.

8. Ibid., 5–6.

9. http://www.recode.net/2016/4/28/11586526/aws-cloud-revenue -growth.

10. Zook and Allen, 39.

11. "What Managers Really Do," *Wall Street Journal*, August 17, 2009, http://www.wsj.com/articles/SB100014240529702049086045743344501 79298822.

12. Mehrdad Baghai, Stephen Coley, and David White, *The Alchemy of Growth* (Perseus Books, 1999).

13. Ibid., 1.

14. Andy Grove, *Only the Paranoid Survive* (Crown Business, 1999), 84–96.

15. Eric Schmidt and Jonathan Rosenberg, *How Google Works* (Grand Central Publishing, 2014), 223.

16. Ibid., 223.

17. Ibid., 227. Also see Paul D. Kretkowski, "The 15% Solution," *Wired*, January 1998.

18. Ibid., 225–26.

19. Brad Stone, "Inside Google's Secret Lab," *Bloomberg*, May 28, 2013, https://www.bloomberg.com/news/articles/2013-05-22/inside-googles -secret-lab.

20. https://backchannel.com/the-secret-to-moonshots-killing-our -projects-49b18dc7f2d6#.poetjip8o.

21. Teller's TED talk can be found at: http://www.ted.com/talks/ astro_teller_the_unexpected_benefit_of_celebrating_failure.

22. Interview with author.

CHAPTER 7

1. David Lieberman, "CEO Forum: Microsoft's Ballmer Having a 'Great Time,'" *USA Today*, April 20, 2007, http://usatoday30.usatoday.com/ money/companies/management/2007-04-29-ballmer-ceo-forum -usat_N.html.

2. http://www.gurufocus.com/financials/MSFT.

3. http://www.forbes.com/sites/gregsatell/2013/04/22/the-blockbuster -microsoft-business-that-nobody-ever-seems-to-talk-about/#412276 d4d0e7.

4. After Microsoft's corporate reorganization in 2015, Azure become part of the Intelligent Cloud division.

5. Microsoft third quarter 2016 press release, https://www.microsoft .com/en-us/Investor/earnings/FY-2016-Q3/press-release-webcast.

6. https://www.aei.org/publication/fortune-500-firms-in-1955-vs-2015 -only-12-remain-thanks-to-the-creative-destruction-that-fuels -economic-growth/.

7. A list for 2016 can be found here: http://www.highsnobiety .com/2016/03/16/nike-innovations-2016/.

8. Kevin Maney, *The Maverick and His Machine* (John Wiley and Sons, 2003), 397–404.

9. Ibid., 43.

10. Ibid., 100–102.

11. Ibid., 137.

12. Ibid., 89.

13. Ibid., 139.

14. Ibid., 154–56.

15. Ibid., 139–40.

16. As it turns out, ENIAC was only the first digital computer that anyone knew of. The first digital computer was actually built by British engineers under the direction of Alan Turing at Bletchley

Park during World War II. However, Winston Churchill ordered the machine destroyed after the war due to national security concerns. It would be decades before that became public knowledge, though.

17. Louis Gerstner, *Who Says Elephants Can't Dance* (Harper Collins, 2002), 116.

18. Ibid., 117.

19. The actual quote is, "No matter who you are, most of the smartest people work for someone else."

20. Kathleen Burton, "Anatomy of a Colossus, Part II," *PC Magazine*, February 1983, 316, https://books.google.com/books?id=7wCi NAUEuAMC&lpg=PA360&pg=PA317#v=onepage&q&f=true.

21. Ibid.

22. Norman McEntire, "The Key to the PC," *PC Magazine*, June–July 1982, 139–40, https://books.google.com/books?id=w_OhaFDePS4C&lpg= RA2-PA18&pg=RA2-PA139#v=onepage&q&f=true

23. Gerstner, 120.

24. Ibid., 4.

25. Ibid., 123.

26. Interview with author.

27. Interview with author.

28. Interview with author.

29. Interview with author.

30. Interview with author.

31. Interview with author.

32. Benoit Mandelbrot, *The Fractalist: Memoir of a Scientific Maverick* (Random House, 2012), 204.

33. Interview with author.

34. Interview with author.

35. Interview with author.

36. Interview with author.

37. https://ycharts.com/companies/IBM/revenues.

38. The five are data and analytics, cloud, mobile, social, and security. IBM Annual Report 2015, Chairman's letter. It can be found at https://www.ibm.com/annualreport/2015/chairmans-letter/.

39. Interview with Eric Brown, director, Watson Technologies.

40. http://www.digitaltonto.com/2013/the-new-era-of-cognitive -collaboration/.

41. http://www.digitaltonto.com/2016/ibm-has-created-a-revolutionary -new-model-for-computing-the-human-brain/.

42. I am indebted to Charlie Bennett, who developed many of the basic principles of quantum computing, for spending the time and patience to explain quantum computing to me.

43. http://www.digitaltonto.com/2016/cloud-computing-just-entered -totally-new-territory/.

CHAPTER 8

1. I am indebted to Moisés Naím for his discussion of Weber and bureaucracy, which can be found in, Moisés Naím, *The End of Power* (Basic Books, 2013), 38–42.
2. Ronald Coase, "The Nature of the Firm," *Economica*, New Series, 4, no. 16. (November 1937), 386–405.
3. Michael Porter, *Competitive Advantage* (The Free Press, 1985), 48.
4. "Markets with Search Frictions" compiled by the Economic Sciences Prize Committee of the Royal Swedish Academy of Sciences, https://www.kva.se/globalassets/priser/ekonomi/2010/sciback_ek_10.pdf.
5. Interview with author.
6. https://www.upwork.com/.
7. https://www.crunchbase.com/organization/innocentive#/entity.
8. Michael Hiltzik, *Dealers of Lightning: Xerox PARC and the Dawn of the Computer Age* (Harper Business, 1999), 272.
9. http://www.digitaltonto.com/2016/the-very-strange-and-fascinating-ideas-behind-quantum-computing/.
10. You can sign up to use the quantum computer at http://www.research.ibm.com/quantum/.
11. Interview with author.
12. Interview with author.
13. Zeynep Ton, *The Good Jobs Strategy* (New Harvest, 2014), 130–42.
14. http://www.marketwatch.com/story/amazon-accounted-for-60-of-online-sales-growth-in-2015-2016-05-03.
15. https://www.census.gov/retail/mrts/www/data/pdf/ec_current.pdf.
16. https://hbr.org/2014/05/strategy-is-no-longer-a-game-of-chess.
17. Neil McAllister, "Redmond Top Man Satya Nadella: 'Microsoft LOVES Linux,'" *The Register*, October 20, 2014.
18. https://blogs.technet.microsoft.com/windowsserver/2015/05/06/microsoft-loves-linux/.

CHAPTER 9

1. Eric Lax, *The Mold in Dr. Florey's Coat: The Story of the Penicillin Miracle* (Henry Holt & Company, 2005), 186–87.
2. David H. Autor, "The 'Task Approach' to Labor Markets: An Overview," National Bureau of Economic Research, http://www.nber.org/papers/w18711.pdf.
3. McKinsey Global Institute, "Help Wanted: The Future of Work in Advanced Economies," March 2012, http://www.mckinsey.com/global-themes/employment-and-growth/future-of-work-in-advanced-economies.
4. Paul Beaudry, David A. Green, and Benjamin M. Sand, "The Great Reversal in the Demand for Skill and Cognitive Tasks," *Journal of Labor Economics* 34(S1) (2016): S199–S247, http://www.nber.org/papers/w18901.

5. http://www.nature.com/nature/history/full/nature06243.html.

6. http://www.nature.com/news/interdisciplinary-research-by-the -numbers-1.18349.

7. Stefan Wuchty, Benjamin F. Jones, and Brian Uzzi, "The Increasing Dominance of Teams in Production of Knowledge," *Science* 316, no. 5827 (May 18, 2007): 1036–39, http://www.kellogg.northwestern.edu/ faculty/jones-ben/htm/Teams.ScienceExpress.pdf.

8. Geoffrey Colvin, *Humans Are Underrated: What High Achievers Know That Brilliant Machines Never Will* (Portfolio Penguin, 2015), 49.

9. J. R. Hackman and M. O'Connor, "What Makes for a Great Analytic Team? Individual vs. Team Approaches to Intelligence Analysis," Washington, DC: Intelligence Science Board, Office of the Director of Central Intelligence, 2004.

10. Lu Hong and Scott Page, "Groups of Diverse Problem Solvers Can Outperform Groups of High-Ability Problem Solvers," *PNAS*, November 16, 2004.

11. Anita Williams Woolley, Christopher F. Chabris, Alex Pentland, Nada Hashmi, and Thomas W. Malone, "Evidence for a Collective Intelligence Factor in the Performance of Human Groups," *Science* 330, no. 6004 (2010): 686–88.

12. Garry Kasparov, "The Chess Master and the Computer," *The New York Review of Books*, February 11, 2010.

13. Martin Heidegger, *A Question Concerning Technology and Other Essays* (Harper Torchbooks, 1977), 3–35.

14. Larry Summers, "The Age of Secular Stagnation: What It Is and What to Do About It," *Foreign Affairs*, February 15, 2016.

15. Robert Gordon, *The Rise and Fall of American Growth* (Princeton University Press, 2016), 605–39.

16. *Science—The Endless Frontier.* A Report to the President by Vannevar Bush, Director of the Office of Scientific Research and Development, July 1945 (Washington: United States Government Printing Office, 1945), https://www.nsf.gov/od/lpa/nsf50/ vbush1945.htm.

17. https://hbr.org/2015/03/stock-buybacks-arent-hurting-innovation.

18. "Report to the President on Ensuring American Leadership in Advanced Manufacturing Technologies," Executive Office of the President, President's Council of Advisors on Science and Technology, June 2011.

AFTERWORD

1. For a good summary of WordPress's history and founding, see Scott Berkun, *The Year Without Pants* (Jossey Bass, 2013), 28–40.

2. Richard Feynman, *"Surely You're Joking, Mr. Feynman!" Adventures of a Curious Character* (W.W. Norton & Company, 1989), 309–17.

3. http://www.inc.com/minda-zetlin/one-simple-strategy-that-helps-you
   -innovate-like-steve-jobs.html.
4. https://www.entrepreneur.com/article/274417.
5. I am indebted to Scott Berkun for making the connection between
   Cargo Cults and corporate culture. See: Scott Berkun, *The Year Without Pants* (Jossey Bass, 2013), 29.
6. Albert Camus, *The Myth of Sisyphus and Other Essays* (Vintage, 1991),
   123.

INDEX

ABOUT THE AUTHOR

Greg Satell is a popular writer, speaker, and consultant whose work has appeared in *Harvard Business Review*, *Forbes*, the *Times of London*, *Fast Company*, *Inc.*, and *Business Insider*. He lives in Gladwyne, Pennsylvania, with his wife, Liliana, his daughter, Ashley, and trusty dog, Spike.